# PRIME
# MERIDIAN

*A CULINARY TOUR OF A
SOUTHERN QUEEN CITY*

# PRIME MERIDIAN

Meridian is a relaxing town in east central Mississippi that retains that hometown country lifestyle feel. Strategically positioned to serve the growing South, Meridian is located at a major transportation junction of US Highway 45, Interstate 20, Interstate 59 and three major railroads.

Lamar Foundation
544 Lindley Road
Meridian, MS 39305

| First Printing | October 2001 | 5,000 copies |
| Second Printing | December 2001 | 5,000 copies |
| Third Printing | December 2003 | 6,000 copies |
| Fourth Printing | June 2007 | 4,000 copies |

ISBN: 978-0-9712056-0-4

Library of Congress Control Number: 2001095273

Copies of *Prime Meridian* may be obtained by sending $22.95 plus $5.00 shipping and handling to the following address. Mississippi residents should add $1.61 sales tax. For your convenience, order forms are located in the back of the book.

*Prime Meridian* Cookbook
P. O. Box 3387
Meridian, MS 39303
601-482-1345 ext. 9 (voice mail)
601-482-7202 (fax)
www.lamarschool.com

WIMMER
COOKBOOKS

ConsolidatedGraphics
1-800-548-2537

# PRIME MERIDIAN

Mississippi's "Queen City" offers history and hospitality to its residents and visitors, and the many individuals who participated in the publication of **Prime Meridian** consider it a special privilege to contribute to this record of the city's many attributes. With Greg Cartmell's colorful depictions of our city's landmarks as a guide, please join us on a culinary tour of Meridian.

Our tour begins with Weidmann's Restaurant, an establishment that proclaims, "It's the food that counts!" This chapter features recipes for the appetizers and beverages that often initiate a dining experience.

Next, the serenity of Dunn's Falls brings us brunch and bread recipes for enhancing tranquil weekend mornings.

Salads appear in the chapter introduced by Merrehope, a home that survived a war to triumph as a tribute to the elegance of past times.

Bonita Lakes Park opens the chapter devoted to soups and sandwiches. Many of these recipes are appropriate for picnics at this superior recreational area.

The Grand Opera House, once a stage for Mississippi's premier cultural attractions, presents the entrées, the limelight of many meals.

Side dishes appear in the chapter featuring Meridian's travel and transportation, which feed its thriving economy much as these dishes support a meal.

The often-decorated gravesites of a gypsy family introduce recipes for embellishing great meals - the desserts.

Finally, an amusement beloved by children of all ages, the Highland Park Carousel, represents a chapter devoted to creative parties and recipes.

We hope that you find our tour featuring Meridian's heritage of hospitality to be a welcome addition to your home and kitchen. We thank you for joining us, and we encourage you to visit often!

# Committee

### Editors
Lallie Bennett
Vicky McDonnell
Kim Waters

### Recipe Editor
Leslie Covington

### Contributing Artist
Greg Cartmell

### Design Coordinator
Aimee Tramontana

### Proofing Coordinator
Kerry Cook

### Marketing Coordinators
Deborah Haggard
Kim Mosley

### Testing Coordinators
Lynn Kimbriel
Barbara Rogers

## Section Chairs

### Appetizers
Jodie Marsalis
Pam Rutherford

### Beverages
Kim Ward

### Brunch
Elyse Thompson

### Breads
Jan Williams

### Soups/Sandwiches
Robin Dungan
Suzanne Thomas

### Salads
Gayle Callahan

### Entrées
Chris Lauderdale
Shelby McRae
Karen Rush
Tanya Thompson
Donna Ulmer
Francie Wilkinson

### Side Dishes
Elsie Jordan
Shelby McRae
Kim Ward

### Desserts
Cindy Blubaugh
Lisa Love
Judy Luquire
Jean Makey
Vicki Mathis
Eileen Neunaber

### Parties
Karen Gates

### Design Committee
Melissa Duggan
Laura Holladay
Debbie Martin
Ricki Tucker
Hallie Ward

### Editorial Committee
Margaret Nicholson
Claudia Pass
Lynn Russell
Cathy Stone

### Typists
Lisa Barrett
Lean Follett
Sharon McMullen

### Proofing Committee
Dee Dee Fouts
Georgette Mosley
Amy Scrivner
Cindy Smith
Donna Ulmer

### Marketing and Publicity
Mary Billups
Amy Branning
Amy Ford
Jeanne Fort
Becky Howard
Greg Jones
Elsie Jordan
Alexa Marcello
Melissa Mabry
Paige McDonald
Pam McKee
Cheryl Richardson
Cathy Shields
Susan Speed
Nita Williams

# TABLE OF CONTENTS

# Lamar School

Chartered in 1964, Lamar School represents the fulfillment of a dream of many Meridianites to provide the area with an independent school that offers an exceptional academic program to its students. The school's name memorializes Lucius Quintus Cincinnatus Lamar, the first Mississippian to serve as a member of the United States Supreme Court. Lamar School provides an educational choice to Meridian's kindergarten through twelfth grade students. The school offers a college preparatory curriculum, small class size, and a variety of extracurricular opportunities for its students. Lamar School receives accreditation through the Southern Association of Colleges and Schools and the Mississippi Private School Association.

Prime Meridian is the third cookbook published by Lamar School patrons. The tradition of good food associated with school functions originates with *Kitchen Gems*, published in the early 1970's and *Lamar School Cookbook,* published in 1991. With Prime Meridian, **Lamar School** volunteers expand upon past successes and pay tribute to the city that represents a future of promise for eastern Mississippi.

# Greg Cartmell

A professional artist for over thirty years, Greg Cartmell is nationally recognized as one of the country's foremost landscape painters. Working in oils in an Alla Prima method, Cartmell uses broken color in true impressionistic style to capture the feeling of light as it illuminates the subject he is painting. A sense of intimacy in his work arises from his preference of painting on location in plain air.

Cartmell shows his paintings throughout the United States, Europe, and the Orient. Over fifteen United States galleries represent his work, and numerous corporate and private collections throughout the world feature it. A resident of Meridian, Cartmell maintains a gallery there. His web site is **cartmellgallery.com**.

# Appetizers & Beverages

# The Finest People on Earth

*"Through this door passes the finest people on earth—my customers" is the motto for Weidmann's Restaurant, a Meridian tradition since 1870. Founded by a Swiss immigrant, Felix Weidmann, this restaurant has achieved international acclaim with such varied specialties as shrimp rémoulade and black bottom pie.*

*Diners at Weidmann's Restaurant expect an experience unique to eastern Mississippi restaurants. While examining the hundreds of historical and celebrity photographs displayed on paneled walls, they enjoy peanut butter from crockery containers at their tables. A dignified and solicitous waiter brings the meals they selected from an extensive menu that proclaims "It's the food that counts." This relaxed dining experience makes Weidmann's Restaurant a popular destination for anyone who wishes to escape the hurried pace of daily life.*

# Bertha's Cheese Tart

*Excellent! This is sure to bring rave reviews!*

### Crust

| | |
|---|---|
| 1 | cup finely chopped onion |
| 1 | cup finely chopped pecans |
| 1 | cup shredded Cheddar cheese |

### Filling

1 cup cooked chopped spinach, well drained
1 (8-ounce) package cream cheese
1 (9-ounce) jar mango chutney
½ teaspoon ground nutmeg
½ teaspoon ground white pepper
½ teaspoon garlic powder
½ teaspoon celery salt
Party crackers

Blend all crust ingredients together and divide into two portions. Spray a 7-inch springform pan with nonstick cooking spray. Press half of crust mixture in the bottom. Press spinach between paper towels to squeeze out excess moisture. In a food processor, blend filling ingredients. Spread over crust. Cover filling with remaining crust mixture. Apply light pressure with a spoon to the top crust to form tart. Refrigerate overnight. Carefully remove the pan's collar. Cover top with a serving plate and invert. Remove the bottom of the pan. Chill until ready to serve. Serve with your choice of party crackers.

*1 (7-inch) tart*

*May substitute 2 (10-ounce) boxes frozen chopped spinach, thawed and well drained, for 1 cup cooked chopped spinach.*

*Note: Recipe must be refrigerated overnight.*

*For a "Big Bertha," use a 9-inch springform pan.*

Bertha Ellington, caterer, Clarksdale, Mississippi

## "Big Bertha"

Bertha Ellington was born and reared in Clarksdale, Mississippi. She began working in the cafeteria of Northwest Mississippi Regional Medical Center in 1981. Bertha, now a successful caterer, often prepares elegant meals for the medical staff and trustees. Dr. M. of Meridian, also an excellent chef, tried to obtain her original recipe. She agreed to share the recipe in exchange for copies of all his original recipes. Doubling this recipe creates a "Big Bertha."

7

# Marinated Cheese

## Beef and Cheddar Dip in Bread Basket

**1 loaf round bread or French bread**

**1 (8-ounce) package cream cheese, softened**

**1 (8-ounce) carton sour cream**

**¼ cup chopped green onion**

**1 (2¼-ounce) jar dried beef, chopped**

**1 tablespoon Worcestershire sauce**

**2 cups shredded sharp Cheddar cheese**

**Tortilla chips**

Preheat oven to 350°F. Cut top off bread, scoop out inside, tearing bread into 1-inch cubes. Reserve top and bread cubes. In a bowl, combine remaining ingredients, except chips and bread. Mix well. Pour into bread and replace top. Place on a baking sheet. Bake 45 minutes. Serve with bread cubes or tortilla chips.

*4½ cups*

| | | | | |
|---|---|---|---|---|
| ½ | cup olive oil | ½ | teaspoon salt |
| ½ | cup white wine vinegar | ½ | teaspoon freshly ground black pepper |
| 1 | (2-ounce) jar diced pimiento, drained | 1 | (8-ounce) block sharp Cheddar cheese, cut into cubes |
| 3 | tablespoons chopped fresh parsley | 1 | (8-ounce) block Monterey Jack cheese with jalapeño pepper, cut into cubes |
| 3 | tablespoons minced green onion | | |
| 3 | cloves garlic, minced | | |
| 1 | teaspoon sugar | | |
| ¾ | teaspoon dried basil | | |

Combine all ingredients, except cheeses in a jar, cover tightly and shake vigorously. Place cheeses in a large zip-top plastic bag. Pour marinade over cheeses and refrigerate a minimum of eight hours. Serve in a shallow dish with toothpicks.

*80 cubes*

*For a beautiful presentation, alternate the cheeses in the serving dish.*

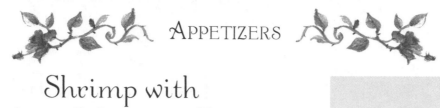
# Shrimp with Herbed Jalapeño Cheese

| | | | | |
|---|---|---|---|---|
| 2 | pounds unpeeled large fresh shrimp | 2 | teaspoons finely chopped fresh chives |
| 6 | cups water | 1 | tablespoon finely chopped fresh parsley |
| 1 | (3-ounce) package shrimp boil | | |
| 1 | (8-ounce) package cream cheese, softened | ⅛ | teaspoon salt, or to taste |
| 1 | clove garlic, minced | ⅛ | teaspoon ground black pepper, or to taste |
| 2 | pickled jalapeño peppers, seeded and finely chopped | | |

Peel shrimp leaving tail and first joint intact. Cut a deep slit down the length of the outside curve of each shrimp and devein. In a large saucepan, combine water and shrimp boil. Bring to a boil. Add shrimp and cook 3 to 5 minutes. Drain well. Rinse with cold water. Pat dry. Chill.

Beat cream cheese with remaining ingredients. Fill a decorator bag fitted with a #32 metal tip with the cream cheese mixture. Pipe filling on curl of shrimp.

*30 to 40 appetizers*

*May also put filling in a zip-top plastic bag, cut off a corner and pipe filling on curl of shrimp.*

## Dilled Carrots

**2 pounds carrots**

**4 teaspoons dill seed**

**4 cloves garlic, scored**

**1 quart white vinegar**

**4 cups water**

**½ cup salt**

**4 quart-size jars, sterilized**

Peel and cut carrots into strips. In a bowl, cover carrots with water and soak in refrigerator 4 hours. In each sterile jar, place 1 teaspoon dill seed and 1 clove garlic. Pack carrot strips upright in the jars. In a saucepan, combine vinegar, water and salt. Bring to a boil. Pour over carrots and cap. Process in boiling water bath 15 minutes.

*4 quarts*

# Mushrooms with Sun-Dried Tomato Pesto

| | | | |
|---|---|---|---|
| ¾ | cup oil packed sun-dried tomatoes, drained, reserve oil | ¼ | cup lightly packed fresh basil or 1 tablespoon dried basil |
| | Olive oil | ½ | teaspoon salt |
| 8 | cloves garlic, or to taste | 20 | fresh medium mushroom caps |
| ¼ | cup pine nuts | | Pine nuts, for garnish (optional) |

Add olive oil to reserved oil to make ½ cup. Place ¼ cup of oil mixture, tomatoes, garlic, pine nuts, basil and salt in a food processor bowl or blender container. Cover and process until finely chopped. With machine running, gradually add remaining oil and process until almost smooth, stopping to scrape sides as needed. Pesto may be made ahead and refrigerated in an airtight container for 1 month.

Preheat oven to 425°F. Clean mushroom caps. Spoon a rounded teaspoon of pesto into each cap. Garnish with additional pine nuts, if desired. Place on a baking sheet. Bake 10 minutes or until hot. Drain on paper towels. Serve warm.

*20 appetizers*

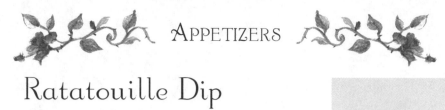

# Ratatouille Dip

*An excellent side dish as well!*

| | | | |
|---|---|---|---|
| ½ | cup olive oil | ⅛ | teaspoon dried thyme |
| 4 | cups unpeeled, cubed eggplant | 1 | bay leaf |
| | | 1 | teaspoon dried basil |
| 4 | cups chopped zucchini or yellow squash | ⅛ | teaspoon dried rosemary |
| | | 1 | tablespoon salt |
| ½ | cup chopped green bell pepper | 1 | teaspoon ground white pepper |
| ¼ | cup chopped red bell pepper | ½ | cup chopped ripe olives |
| ½ | cup chopped onion | 2 | tablespoons chopped fresh parsley |
| 2 | tablespoons minced garlic | | French bread rounds |
| ½ | cup white wine | | Olive oil |
| 4 | fresh tomatoes, peeled and chopped | | Grated Parmesan cheese |

Preheat oven to 350°F. In a large skillet, heat olive oil. Sauté eggplant and squash 8 minutes. Add bell peppers and onion. Simmer, uncovered, 6 minutes. Add garlic. Simmer 2 minutes. Add wine, tomatoes, thyme, bay leaf, basil, rosemary, salt, white pepper and olives. Transfer to a 2-quart baking dish. Bake covered 20 minutes or until eggplant is tender. Sprinkle with parsley. Serve with French bread rounds that have been brushed with olive oil, sprinkled with Parmesan cheese and toasted.

*2 quarts*

## Pumpkin Dip

2 (8-ounce) packages
cream cheese, softened

4 cups powdered
sugar, sifted

1 (15-ounce) can
pumpkin pie filling

2 teaspoons
ground cinnamon

1 teaspoon ground ginger

Gingersnaps

In a large mixing bowl,
beat cream cheese and sugar
with an electric mixer until
well blended. Beat in
remaining ingredients. Store
in an airtight container in the
refrigerator until ready
to serve. Serve with
gingersnaps. Freezes well.

*1 quart*

*For a festive presentation,
scoop out a small baking
pumpkin and fill with the dip.*

# Warm Crab
# and Artichoke Dip

| | | | |
|---|---|---|---|
| 2 | ounces cream cheese, softened | 2 | tablespoons chopped green onion |
| ½ | cup mayonnaise | 2 | tablespoons diced red bell pepper |
| ⅛ | teaspoon salt, or to taste | 2 | tablespoons diced celery |
| ⅛ | teaspoon ground black pepper, or to taste | 1 | tablespoon finely chopped fresh parsley |
| ¾ | cup crabmeat, picked over for shells | 1½ | tablespoons sherry wine vinegar |
| ¼ | cup plus 2 tablespoons grated Parmesan cheese, divided | ½ | teaspoon hot pepper sauce |
| 3 | tablespoons chopped, drained marinated artichoke hearts | | Toasted baguette slices |

Preheat oven to 400°F. In a large bowl, beat cream cheese with an electric mixer until smooth. Add mayonnaise. Beat until blended. Season with salt and pepper. Using a rubber spatula, fold in crabmeat, ¼ cup Parmesan, artichokes, onion, bell pepper, celery, parsley, vinegar and pepper sauce. Transfer crab mixture into a lightly greased 3-cup soufflé dish. Top with remaining 2 tablespoons Parmesan cheese. Bake 15 minutes or until crab mixture is warm and cheese melts. Serve immediately with toasted baguette slices.

*2½ cups*

*May be served in a chafing dish.*

# Flan with Praline Sauce

| | | | |
|---|---|---|---|
| 4 | (3-ounce) packages cream cheese, softened | 1 | (¼-ounce) package unflavored gelatin |
| ½ | cup butter, softened | ¼ | cup cold water |
| ½ | cup sour cream, room temperature | 1 | cup Praline Sauce (see accompanying recipe) |
| ½ | cup sugar | | Roll Out Sugar Cookies (see index) |

Beat cream cheese, butter and sour cream. Add sugar and blend well. Soften gelatin in cold water, dissolve over a bowl of hot water. Add to cream cheese mixture. Pour into a 1-quart mold or plastic bowl sprayed with nonstick cooking spray. Refrigerate until firm. To serve, unmold onto a rimmed serving plate. Top with Praline Sauce. Serve with cookies. May be frozen.

*1 flan*

# Elegant Caviar Mousse

| | | | |
|---|---|---|---|
| 4 | ounces red lumpfish caviar, divided | ¼ | teaspoon freshly ground black pepper |
| 3 | tablespoons chopped fresh parsley, divided | 1½ | teaspoons unflavored gelatin |
| 2 | tablespoons finely minced onion, divided | 2 | tablespoons water |
| 1 | cup sour cream | ½ | cup whipping cream, whipped |
| | | | Water crackers |

Set aside 2 tablespoons caviar, 1 tablespoon parsley and 1 tablespoon onion for garnish. Cover and refrigerate. In a medium nonmetallic bowl, combine remaining caviar, parsley, onion, sour cream and pepper. Blend well. In a small saucepan, sprinkle gelatin over water. Stir over low heat until gelatin dissolves completely. Remove from heat and stir into caviar mixture. Fold in whipped cream. Turn into a 3-cup nonmetallic mold. Cover and refrigerate until set. When ready to serve, invert mold on a platter. Serve with water crackers.

*3 cups*

## Praline Sauce

3 tablespoons butter or margarine

1 cup firmly packed brown sugar

½ cup half-and-half

1 cup chopped pecans

1 teaspoon vanilla

In a heavy saucepan over low heat, melt butter. Add brown sugar. Stirring constantly, cook 5 to 8 minutes or until mixture is smooth. Gradually stir in half-and-half. Cook 1 minute and remove from heat. Stir in pecans and vanilla. Cool to room temperature and pour 1 cup over flan. May be made ahead and refrigerated. Bring to room temperature.

*2 cups*

*This praline sauce is great served over vanilla ice cream!!!*

# Regal Caviar Mold

### Egg Layer

| | | | | |
|---|---|---|---|---|
| 4 | hard-boiled eggs, peeled and chopped | ¼ | teaspoon salt, or to taste | |
| ¼ | cup finely chopped onion | ⅛ | teaspoon ground black pepper, or to taste | |
| 2 | tablespoons sour cream | | | |

### Avocado Layer

| | | | | |
|---|---|---|---|---|
| 1 | small avocado, peeled and pit removed | 1 | teaspoon fresh lemon juice | |
| 2 | ounces cream cheese, softened | ⅛ | teaspoon salt, or to taste | |
| 1 | tablespoon finely chopped onion | ⅛ | teaspoon ground black pepper, or to taste | |

### Topping

| | | | |
|---|---|---|---|
| ¾ | cup sour cream | Assorted crackers or baguette slices | |
| 2 | ounces black, gold or red caviar | | |

For egg layer, stir together eggs, onion, sour cream, salt and pepper until combined. Set aside. To prepare avocado layer, mash avocado with cream cheese until smooth. Stir in onion, lemon juice, salt and pepper. Set aside.

In the center of a round serving platter, spread egg layer in a 6-inch circle. Flatten the top. Over the egg mixture, spread avocado mixture creating a slight dome. Spread sour cream over top and sides. Cover with plastic wrap. Refrigerate until firm or overnight. Just prior to serving, cover top with caviar. Surround with crackers or baguette slices.

*3 cups*

## Crawfish Edine

1   pound crawfish tails
¾   cup butter or
    margarine, divided
1   small bunch green
    onions, chopped
½   cup chopped parsley
3   tablespoons all-purpose
    flour

1   pint half-and-half
3   tablespoons sherry
⅛   teaspoon salt, or to
    taste
⅛   teaspoon cayenne
    pepper, or to taste
    Mini phyllo shells or
    Melba rounds

Lay crawfish tails on paper towels and wipe gently to remove some of the fat. In a skillet, sauté crawfish tails in ¼ cup butter. Remove with a slotted spoon being careful not to include fat from pan. Set aside. In another skillet, sauté green onions and parsley in ½ cup butter. Blend in flour and gradually add half-and-half, stirring constantly to make a thick sauce. Stir in sherry. Add crawfish tails. Season with salt and pepper to taste. Serve in mini phyllo shells or in a chafing dish with Melba rounds. Freezes well.

*1½ quarts*

## Marinated Crab Claws

1   cup olive oil
½   cup red wine vinegar
¼   cup fresh lemon juice
1   teaspoon tarragon
    leaves
10   cloves garlic, minced
1   cup chopped green
    onion

1   cup chopped parsley
1   cup chopped celery
¾   teaspoon salt
¾   teaspoon sugar
¾   teaspoon ground black
    pepper
32   crab claws, cooked

Mix all ingredients except crab claws and refrigerate. When ready to serve, place crab claws on a serving platter. Pour marinade over crab claws.

*32 appetizers*

### Bleu Cheese Vegetable Dip

**1 (8-ounce) package cream cheese, softened**

**1 cup sour cream**

**4 ounces bleu cheese, crumbled**

**2 teaspoons Worcestershire sauce**

**Raw vegetables**

Blend all ingredients except vegetables. Serve with raw vegetables.

*2½ cups*

*For a lower fat dip, use Neufchâtel cheese and light sour cream.*

# Marinated Shrimp and Vegetables

## Tarragon Marinade

¾ cup tarragon vinegar

½ cup finely chopped onion

1 tablespoon crushed garlic

1½ teaspoons fresh lemon juice

½ teaspoon brown sugar

½ teaspoon salad herbs or Italian seasoning

⅛ teaspoon prepared mustard

¼ teaspoon salt

¼ teaspoon ground black pepper

2 cups vegetable oil

½ cup olive oil

Combine all ingredients, except oils. Add oils slowly while whisking.

*4 cups*

3 pounds large shrimp, cooked, peeled and deveined

2 (8½-ounce) cans artichoke hearts, drained and cut into bite-size pieces

½ pound fresh mushrooms, cleaned and cut into bite-size pieces

1 pint cherry tomatoes, halved
   **Tarragon Marinade (see accompanying recipe)**
   **Leaf lettuce (optional)**

In an airtight plastic container, combine shrimp, artichokes, mushrooms and tomatoes. Add Tarragon Marinade. Cover tightly and chill 18 to 24 hours. Drain before serving. Spoon mixture over lettuce, if desired.

*3 quarts*

*Note: Must marinate 18 hours.*

## Hot Shrimp Canapés

2   (8-ounce) packages cream cheese, softened
4   teaspoons grated onion
1   cup Hellmann's mayonnaise
2   tablespoons chopped chives
¼-½  teaspoon cayenne pepper
½   cup grated Parmesan cheese

2   cups boiled shrimp, peeled, deveined and chopped
2   (16-ounce) loaves thin white bread, crust removed
   Fresh dill weed, for garnish
   Shrimp, cooked and peeled, for garnish (optional)

Preheat oven to 350°F. Combine all ingredients except bread and garnishes. Cut bread into 1½ inch rounds. Lightly toast one side. Cool. On the other side, spread with shrimp mixture. Bake 15 minutes or longer for crispier puffs. Garnish with dill weed and shrimp. Freezes well.

*4 dozen*

## Baked Oysters

¼   cup butter
¼   cup olive oil
⅔   cup Italian bread crumbs
½   teaspoon salt
½   teaspoon freshly ground black pepper
2   tablespoons finely chopped green onion tops

⅛   teaspoon cayenne pepper
½   teaspoon dried tarragon
½   teaspoon dried oregano
2   tablespoons minced fresh parsley
2   teaspoons minced garlic
1½  pints fresh small oysters
   Melba toast rounds

Preheat oven to 450°F. In a heavy saucepan melt butter over low heat. Mix in olive oil and heat. Add remaining ingredients, except oysters and Melba toast. Mix well. Remove the pan from heat. Place well drained oysters in an ovenproof serving dish. Cover with sauce. Bake 20 minutes or until top is lightly browned. Serve with Melba toast rounds.

*8 servings*

### New Year's Day Dip

2 cups cooked black-eyed peas, drained

1 cup chopped onion

1 (4½-ounce) can chopped green chiles (optional)

12 ounces salsa

1 cup shredded Monterey Jack cheese

2 cups shredded sharp Cheddar cheese

Large corn chips

Preheat oven to 350°F. Mash peas and place in a 2-quart greased baking dish. Layer onion, chiles, salsa and cheeses. Bake 25 minutes. Serve with corn chips.

*6 cups*

*May use drained canned black-eyed peas.*

# APPETIZERS

## Italian Cream Cheese Spread

*Quick!*

1 (8-ounce) package
cream cheese, softened

1 (0.7-ounce) package
dried Italian dressing mix

Water crackers
or fresh vegetables

Combine cream cheese
and Italian dressing mix.
Serve with crackers or
fresh vegetables.

*24 to 36 servings*

# Layered Shrimp Delight

*Easy to make and so delicious!*

| | | | |
|---|---|---|---|
| 1½ | pounds shrimp, cooked, peeled and deveined | 1 | (12-ounce) bottle cocktail sauce or chili sauce |
| 1 | (8-ounce) package cream cheese, softened | ¼-½ | cup chopped green onion |
| 2 | tablespoons sour cream | ¾ | cup sliced ripe olives |
| 2 | teaspoons Worcestershire sauce | 1 | small green bell pepper, seeded and finely chopped |
| 1 | teaspoon fresh lemon juice | 2 | cups shredded mozzarella cheese |
| ½ | teaspoon ground cayenne pepper | | Corn chips, tortilla chips or assorted crackers |
| 1 | clove garlic, minced | | |

Reserve 6 whole shrimp for garnish. Chop remaining shrimp; set aside. In a medium bowl, combine cream cheese and sour cream. Stir in Worcestershire, lemon juice, cayenne pepper and garlic. Spread mixture on the bottom of an 8-inch round serving dish. On top, layer cocktail sauce, onion, chopped shrimp, olives, bell pepper and cheese. Garnish with whole shrimp. Serve with corn chips, tortilla chips or assorted crackers.

*10 to 12 servings*

*May add pimiento stuffed green olives or substitute Cheddar cheese for mozzarella cheese.*

## Shrimp Mango Dip
*Delicious and low-fat*

| | | | |
|---|---|---|---|
| 1½ | pounds shrimp, cooked, peeled and deveined | ¼ | teaspoon ground white pepper |
| 1 | large or 2 small mangoes | ⅓ | cup chopped green onion |
| 12 | ounces fat-free cream cheese, softened | | Green onion fan, for garnish |
| ¾ | cup fat-free sour cream | | Shrimp, cooked, peeled with tail intact, for garnish |
| 2 | cloves garlic, minced | | |
| 1 | teaspoon curry powder | | Party crackers, pita chips or raw vegetables |
| ½ | teaspoon salt | | |

Chop shrimp. Chill and set aside. Peel and chop mangoes, reserving all juice, including juice from flesh surrounding pit. Set aside.

In a medium bowl, beat cream cheese, sour cream, garlic, curry, salt and pepper with an electric mixer on medium speed until well blended. Fold in shrimp, mangoes, onion and enough reserved juice to reach desired consistency. Chill well. Garnish with green onion fan and whole shrimp. Serve with crackers, chips or raw vegetables.

*5 cups*

## Hot Swiss and Bacon Dip

| | | | |
|---|---|---|---|
| 1 | (8-ounce) package cream cheese, softened | 2 | tablespoons chopped onion |
| ½ | cup mayonnaise | 10 | slices bacon, cooked and crumbled, divided |
| 1 | cup shredded Swiss cheese | | Round buttery crackers |

Preheat oven to 350°F. Mix cream cheese and mayonnaise. Add Swiss cheese, onion and bacon, reserving 3 tablespoons of bacon. Place in a greased 1½-quart baking dish. Crumble 15 to 20 crackers. Sprinkle cracker crumbs and remaining bacon on top. Bake 15 to 20 minutes. Serve with remaining crackers.

*3 cups*

### Bleu Cheese Bits

**3 ounces crumbled bleu cheese**

**1 tablespoon butter**

**1 (10-count) can refrigerated biscuits**

Preheat oven to 400°F. In a 9-inch baking pan, place cheese and butter. Bake 4 to 6 minutes or until melted. Remove from oven and blend. Cut biscuits into quarters. Layer on top of cheese mixture. At this point, you may cover with aluminum foil and refrigerate for several hours. Bring to room temperature. Bake 12 to 15 minutes or until golden brown. Invert onto a serving dish and serve warm.

*40 bits*

## Hot Bleu Cheese Dip

1 (8-ounce) package cream cheese, softened

4 ounces crumbled bleu cheese

¼ cup milk or half-and-half

½ teaspoon minced garlic

7 slices crisp bacon, crumbled

Granny Smith apple slices

Preheat oven to 350°F. Combine all ingredients, except apple slices. Spoon mixture into a greased 1-quart baking dish. Bake 30 minutes. Serve with chilled Granny Smith apple slices.

*2 cups*

*For Christmas, alternate red and green apple slices in a wreath pattern around dip.*

# Sausage Puffs

*Wonderful for a morning meeting*

| | | | |
|---|---|---|---|
| 1 | (12-ounce) package reduced fat breakfast sausage | ⅛ | teaspoon ground black pepper |
| ¾ | cup chopped onion | 4 | ounces reduced fat cream cheese, softened |
| ⅛-¼ | cup finely chopped jalapeño pepper | | |
| ½ | teaspoon salt | 2 | (8-ounce) cans reduced fat refrigerated crescent rolls |

In a skillet, heat sausage. When sausage begins to brown, add onion and jalapeño pepper. Cook until sausage is browned and onion becomes translucent. Season with salt and pepper. Drain well and transfer to a bowl. Blend in cream cheese.

Preheat oven to 375°F. Separate crescent rolls into triangles. Place 1 tablespoon filling onto wide edge of triangle. Roll wide edge toward the point, enveloping the filling. Fold in edges of dough so filling is completely enclosed. Bake 11 to 13 minutes or until golden brown.

*16 puffs*

*For bite-size puffs, cut crescent roll triangles in half and reduce filling to ½ tablespoon per puff.*

## Hearty Nacho Dip

*Great crockpot recipe! Teenagers love this!*

| | |
|---|---|
| 1 | pound ground beef |
| ½ | cup chopped onion |
| ¼ | cup chopped green bell pepper |
| 1 | (10¾-ounce) can cream of mushroom soup |
| 1 | (10¾-ounce) can tomato soup |
| 1 | (1-pound) loaf processed cheese, cut into cubes |
| | Sliced jalapeño peppers (optional) |
| | Corn chips or tortilla chips |

In a skillet, brown ground beef and drain well. Add onion and bell pepper. Cook until tender. Transfer beef mixture to a crockpot. Add soups and cheese cubes. Stir well. Cook on high 1 hour, stirring occasionally. Reduce heat to low to keep warm. May add jalapeño peppers for a spicier flavor. Serve warm with large corn chips or tortilla chips.

*6 cups*

## Hot Reuben Dip

| | |
|---|---|
| 1 | (8-ounce) package cream cheese, softened |
| ½ | cup sour cream |
| 1 | cup well drained sauerkraut, chopped |
| ½ | pound cooked lean corned beef, finely chopped |
| 2 | teaspoons finely chopped onion |
| 1 | tablespoon ketchup |
| 2 | teaspoons spicy brown mustard |
| 1 | cup shredded Swiss cheese |
| | Rye crackers or rye Melba rounds |

Preheat oven to 375°F. In a large bowl combine all ingredients, except crackers. Transfer to a lightly greased 1½-quart baking dish. Bake, covered, 30 minutes or until edges bubble. Uncover and bake 5 minutes or until lightly golden. Serve warm with crackers.

*2 cups*

### Toasted Cheese Tortillas

16 (8-inch) corn tortillas

Vegetable oil

1 teaspoon salt

1 teaspoon dried oregano

¼ teaspoon cayenne pepper

1½ cups shredded sharp Cheddar cheese

Preheat oven to 400°F. Brush 1 side of tortillas with vegetable oil. Cut each tortilla into quarters. Arrange on nonstick baking sheets. Mix salt, oregano and cayenne pepper. Sprinkle on each tortilla. Top with cheese. Bake 10 to 12 minutes or until golden and crisp.

*64 chips*

# Hot Venison Dip

*Always disappears first at tailgate parties!*

| | | | |
|---|---|---|---|
| 1 | pound ground venison | 2 | (6-ounce) rolls garlic cheese, cubed |
| 1 | (10¾-ounce) can cream of mushroom soup | 2 | (6-ounce) rolls jalapeño cheese, cubed |
| 1 | (10¾-ounce) can cream of celery soup | 2 | (4½-ounce) cans chopped green chiles |
| | | | Corn chips |

Brown ground venison. Drain if necessary. Add remaining ingredients, except corn chips, and heat, stirring frequently, until cheese is melted. Serve hot in a chafing dish with corn chips.

*1½ quarts*

*May substitute 12 ounces Mexican process cheese loaf for jalapeño cheese rolls.*

*Ground beef may be substituted for the venison, but people who don't like venison love this dip.*

Tailgating at Mississippi State University is a fall tradition. Meridian Dawg Pound tailgaters enjoy this venison dip. Hamburger may be substituted, but it spoils C.L.'s pleasure of telling venison haters all about the recipe... after they have just eaten a bowl of it!

# California Caviar

| | | | |
|---|---|---|---|
| 1 | (15-ounce) can black beans, drained | 2 | stalks celery, chopped |
| 1 | (11-ounce) can niblet corn, drained | ¼ | cup chopped onion |
| 1 | (16-ounce) jar hot, medium or mild salsa | 1 | teaspoon ground cumin |
| | | | Tortilla chips |

Combine all ingredients, except chips. Chill. For best flavor, marinate at least 6 hours. Serve with tortilla chips.

*6 cups*

This recipe came from "Navy Wives" stationed at the Meridian Naval Air Station. It was very popular in San Diego. We feel like California beach people whenever we serve it!

# Carnival Flans

*A very different "pick up" item.*

| | | | |
|---|---|---|---|
| 2 | quarts water | ⅛ | teaspoon freshly |
| 2½ | teaspoons salt, divided | | ground black pepper, |
| 3 | ounces angel hair | | or to taste |
| | pasta | 1¼ | cups shredded |
| ½ | cup finely diced mixed | | Monterey Jack |
| | sweet red and green | | cheese with jalapeño |
| | bell peppers | | pepper |
| 4 | large eggs | 3 | tablespoons chopped |
| 1⅓ | cups whipping cream | | fresh parsley |

Preheat oven to 350°F. Spray miniature muffin tins with nonstick vegetable cooking spray. In a saucepan, bring water to a boil. Add 2 teaspoons salt and pasta. Boil 4 to 5 minutes or until tender. Drain pasta and pat dry with a clean kitchen towel. Divide pasta evenly among the tins. Sprinkle diced bell peppers evenly over pasta.

In a mixing bowl, whisk eggs, cream, remaining salt, pepper and cheese to blend. Ladle into the muffin tins. On the center shelf of the oven, bake 15 to 20 minutes or until set, puffed and lightly browned. Remove and cool 10 minutes. Flans will deflate and lose puffiness. To serve, gently remove from the muffin tins. Arrange on a serving plate. Sprinkle with parsley.

*36 flans*

*May be made three days in advance. Cover cooled, unmolded flans with plastic wrap and refrigerate. To serve, preheat oven to 350°F. Place flans on a baking sheet. Bake 10 to 15 minutes or until thoroughly heated.*

## Toasted Pecans with Rosemary

**1½ pounds pecan halves**

**2-3 tablespoons melted butter, divided**

**Salt**

**2½ tablespoons coarsely chopped fresh rosemary**

**¾ teaspoon cayenne pepper**

**1 tablespoon dark brown sugar**

Preheat oven to 250°F. Spread pecans on a large baking sheet. Toast 30 minutes to dry. Drizzle 2 tablespoons butter over pecans and mix well. Return to oven 10 minutes. Sprinkle pecans with salt and drizzle remaining butter, if needed. Stir well. Return to oven 10 minutes. Mix rosemary, cayenne pepper and brown sugar. Toss with warm nuts. Serve warm or at room temperature.

*1½ pounds pecans*

## Toasted Pecans

*Wonderful! Great Christmas Gift!*

½ cup margarine, melted

4 teaspoons
Worcestershire sauce

1 tablespoon garlic salt

½ teaspoon Tabasco sauce

4 cups pecan halves

Preheat oven to 300°F.
Combine margarine,
Worcestershire, garlic salt and
Tabasco until well blended.
Mix with pecans, coating
thoroughly. Spread pecans
onto a 15x10-inch jelly-roll
pan or cookie sheet with
sides. Toast 30 minutes.
Drain on paper towels.

*4 cups*

# Artichoke and Olive Tapenade

*A tangy and unique flavor.*

| | | | |
|---|---|---|---|
| 1 | (14-ounce) can artichoke hearts, well drained | 2 | tablespoons chopped fresh parsley, divided |
| ¼ | cup walnuts, toasted | 1 | tablespoon extra virgin olive oil |
| 8 | large brine-cured green olives, pitted | ⅛ | teaspoon salt |
| ½ | teaspoon lemon zest | ⅛ | teaspoon ground black pepper |
| 1 | teaspoon fresh lemon juice | | Toasted baguette slices |

In a food processor, process artichoke hearts, walnuts, olives, lemon zest and juice until finely chopped. Add 1 tablespoon parsley and oil. Purée until coarse paste forms. Season with salt and pepper. Transfer to a small bowl. Sprinkle with remaining parsley. Serve as a spread on toasted baguette slices.

*1 cup*

*May be made one day ahead and refrigerated.*

# Hummus Bi Tahini

| | | | |
|---|---|---|---|
| 1 | (15-ounce) can garbanzo beans, drained | ¾ | teaspoon salt |
| | | 2 | tablespoons water |
| 3 | tablespoons tahini | 2 | tablespoons olive oil, for garnish |
| ½ | cup fresh lemon juice | | Finely chopped parsley, for garnish |
| 2 | cloves garlic, minced, or to taste | | Pita bread triangles |

In a food processor, process beans, tahini, lemon juice, garlic, salt and water until smooth and creamy. If thinner consistency is desired, add more water. Place in a serving dish. Garnish with olive oil and parsley. Serve cold or at room temperature with warm pita bread triangles.

*2 cups*

# Stuffed Grape Leaves

*Well worth the preparation time*

1½ cups long grain rice, prepared according to package directions
1½ tablespoons minced fresh mint
½ cup chopped fresh parsley
1½ bunches green onions, chopped
¼ cup olive oil
1½ teaspoons salt
¾ teaspoon ground black pepper
1½ tablespoons fresh lemon juice
1 (16-ounce) jar grape leaves

In a bowl, combine all ingredients, except grape leaves. Blend well. Wash grape leaves and pat dry with paper towels. Remove tough stems. Place leaves on counter with stem end facing you. Place 1 tablespoon filling across middle of each leaf. Fold both sides to the middle and roll away from you into a small firm roll. Refrigerate until ready to serve.

*40 to 45 rolls*

## Sugar and Spice Nuts

*Delicious sprinkled over ice cream!*

1 cup sugar

1 teaspoon ground cinnamon

¼ teaspoon salt

6 tablespoons milk

1 teaspoon vanilla

2 cups pecans or walnuts

In a saucepan, mix sugar, cinnamon, salt and milk. Cook to soft-ball stage (235°F). Remove from heat. Add vanilla and nuts. Turn out onto wax paper and separate with a fork.

*2 cups pecans or walnuts*

*Wonderful sprinkled over mixed greens tossed in a vinaigrette and topped with chèvre cheese.*

# Stuffed Mushrooms

| | | | | |
|---|---|---|---|---|
| 12 | large fresh mushrooms | 3 | tablespoons grated Parmesan cheese |
| 2 | tablespoons butter | | |
| ¾ | cup chopped onion | 1 | tablespoon finely chopped parsley |
| 2 | ounces pepperoni, chopped | | |
| | | ½ | teaspoon salt |
| ¼ | cup chopped green bell pepper | ⅛ | teaspoon ground black pepper |
| 1 | small clove garlic, minced | ¼ | teaspoon dried oregano |
| | | ⅓ | cup chicken broth |
| ½ | cup crushed saltine crackers | | |

Preheat oven to 325°F. Remove mushroom stems and chop. In a skillet, melt butter. Sauté onion, pepperoni, bell pepper, garlic and mushroom stems until tender. Add saltines, cheese, parsley, salt, pepper and oregano. Stir in chicken broth. Spoon stuffing into mushroom caps. Place in a shallow pan with ¼ inch of water. Bake 25 minutes. Dry on paper towels and serve warm.

*1 dozen appetizers*

## Sassy Salsa

*Totally fat-free and delicious.*

2 (28-ounce) cans diced tomatoes

4 green onions, chopped

1 clove garlic, minced

1 (10-ounce) can diced tomatoes with green chiles

2 tablespoons chopped fresh cilantro or parsley

½ teaspoon dried oregano

¼ teaspoon ground cumin

4 teaspoons white vinegar

1 tablespoon fresh lime juice

1 tablespoon Greek seasoning

Tortilla chips

Combine all ingredients except chips. Chill. Serve with tortilla chips.

*1½ quarts*

# Toasted Parmesan Pitas

| | | | | |
|---|---|---|---|---|
| 4 | (6-inch) pita rounds | ½ | cup grated Parmesan cheese |
| 6 | tablespoons olive oil | | |
| 1 | teaspoon dried oregano | 1½ | tablespoons sesame seeds |
| 1 | teaspoon garlic powder | | |

Preheat oven to 425°F. Separate each pita round into 2 circles. Cut each circle into 6 wedges. Place wedges, rough side up, on ungreased baking sheet. In a small bowl, combine oil, oregano and garlic powder. Stir well. Brush lightly onto wedges. In another bowl, combine cheese and sesame seeds. Sprinkle on wedges. Bake 5 to 10 minutes or until lightly browned. Watch carefully. Cool. Store in airtight containers.

*4 dozen crackers*

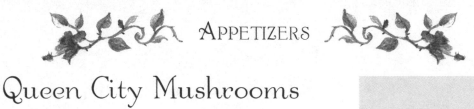

# Queen City Mushrooms

| | | | | |
|---|---|---|---|---|
| 15 | slices white or wheat bread | 2 | egg yolks | |
| 1 | (8-ounce) package cream cheese, softened | 1 | clove garlic, minced | |
| | | ⅛ | teaspoon salt | |
| | | 1 | pound mushroom caps | |
| | | ¼ | cup butter | |

Cut four 1-inch bread rounds from each slice of bread. On a cookie sheet, broil until lightly toasted on 1 side. Set aside. In a food processor or medium bowl, combine cream cheese and egg yolks. Add garlic and salt. Blend well. Thinly coat untoasted side of rounds with cheese mixture. Sauté mushroom caps in butter. Drain on paper towels. Place 1 cap on top of each round and fill with remaining cheese mixture. To serve, broil until lightly browned. Serve immediately.

*60 appetizers*

*Mushroom rounds may be prepared and refrigerated 8 hours before broiling.*

# Greek Tomato Pastries

| | | |
|---|---|---|
| 4 | (9-inch) refrigerated pie crusts | Olive oil or olive oil spray |
| 8 | ounces crumbled herbed feta cheese | Greek seasoning |
| 1 | pint cherry tomatoes, thinly sliced | Fresh basil, finely chopped |

Preheat oven to 350°F. Slightly roll out pie crusts. Cut with a 2½-inch biscuit cutter. Spray miniature muffin pans with nonstick cooking spray. Press crust into the muffin pans. Bake 5 to 8 minutes or until lightly browned. Crumble cheese onto crusts. Top with tomato slice. Brush or spray with olive oil. Sprinkle with Greek seasoning and fresh basil. Bake 10 minutes or until heated.

*80 appetizers*

## Hot Taco Dip

1 (1-pound) package mild or hot bulk sausage, cooked and drained

1 (16-ounce) can refried beans

2 (8-ounce) jars taco sauce

1 (4½-ounce) can chopped green chiles

1 (4¼-ounce) can chopped ripe olives, drained

12 ounces Monterey Jack cheese, shredded

Tortilla or corn chips

Preheat oven to 350°F. Mix all ingredients except cheese and chips. Place in a 2-quart ovenproof serving dish. Top with cheese. Bake 30 minutes. Serve with chips.

*2 quarts*

27

# Spinach Tortilla Pinwheels

1   cup mayonnaise

1   cup sour cream

1   (1-ounce) package
    ranch salad dressing
    mix

½   (3-ounce) jar real
    bacon bits

3   green onions, finely
    chopped

4-5  cups fresh spinach,
    washed with stems
    removed

1   (13½-ounce) package
    8-inch flour tortillas

Combine all ingredients, except spinach and tortillas. Evenly spread mixture on tortillas. Top mixture with a single layer of spinach. Roll up tortillas. Cover completely with plastic wrap. Refrigerate for several hours. Slice into bite-size pieces.

*10 to 12 dozen pinwheels*

## Guacamole Dip

1 medium tomato,
  finely chopped

1 small purple onion,
  finely chopped

3 avocados, mashed

Juice of 1 lemon

¼ teaspoon olive oil

1 tablespoon mayonnaise

⅛ teaspoon salt, or to taste

⅛ teaspoon ground black
  pepper, or to taste

Tortilla chips

In a bowl, combine all ingredients except chips. Mix well. Refrigerate. Serve with tortilla chips.

*3 cups*

# Garden Vegetable Mousse
*Light and delicious!*

¾  cup chopped onion

1   cup chopped celery

¾  cup chopped tomato

¾  cup chopped green bell
    pepper

¾  cup chopped cucumber

1   (¼-ounce) package
    unflavored gelatin

¼  cup cold water

¼  cup boiling water

2   cups mayonnaise

1   teaspoon garlic salt

1   teaspoon ground white
    pepper

    Shredded wheat
    crackers

Drain onion, celery, tomato, bell pepper and cucumber very well on paper towels. Soak gelatin in cold water 3 to 5 minutes. Add boiling water to dissolve gelatin. Let cool. Add mayonnaise, garlic salt and white pepper. Mix well. Stir in vegetables. Pour into a 4-cup ring mold that has been sprayed with nonstick cooking spray. Refrigerate several hours or overnight. Unmold and serve with crackers.

*4 cups*

*For a dip, pour mixture into a 1-quart serving bowl and chill. To serve, toss with a fork.*

# Gourmet Nachos

| | | | |
|---|---|---|---|
| 4 | ounces chèvre cheese | 2 | tablespoons chopped fresh cilantro |
| 4 | ounces sun-dried tomatoes packed in olive oil, drained and chopped | 8 | ounces blue corn chips or tortilla chips |
| 1 | clove garlic, minced | | Cilantro sprigs, for garnish |
| ⅛ | teaspoon freshly ground black pepper | | |

Preheat oven to 300°F. Crumble cheese and toss with sun-dried tomatoes, garlic, pepper and cilantro. Sprinkle over chips. Bake 20 minutes or until cheese is warmed through. Cheese will not melt. Garnish with cilantro sprigs and serve immediately.

*6 servings*

# Mexican Rollups

| | | | |
|---|---|---|---|
| 8 | (8-inch) flour tortillas | ½ | bunch fresh cilantro or parsley, chopped |
| 1 | (8-ounce) package cream cheese, softened | 2 | cups shredded Cheddar cheese |
| 1 | (8-ounce) jar salsa | 1 | (6-ounce) can large pitted ripe olives |
| 1 | bunch green onions, chopped | | |

Spread each tortilla, almost to the edge, with cream cheese. Cover each with 2 tablespoons salsa. Sprinkle each with green onions and cilantro. Sprinkle cheese on top. Be careful to keep tortilla edges clean. In a single row, lay olives about ¼ of the way down each tortilla. Roll tortillas very tightly starting at the olive end. Cover completely with plastic wrap and refrigerate. Slice into thin pinwheels before serving.

*7 to 8 dozen pinwheels*

---

*Chèvre cheese is a pure white goat's milk cheese with a delightfully tart flavor.*

## Salsa Fantastica

**1 (8-ounce) package cherry tomatoes, cut in fourths**

**1 (10-ounce) can diced tomatoes with green chiles**

**1 (4¼-ounce) can chopped ripe olives, drained**

**1 (7-ounce) can hot jalapeño relish**

**4 green onions, chopped**

**3 tablespoons oil**

**1½ tablespoons white vinegar**

**1 tablespoon garlic salt**

**Tortilla chips**

Combine all ingredients. Chill for eight hours. Serve with tortilla chips.

*3 cups*

## Spinach and Artichoke Dip

| | | | |
|---|---|---|---|
| 1 | (10-ounce) package frozen chopped spinach, thawed and drained well | 12 | ounces cream cheese, softened |
| 1 | (12-ounce) jar marinated artichoke hearts, chopped, drained, reserve marinade | 2 | teaspoons fresh lemon juice |
| | | 1 | cup grated Parmesan cheese |
| 3 | cloves garlic, chopped | 1 | cup chopped pecans |
| ½ | cup mayonnaise | 1 | cup bread crumbs |
| | | | Melba rounds or crackers |

Preheat oven to 375°F. Mix all ingredients, except bread crumbs and crackers. Pour into a buttered 9x9-inch baking dish. Sprinkle with bread crumbs. Bake 25 minutes. Serve with Melba rounds or a variety of crackers.

*2½ quarts*

## Tailgate Crostini Dip

| | | | |
|---|---|---|---|
| 10 | Roma tomatoes, chopped | 2 | tablespoons white wine vinegar |
| 3-6 | green onions, chopped | 1 | tablespoon sugar |
| ½ | cup chopped purple or Vidalia onion | ¼ | teaspoon salt |
| ¼-½ | cup fresh chopped basil | ¼ | teaspoon ground black pepper |
| 2 | teaspoons minced garlic | 1 | (4-ounce) package feta cheese |
| 1 | tablespoon olive oil | | Toasted French bread rounds |
| 2 | tablespoons balsamic vinegar | | |

Mix all ingredients except feta cheese and bread rounds. Chill for several hours. Place in a serving bowl. Top with feta cheese prior to serving. Serve with toasted French bread rounds.

*3 cups*

### Easy Marinated Shrimp

2 pounds fresh shrimp, boiled and peeled

1 large white onion, finely sliced

1 (3.5-ounce) jar capers

1 bay leaf

1 (16-ounce) bottle Italian salad dressing

In a bowl, combine all ingredients. Cover and refrigerate 24 hours. Remove bay leaf before serving.

*2 pounds*

*Note: Must marinate 24 hours.*

# Amaretto Cheese Mold

| | | | |
|---|---|---|---|
| 1 | pound Cheddar cheese, shredded | 1 | (16-ounce) carton cottage cheese |
| 2 | (8-ounce) packages cream cheese, softened | 1 | cup butter, softened |
| | | 3 | green onions, chopped |
| | | ⅓ | cup amaretto liqueur |
| | | | Crackers |

In a bowl, combine all cheeses until well blended. Stir in butter, onions and amaretto. Mix well. Line a 1½-quart mold with a damp piece of cheesecloth. Press mixture firmly and evenly into mold. Cover with cheesecloth and chill several hours. Unmold and remove cheesecloth. Serve with crackers.

*1½ quarts*

# Festive Brie

*Gorgeous at Christmas!*

| | | | |
|---|---|---|---|
| 1 | (8-ounce) wheel Brie cheese | ¼ | teaspoon orange extract |
| ⅓ | cup whole berry cranberry sauce, crushed | ⅛ | teaspoon ground nutmeg |
| | | ½ | cup chopped pecans |
| 2 | tablespoons brown sugar | | Water crackers |

Preheat oven to 400°F. Carefully remove rind from top of Brie leaving a small margin around edge. Place on an ovenproof serving dish. Combine cranberry sauce, sugar, orange extract and nutmeg. Spread over Brie. Top with pecans. Bake 10 minutes. Serve with water crackers.

*1 (8-ounce) Brie*

*For Valentine's Day, cut top of Brie out in a heart shape and spread sauce in the shape of a heart.*

## Different Chicken Salad Filling

**1 cup cooked and diced chicken**

**½ cup finely chopped dates**

**¼ cup chopped pecans**

**¼ cup crumbled crisp bacon**

**½ cup mayonnaise**

**¼ teaspoon salt**

In a medium bowl, combine all ingredients.

*2½ cups*

*Stuff celery sticks with filling or use for tea sandwiches.*

# Italian Torta

Pesto is an uncooked Italian sauce traditionally made from basil, olive oil, garlic, Parmesan cheese and sometimes pine nuts.

## Basil Pesto

2 large cloves garlic

2 cups packed fresh basil leaves

⅔ cup grated Parmesan cheese

⅔ cup chopped walnuts

¼ cup olive oil

In a food processor fitted with a metal blade, process garlic until minced. Add basil, cheese and walnuts. Process until ground. Slowly add oil and process until mixture is a thick paste. Pesto may be refrigerated in an airtight container for one month.

*2 cups*

| | | | |
|---|---|---|---|
| 2 | (8-ounce) packages cream cheese, softened | ¼ | cup prepared basil pesto (or see accompanying recipe) |
| 8 | ounces chèvre cheese | 1 | (7-ounce) jar oil packed sun-dried tomatoes, drained |
| 1¼ | teaspoons dried oregano | | Parsley, for garnish |
| 2 | cloves garlic, minced | | Stone ground wheat crackers |
| ⅛ | teaspoon ground black pepper | | |

In a food processor or mixer, mix cream cheese, chèvre cheese, oregano, garlic and pepper until smooth. Line a 4-cup container with plastic wrap. Layer ⅓ of cheese mixture in the dish. Top with basil pesto. Repeat cheese layer.

Reserve 1 tomato for garnish. Coarsely chop remaining tomatoes. Layer over cheese mixture. Top with remaining cheese mixture. Cover with plastic wrap and refrigerate several hours. Unmold and garnish with reserved tomato and parsley. Serve with stone ground wheat crackers.

*16 servings*

*Sun-dried tomato pesto may be substituted for sun-dried tomatoes. Feta cheese may be substituted for chèvre cheese.*

*Instead of a pesto layer, add a layer of chopped kalamata olives, marinated artichoke hearts and roasted red bell peppers.*

# Brie with Walnut Glaze

| | | | |
|---|---|---|---|
| ⅔ | cup walnuts, finely chopped | ½ | teaspoon vanilla |
| ¼ | cup coffee liqueur | 1 | (14-ounce) round Brie cheese |
| 3 | tablespoons brown sugar | | Assorted crackers |
| | | | Pear slices |

Preheat oven to 350°F. Spread chopped walnuts in a baking pan. Bake 10 to 12 minutes or until toasted, stirring occasionally. Stir in liqueur, brown sugar and vanilla. Set aside.

Reduce oven temperature to 325°F. Remove the top rind of the Brie. Place Brie in a shallow baking dish. Top with walnut mixture. Bake 8 to 10 minutes or until the Brie is soft and thoroughly heated. Serve immediately with assorted crackers and pear slices.

*1 (14-ounce) Brie*

# Creamy Mango Chutney Spread

*Easy and elegant!*

| | | | |
|---|---|---|---|
| 1 | (8-ounce) package cream cheese, softened | 1 | (9-ounce) jar mango chutney |
| ½ | cup shredded sharp Cheddar cheese | 1 | bunch green onions, chopped |
| 2 | tablespoons sherry | | Thin wheat crackers |

Combine cheeses and sherry until well blended. Spread very thinly on a rimmed glass serving plate. Spread chutney over cheese mixture. Sprinkle with onions. Cover with plastic wrap and chill. Serve with wheat crackers.

*50 to 60 servings*

*Add cooked, crumbled bacon as a topping.*

## Sun-Dried Tomato Pesto

½ cup oil packed sun-dried tomatoes, drained and reserve ¼ cup oil

2 cloves garlic

¼-½ teaspoon cayenne pepper (optional)

1 teaspoon drained capers (optional)

6-8 pitted ripe olives (optional)

1 teaspoon red wine vinegar (optional)

1 teaspoon chopped parsley (optional)

In a food processor, process all ingredients until mixture is the consistency of butter.

*¾ cup*

# Wrapped Gouda

## Cheese Ball

4 (8-ounce) packages cream cheese, softened

1 (4¼-ounce) can chopped ripe olives, drained

1 (4.5-ounce) jar dried beef, chopped

1 bunch green onions, chopped

1 (4-ounce) can chopped mushrooms, drained

3 teaspoons Accent

1 cup finely chopped pecans

Round buttery crackers

Combine all ingredients except pecans and crackers in a mixing bowl. Blend well. Divide into 2 portions and roll each into a ball. Roll balls in chopped pecans. Serve with round buttery crackers.

*2 cheese balls*

| | | | |
|---|---|---|---|
| 1 | (8-ounce) can crescent rolls | 1 | (7-ounce) round Gouda cheese |
| | | 1 | egg, beaten |

Preheat oven to 350°F. Cut cheese round in half horizontally to form 2 circles. Remove wax. Separate crescent roll dough. Press 2 triangles together, sealing perforations well, to form 1 rectangle. Repeat process for remaining triangles. Stack 2 rectangles on top of each other. Roll out into a 6-inch square. Wrap around 1 cheese circle. Press dough tightly around cheese and twist ends to seal, removing and reserving excess dough. Repeat process for other cheese circle. Roll out reserved dough and cut out decorative shapes. Place on top of each wrap. Brush wraps with beaten egg. Place on an ungreased cookie sheet 3 inches apart. Bake 18 to 22 minutes or until golden brown. Cool 10 minutes before serving. Serve with crackers.

*2 wraps*

*May top with pepper jelly after baking.*

*Different cheeses, such as Havarti, may be substituted for Gouda cheese.*

# Savory Cheesecake Royale

*Superb!*

### Crust

| | | | |
|---|---|---|---|
| ¼ | cup fine bread crumbs | ¼ | cup finely shredded sharp Cheddar cheese |

### Filling

| | | | |
|---|---|---|---|
| 6 | ounces thinly sliced ham, divided | 4 | eggs |
| 3 | (8-ounce) packages cream cheese, softened | 3 | tablespoons finely chopped jalapeño pepper |
| 12 | ounces shredded sharp Cheddar cheese | 2 | tablespoons milk |
| 1 | cup cottage cheese | 1 | clove garlic, minced |
| ¾ | cup chopped green onion | 5 | dashes hot pepper sauce |
| | | | Chopped green onion, for garnish |
| | | | Crackers |

Preheat oven to 325°F. Spray a 9-inch springform pan with nonstick cooking spray. In a medium bowl, mix bread crumbs and ¼ cup Cheddar cheese. Press into bottom of the pan and refrigerate.

Dice half of ham and reserve remaining slices. In a large bowl, combine diced ham and remaining filling ingredients until smooth. Pour half of filling into the pan. Top with reserved ham slices. Cover with remaining filling. Set the pan on a baking sheet. Bake 1 hour 15 minutes. Turn oven off. Let cake cool 1 hour with oven door ajar. Remove from oven and cool completely.

To serve, release cake from pan and place on a serving platter. Sprinkle green onion over top. Serve with crackers.

*24 servings*

## Chocolate Fondue

6 (1-ounce) squares semisweet chocolate

1 cup butter

1½ cups sugar

1 cup whipping cream

2 teaspoons vanilla

⅛ teaspoon salt

Bananas, strawberries, apples, cherries or pineapple

In a saucepan, melt chocolate and butter. Add sugar and stir until dissolved. Stir in cream, vanilla and salt. Heat thoroughly. Serve in a fondue pot or a chafing dish. Spear fruit for dipping.

*3½ cups*

## Fresh Fruit Dip

¼ cup sugar

¾ cup firmly packed
light brown sugar

1 tablespoon vanilla

1 (8-ounce) package cream
cheese, softened

Fresh fruit slices

Combine sugars, vanilla
and cream cheese until well
blended. Serve with fresh
fruit such as pineapple,
strawberries, apples
and pears.

*1¼ cups*

# Triple Layer Cheesecake

*Sure to be a hit!*

| | | | |
|---|---|---|---|
| 3 | (8-ounce) packages cream cheese, softened and divided | 1 | teaspoon grated onion |
| | | ¼ | cup butter or margarine, softened |
| 3 | tablespoons chopped pimiento stuffed green olives | 2 | cloves garlic, pressed |
| | | 1 | teaspoon dried Italian seasoning |
| 2 | teaspoons olive juice | | Wheat crackers, air baked crackers or toasted baguette slices |
| 1 | tablespoon mayonnaise | | |
| 1 | cup shredded sharp Cheddar cheese | | |
| 1 | (2-ounce) jar diced pimiento, drained | | |

With an electric mixer on medium speed, beat 1 package cream cheese until creamy. Stir in olives and olive juice. Line an 8x4-inch loaf pan with plastic wrap. Spread olive mixture over bottom. For 2nd layer, beat 1 package cream cheese. Beat in mayonnaise and Cheddar cheese until blended. Stir in pimiento and onion. Spread over olive mixture. Beat remaining cream cheese and butter until creamy. Beat in garlic and Italian seasoning until blended. Spread garlic mixture over pimiento mixture. Cover and chill 3 hours or until firm. Unmold onto a serving plate. Serve with wheat crackers, air baked crackers or toasted baguette slices.

*24 servings*

# Cucumber Tea Sandwiches

*Perfect for an afternoon tea*

| | | | |
|---|---|---|---|
| 3 | (3-ounce) packages cream cheese, softened | 1 | loaf thinly sliced white bread |
| 1½ | teaspoons garlic salt | 2 | cucumbers, peeled and thinly sliced |
| 3 | teaspoons chopped chives | | Fresh dill weed, for garnish |
| 1½ | teaspoons dried chervil | | |

Combine cream cheese, garlic salt, chives and chervil. Blend well. Refrigerate at least 2 hours. Cut bread into rounds with a biscuit cutter. Spread rounds with cream cheese mixture. Top with a cucumber slice. Garnish each open-faced sandwich with a sprig of dill weed.

*24 to 48 sandwiches depending on size of bread rounds*

# BLT Bites

*Simple to prepare and delicious!*

| | | | |
|---|---|---|---|
| 1 | (3-ounce) jar real bacon bits | 40 | thin wheat crackers or bread rounds |
| 3 | tablespoons mayonnaise, or to taste | 20 | grape tomatoes, halved Lettuce, for garnish |

Combine bacon bits and mayonnaise. Mound 1 teaspoon mixture onto cracker. Top with tomato half. For color, add a tiny sliver of lettuce. Pop into mouth!

*40 appetizers*

*May also use bacon and mayonnaise mixture to stuff cherry tomatoes. So tomato will sit up, cut a thin slice off the bottom. Carefully scoop out pulp. Place upside down on paper towels to drain. Spoon mixture into tomatoes. Sprinkle with snipped parsley.*

Chervil is a member of the parsley family. Sometimes referred to as "gourmet parsley," chervil is sweeter and more fragrant than parsley.

## Stuffed Dates

1 (6-ounce) package pitted dates

1 (8-ounce) package cream cheese, softened

30-35 pecan halves

Powdered sugar

Fill each date with 1 teaspoon cream cheese. Top with pecan half. Roll in powdered sugar.

*30 to 35 dates*

## No Bake Snack Mix

3 tablespoons olive oil

1 tablespoon
Italian seasoning

1 (7-ounce) box baked
snack crackers

4 cups small pretzels

1 (12-ounce) can peanuts

¼ cup grated
Parmesan cheese

In a large zip-top plastic bag, combine oil and seasoning. Knead well. Add crackers, pretzels and peanuts. Gently shake to coat well with oil mixture. Add cheese and gently shake to mix ingredients. May be stored in the bag for 5 days.

*2 quarts*

# Shrimp Tea Sandwiches

| | | | |
|---|---|---|---|
| 1 | (8-ounce) package cream cheese, softened | 1½ | tablespoons mayonnaise |
| 1 | (7½-ounce) can shrimp, rinsed, drained and chopped | 2 | tablespoons chili sauce |
| | | 1½ | tablespoons dill pickle relish |
| 1 | teaspoon Worcestershire sauce | 3 | dashes Tabasco sauce, or to taste |
| ½ | teaspoon curry powder | 1 | teaspoon fresh lemon juice |
| 2 | dashes cayenne pepper, or to taste | 2 | loaves thinly sliced white bread, crusts removed |

In a medium bowl, combine all ingredients, except bread. Spread mixture on 1 bread slice and top with another slice. With a serrated knife, cut sandwich on the diagonal both ways to make 4 triangles. Cut ⅛ inch off each corner to make a neater edge. Serve sandwich standing up on a platter.

*96 sandwiches*

# SNACK!

| | | | |
|---|---|---|---|
| 1 | (16-ounce) box toasted oatmeal squares cereal | 2 | cups chow mein noodles |
| 2 | cups round toasted oat cereal | 4 | tablespoons butter |
| | | 1 | cup white corn syrup |
| 2 | cups small pretzels, broken, if desired | 1 | cup firmly packed light brown sugar |
| 2 | cups nuts | 1 | teaspoon vanilla |
| | | ½ | teaspoon baking soda |

Preheat oven to 250°F. In a large bowl, mix cereals, pretzels, nuts and noodles. Transfer to a roasting pan sprayed with nonstick cooking spray. In a heavy saucepan over medium heat, combine butter, corn syrup and brown sugar. Bring mixture to a boil. Remove from heat. Add vanilla and baking soda. Stir well. Pour over cereal mixture, stirring well. Bake 1 hour, stirring every 15 minutes.

*4 quarts*

*For oatmeal squares cereal, may substitute 7 cups popped popcorn or substitute 3 cups rice squares cereal for pretzels.*

# Old-Fashioned Ice Box Cheese Wafers

*Ideal for Christmas gifts!*

| | | | |
|---|---|---|---|
| 8 | ounces shredded sharp Cheddar cheese, room temperature | ¼ | teaspoon cayenne pepper, or to taste |
| ½ | cup butter, softened | 1½ | cups sifted all-purpose flour |
| ½ | teaspoon salt | | Pecan halves (optional) |

Cream cheese, butter, salt and cayenne pepper until blended. Add flour. Work dough with your hands until mixture forms a ball. Roll into a long roll about the diameter of a quarter. Wrap in wax paper. Store in refrigerator 8 hours.

Preheat oven to 350°F. Slice roll into ¼-inch thick slices. Place on a baking sheet. Top with pecan half. Bake 10 minutes or until lightly browned. May serve warm or at room temperature. Store in an airtight container. Freezes well.

*5 dozen*

*May keep in refrigerator for 2 weeks before baking.*

# Bleu Cheese Frosted Grapes

| | | | |
|---|---|---|---|
| 4 | ounces bleu cheese, crumbled | 30 | seedless green grapes |
| 1 | (3-ounce) package cream cheese, softened | 1 | cup finely chopped pecans, toasted |

With an electric mixer on medium speed, beat bleu cheese and cream cheese until smooth. Chill 1 hour. Remove and discard grape stems. Wash grapes and pat completely dry. Wrap enough cheese mixture around each grape to cover. Roll in pecans and chill 1 hour.

*30 grapes*

## Ambrosia Spread

1 (8-ounce) container cream cheese with pineapple, softened

¼ cup flaked coconut, toasted

¼ cup chopped pecans, toasted

1 (11-ounce) can Mandarin oranges, drained and chopped

Banana Tea Bread (see index)

Combine cream cheese, coconut and pecans. Fold in chopped oranges. Cover and chill. Serve as a spread for Banana Tea Bread. Also good for finger sandwiches.

*1⅔ cups*

## Lamar Graduation Punch

| | | | |
|---|---|---|---|
| ½ | gallon pineapple juice, save carton | 1 | (12-ounce) can frozen lemonade concentrate, undiluted |
| ½ | gallon orange juice, save carton | 1 | cup sugar |
| | | 2 | (2-liter) bottles ginger ale |

Mix juices, lemonade concentrate and sugar. Pour into the saved cartons. Freeze solid. Place in refrigerator 6 hours. Let stand at room temperature 2 hours. To serve, break mixture into chunks. Add ginger ale and stir until slushy.

*3 gallons*

*Note: Must be prepared at least one day in advance.*

## Frozen Margarita Punch

*Great way to serve margaritas to a crowd!*

| | | | |
|---|---|---|---|
| 4 | (12-ounce) cans frozen limeade, thawed | 2 | (2-liter) bottles lemon-lime soda |
| 3 | quarts water | | Margarita salt, for garnish |
| 3 | cups triple sec | | Limes, for garnish |
| 3 | cups tequila | | |

Combine limeade, water, triple sec and tequila in zip-lock plastic bags or a wide mouth container. Freeze at least 8 hours stirring at least twice. Remove from freezer, 30 minutes prior to serving. Break into chunks. Add lemon-lime soda. Stir until slushy. Wet rims of margarita glasses with lime wedge. Dip glass rim into margarita salt. Pour in punch. Garnish with lime slices.

*2½ gallons*

May in Mississippi is usually pleasant and warm. Some years, however, summer begins early, and high school graduation in an unairconditioned gymnasium can poach even the sturdiest grandparent. Each year the Lamar School graduation refreshments committee prepares a traditional punch, an heirloom recipe, said to have saved numerous relatives from severe dehydration in years of high temperatures and long speeches. In more recent years, the recipe, carefully preserved on an old typewritten recipe card, has posed a unique "ginger ale" problem for the committee. Old bottles of ginger ale were not the same size as new

# Cranberry Pineapple Punch

| | | | | |
|---|---|---|---|---|
| 1 | quart pineapple juice | | 1 | tablespoon almond extract |
| 1 | quart cranberry juice cocktail | | 1 | (2-liter) bottle ginger ale |
| 1 ½ | cups sugar | | | |

Combine juices, sugar and almond extract. Refrigerate until ready to use. Prior to serving, combine juice mixture and ginger ale in a punch bowl.

*1 gallon*

*Use a ginger ale ice float, if desired.*

# Sparkling Peach Punch

**Frozen Ring Mold**

| | | | |
|---|---|---|---|
| | Fresh whole strawberries | | Kiwi, sliced |
| | White grapes | 1 | (32-ounce) bottle white grape juice |

**Punch**

| | | | |
|---|---|---|---|
| 2 | (10-ounce) cans frozen peach daiquiri mix, thawed | 1 | (2-liter) bottle ginger ale |
| 2 | (25.4-ounce) bottles sparkling white grape juice | 1 | (1-liter) bottle club soda |

Layer fresh fruit in a ring mold. Pour white grape juice over fruit. Freeze until solid. For punch, pour daiquiri mix, juice, ginger ale and club soda in a large punch bowl. Float frozen mold in punch bowl.

*1½ gallons*

*For alcoholic punch, substitute 2 bottles of champagne for 2 bottles of sparkling white grape juice.*

## Mock Champagne Punch

Combine equal portions of chilled white grape juice and chilled ginger ale. For a pretty visual presentation, float fresh strawberries in the punch.

## Iced Tea Punch

|   | Water | 1 | (6-ounce) can frozen |
|---|-------|---|----------------------|
| 8 | regular sized tea bags |  | orange juice |
| 1½ | cups sugar |  | concentrate |
| 1 | (6-ounce) can frozen lemonade concentrate |  |  |

Bring 1 quart water to a boil. Add tea bags and steep 15 to 20 minutes. Discard tea bags. Dissolve sugar and concentrates in tea. Add water to make 1 gallon.

*1 gallon*

## Summer Fruit Smoothie

| ½ | cup milk | 2 | tablespoons sugar |
|---|----------|---|-------------------|
| ½ | cup cold apple juice | ½ | teaspoon vanilla |
| 2 | cups fresh fruit chunks, strawberries, bananas or peeled peaches | 10 | ice cubes |

Place all ingredients except ice cubes in blender. Blend until smooth. Add ice cubes and blend until thickened. Serve immediately.

*3 cups*

---

### Blueberry Lemonade

**2 cups fresh blueberries**

**⅓ cup water**

**½ gallon prepared lemonade**

**Sugar to taste**

Place blueberries and water in a saucepan. Simmer while stirring 5 minutes or until juices have formed. Strain blueberry juice and combine with lemonade. Add sugar to desired sweetness. Serve over ice.

*9 cups*

### Hot Chocolate Mix
*Great for Christmas presents*

| 1 | (25.6-ounce) box dry milk powder |
|---|--------------------------------|
| 1 | (16-ounce) carton chocolate flavored powdered drink mix |
| 1 | cup powdered sugar |
| 1 | cup powdered non-dairy coffee creamer |

Combine all ingredients well. Store in an airtight container. For hot chocolate, fill cup half full with chocolate mix. Add hot water to fill cup and stir.

*7 cups dry mix*

*Wonderful to have around the house during cold weather! The kids love it!*

# Brunch & Breads

# A Place Where Serenity Reigns

*In 1854, Irish immigrant John Dunn recognized the natural beauty and the energy-producing potential of the Chunky River and its over sixty-foot falls. There, he built a cotton mill that the Confederate government confiscated and used for manufacturing blankets, hats, and knives.*

*After the Civil War ended, Dunn's building became a grist mill for grinding flour and corn meal and served as a site for many area dances. Today, the industrial enterprises have closed, and a relocated grist mill marks the site of Dunn's original mill. The area's beauty and serenity remain. The sixty-nine acre Dunn's Falls Waterpark is now a peaceful wildlife refuge and popular picnic destination where many families enjoy afternoons of wading, swimming, fishing, and hiking.*

# Caramel French Toast

*Impress your overnight guest with this fabulous dish!*

| | | | |
|---|---|---|---|
| 1½ | cups firmly packed brown sugar | 2½ | cups milk |
| ¾ | cup butter or margarine | 1 | tablespoon vanilla |
| 6 | tablespoons light corn syrup | ¼ | teaspoon salt |
| 10 | (1¼-inch) French bread slices | 3 | tablespoons sugar |
| 4 | eggs, beaten | 1½ | teaspoons ground cinnamon |
| | | ¼ | cup butter or margarine, melted |

In a medium saucepan, combine brown sugar, ¾ cup butter and corn syrup. Cook over medium heat, stirring constantly for 5 minutes or until bubbly. Pour syrup evenly into a lightly greased 13x9-inch baking dish. Place bread slices over syrup. Combine eggs, milk, vanilla and salt. Stir well and pour over bread. Cover and refrigerate at least 8 hours.

Preheat oven to 350°F. Combine sugar and cinnamon. Sprinkle evenly over soaked bread. Drizzle ¼ cup melted butter over top. Bake, uncovered, 45 to 50 minutes or until golden and bubbly.

*10 servings*

*Note: Must be refrigerated 8 hours before baking.*

Caramel French Toast is also a fabulous dessert! Just add 1 cup chopped pecans to syrup mixture. To serve, top each serving with whipped cream and fanned strawberry.

# Bacon Batons

| | | | |
|---|---|---|---|
| 1 | pound regular sliced bacon, room temperature | 1¼ | cups firmly packed brown sugar |
| | | 1 | tablespoon ground cinnamon (optional) |

Preheat oven to 350°F. Cut each slice of bacon in half, crosswise. Mix brown sugar and cinnamon together and thoroughly coat each slice of bacon. Twist slices and place on a rack in a broiler pan or jelly-roll pan. Bake 15 to 20 minutes or until bacon is crisp and sugar is bubbly. Watch closely as sugar burns quickly. Cool on foil. Serve at room temperature.

*8 to 10 servings*

*May be made hours ahead and left at room temperature.*

# Sun-Dried Tomato and Basil Egg Soufflé

## Sausage Balls

2 cups biscuit baking mix

1 pound hot sausage

1 (8-ounce) package extra sharp Cheddar cheese, shredded

Preheat oven to 350°F. In a bowl, combine all ingredients. Roll into 1-inch balls. Bake on cookie sheets 25 minutes.

*40 to 50 sausage balls*

| | |
|---|---|
| 4 | tablespoons butter, softened and divided |
| 8 | slices dry bread with crust |
| 6 | ounces sharp Cheddar cheese, shredded |
| 5 | eggs, beaten |
| 2½ | cups milk |
| ¼ | teaspoon Tabasco sauce |
| ⅛ | teaspoon ground white pepper |
| ½ | teaspoon salt |
| 1½ | tablespoons prepared basil pesto (or see index) |
| 4 | sun-dried tomatoes, oil-packed, drained and chopped |

Butter an 8x8-inch baking dish. Spread remaining butter on bread slices. Put one layer of bread in the pan, buttered side up. Top with half of cheese. Repeat layers. Whisk together eggs and remaining ingredients and pour over layers. Cover and refrigerate overnight.

Preheat oven to 350°F. In the upper one-third of the oven, bake 30 to 40 minutes or until puffy and brown.

*4 servings*

*Note: Must be refrigerated 8 hours.*

# Texas Breakfast Taquitos

| | | | |
|---|---|---|---|
| 12 | large flour tortillas | ½ | cup chopped red or green bell pepper |
| 8 | eggs, scrambled | ½ | cup sliced ripe olives |
| 1 | pound bulk sausage, browned and drained | 6 | ounces sour cream |
| ½ | cup chopped tomato | 1 | (8-ounce) jar salsa |
| ½ | cup chopped onion | 1 | cup shredded Cheddar cheese, divided |

Preheat oven to 325°F. Lightly moisten each tortilla with water. Fill each tortilla with equal portions of egg, sausage and vegetables. Add 1 tablespoon sour cream and 1 tablespoon salsa to each tortilla. Sprinkle with half of the cheese, rollup and secure with toothpick if needed. Place rolled tortillas in a lightly greased 13x9-inch baking dish. Sprinkle with remaining cheese. Bake 20 to 30 minutes. Top with remaining salsa.

*12 servings*

# Herbed Brunch Casserole

| | | | |
|---|---|---|---|
| 2 | cups herbed seasoned croutons | 3¼ | cups milk, divided |
| | | 1 | teaspoon dry mustard |
| 1½ | cups shredded Cheddar cheese | 1 | teaspoon salt |
| | | ¼ | teaspoon onion salt |
| 1¼ | pounds mild bulk sausage, cooked and drained | 1 | (10¾-ounce) can cream of mushroom soup |
| 5 | eggs | | |

Grease a 13x9-inch baking dish. In order, layer croutons, cheese and sausage. Mix eggs, 3 cups milk, mustard and salts together. Pour over layers. Cover and refrigerate 8 hours or overnight.

Preheat oven to 325°F. Combine soup with remaining ¼ cup milk. Pour over top of casserole. Bake 1½ hours.

*8 servings*

*Note: Must be refrigerated 8 hours before cooking.*

## Orange Toast

½ cup butter, softened

½ cup sugar

2 tablespoons orange zest

2 tablespoons
orange juice concentrate

1 loaf very thinly sliced
white bread, crusts removed

Preheat oven to 350°F.
Combine all ingredients
except bread. Spread on
bread and cut into thirds.
Bake 15 to 20 minutes or
until bubbly.

*60 servings*

Pretty Presentations Catering,
Newton, MS

During "Hollydays" in
Baton Rouge, the food
columnist for
The Times-Picayune
eagerly shared this
recipe. Orange Toast is
a simple, yet elegant
recipe for a morning
brunch or ladies' coffee.

# Ham and Cheese Breakfast Casserole

*Children love this for breakfast or dinner*

| | | | |
|---|---|---|---|
| 6 | frozen hash brown patties | 7 | eggs |
| 2 | cups shredded Cheddar cheese | 1 | cup milk |
| 1 | pound cooked ham, cubed | ½ | teaspoon salt |
| | | ½ | teaspoon dry mustard |

Preheat oven to 350°F. Place hash brown patties in a greased 13x9-inch baking dish. Sprinkle with cheese and ham. In a bowl, beat eggs, milk, salt and mustard. Pour over ham. Cover and bake 1 hour. Uncover and bake an additional 15 to 20 minutes or until edges are golden brown and a knife inserted in the center comes out clean.

*10 to 12 servings*

# Crab Quiche

*Perfect for a ladies luncheon!*

| | | | |
|---|---|---|---|
| 1 | (9-inch) deep-dish pie crust | 2 | green onions, minced |
| 4 | ounces shredded Swiss cheese | ½ | cup sliced mushrooms |
| 3 | eggs | ¼ | cup blanched or slivered almonds |
| 1 | cup half-and-half | 1 | tablespoon fresh lemon juice |
| ¼ | cup all-purpose flour | ¾ | cup fresh lump crabmeat, picked over for shells |
| ¼ | teaspoon dry mustard | | |
| ½ | teaspoon salt | | |

Preheat oven to 350°F. Sprinkle cheese over bottom of pie crust. In a bowl, mix eggs, half-and-half, flour, mustard and salt well with a mixer. Add onions, mushrooms, almonds and lemon juice. Blend well. Fold in crabmeat. Pour into prepared pie crust. Bake 40 minutes or until set. Let stand 15 to 20 minutes before serving to allow setting.

*6 servings*

# Three Cheese Spinach Quiche

| | | | |
|---|---|---|---|
| 2 | (10-ounce) packages frozen chopped spinach, thawed | ¼ | teaspoon ground nutmeg |
| ¼ | cup butter or margarine, divided | ¼ | teaspoon ground black pepper |
| 4 | green onions, chopped | 2 | (9-inch) baked pie shells |
| 2 | (15-ounce) cartons ricotta cheese | 2 | tablespoons Dijon mustard |
| 1 | cup whipping cream | 2 | cups shredded Cheddar cheese |
| 6 | large eggs, beaten | ½ | cup shredded Swiss cheese |
| 1 | teaspoon salt | | |

Preheat oven to 375°F. Drain spinach well. Squeeze out excess moisture by pressing it between layers of paper towels. Melt 2 tablespoons butter in a large skillet over medium heat. Add green onions and sauté 2 minutes or until tender. Add spinach and cook 2 minutes. Remove from heat. Stir in ricotta, cream, eggs, salt, nutmeg and pepper. Brush prepared pie shells with mustard. Pour spinach mixture evenly into pie shells. Sprinkle with cheeses. Dot with remaining butter. Bake 40 to 45 minutes or until set. Let stand 10 to 15 minutes before serving.

*12 to 16 servings*

# Garlic Cheese Grits

| | | | |
|---|---|---|---|
| 1 | cup quick-cooking grits | 1 | (6-ounce) roll garlic cheese, cut into small pieces |
| 4 | cups water | | |
| 1 | teaspoon salt | | |
| 1 | (6-ounce) roll jalapeño cheese, cut into small pieces | ¼ | cup butter or margarine |

Preheat oven to 350°F. Add grits to boiling salted water and reduce heat. Cook 4 to 5 minutes, stirring frequently. Add cheeses and remove from heat. Add butter. Stir until cheeses and butter are melted and well blended. May serve immediately or bake, uncovered in a 1½-quart greased baking dish, 30 minutes.

*4 to 6 servings*

# Shrimp Jambalaya Grits

*Terrific as a casual entrée also!*

| | | | |
|---|---|---|---|
| 1 | tablespoon olive oil | ½ | pound medium shrimp, peeled and deveined |
| 1 | cup chopped yellow onion | 1 | tablespoon minced garlic |
| ½ | cup chopped green bell pepper | ½ | cup peeled, seeded and chopped tomato |
| ½ | cup chopped celery | 6 | cups milk |
| 1½ | teaspoons salt | 2 | cups quick-cooking white grits |
| ⅛ | teaspoon ground black pepper | | |
| ⅛-¼ | teaspoon cayenne pepper | ¼ | cup chopped green onion tops |
| ¼ | pound boiled ham, diced | ¼ | pound sharp Cheddar cheese, shredded |

In a large heavy pot, heat olive oil over medium heat. Add yellow onion, bell pepper, celery, salt and peppers. Cook until vegetables are soft, about 4 minutes. Add ham and shrimp and continue cooking 2 minutes. Add garlic and tomato. Cook for an additional 2 minutes. Add milk and bring to a boil. Stir in grits. Reduce heat. Cover and cook 9 to 10 minutes or until grits are creamy. Add green onion and cheese. Stir until cheese is melted.

*8 servings*

Once upon a time, T.B.'s mother-in-law gave his new bride a simple, handwritten cookbook. The cookbook contained all her new husband's favorite recipes. Fifteen years later, the couple still "lives happily ever after!"

# Fruit and Granola Parfait

*Perfect breakfast for teenage girls*

| | | | |
|---|---|---|---|
| ½ | cup low-fat vanilla yogurt | 1 | medium banana, sliced |
| ¼ | cup nonfat soft-style cream cheese | 1 | medium orange, sectioned |
| 1 | tablespoon honey | 1½ | cups frozen red raspberries, thawed and drained |
| ¼ | teaspoon ground cinnamon | 1 | cup low-fat granola cereal without raisins |
| 2 | kiwis, peeled and sliced | | |

In a small mixing bowl, combine yogurt, cream cheese, honey and cinnamon. Beat with an electric mixer on medium speed until combined. Chill.

To assemble, stir together fruit in another small bowl. Divide one-third of fruit mixture among four parfait glasses. Spoon 2 tablespoons each of cream cheese mixture and granola on top of fruit. Repeat layers. Top with remaining fruit. Chill until serving.

*4 servings*

*Rinsed fresh red raspberries may be substituted for frozen red raspberries.*

# Ham Biscuits with Currant Jelly

*A.E.'s mother makes these biscuits for her four boys and their many cousins. Within minutes they are history!*

### Biscuits

| | | | |
|---|---|---|---|
| 2 | cups all-purpose flour | 2 | teaspoons sugar |
| 1 | tablespoon baking powder | 1 | teaspoon salt |
| | | 1 | cup whipping cream |

### Ham Mixture

| | | | |
|---|---|---|---|
| 1 | pound precooked ham, cut in large pieces | 6 | tablespoons yellow mustard |
| 6 | ounces red currant jelly | | |

Preheat oven to 425°F. For the biscuits combine flour, baking powder, sugar and salt. Stir in cream. On a floured surface, roll out biscuits and cut with a 1-inch biscuit cutter. Place biscuits on a cookie sheet. Bake 15 minutes. For ham mixture, place ham in a food processor and finely chop. Add jelly and mustard. Process until mixed. Slice biscuits. Spread ham mixture on bottom half of biscuit and replace top. Place on a cookie sheet and top with dot of butter. Preheat oven to 325°F. Bake until warm.

*20 biscuits*

## Tomato Bacon Rounds

| | | | |
|---|---|---|---|
| 10 | slices cooked bacon, crumbled | 1 | cup shredded Swiss cheese |
| ½ | cup mayonnaise | ⅛ | teaspoon garlic powder, or to taste |
| 1 | medium tomato, chopped and drained | 1 | (10-count) can flaky butter-tasting biscuits |
| 1 | tablespoon chopped onion | | |

Preheat oven to 350°F. Mix all ingredients except biscuits. Divide each biscuit into two rounds. Top each round with a spoonful of mixture and bake on a pizza stone or a cookie sheet in the oven 15 minutes or until brown.

*20 rounds*

## Light, Crisp Waffles

| | | | |
|---|---|---|---|
| ¾ | cup all-purpose flour | ¼ | cup milk |
| ¼ | cup cornstarch | 6 | tablespoons vegetable oil |
| ½ | teaspoon salt | | |
| ½ | teaspoon baking powder | 1 | egg, separated |
| ½ | teaspoon baking soda | 1 | tablespoon sugar |
| ¾ | cup buttermilk | ½ | teaspoon vanilla |

Preheat oven to 200°F and preheat waffle iron. Sift together flour, cornstarch, salt, baking powder and baking soda. Set aside. Measure buttermilk, milk and oil in a 2-cup measuring cup. Mix in egg yolk and set aside. Beat egg white in a small bowl with an electric hand mixer until soft peaks almost form. Sprinkle in sugar and continue to beat until white and glossy. Beat in vanilla. Pour buttermilk mixture into flour mixture. Whisk until just mixed. Fold in egg white. Pour ¼ to ½ cup batter onto hot waffle iron and cook until browned. Set waffles directly on oven rack to keep warm. Do not stack.

*4 to 5 waffles*

### Belgian Waffles

3 eggs

1½ cups buttermilk

1 teaspoon baking soda

1¾ cups all-purpose flour

2 teaspoons baking powder

½ teaspoon salt

½ cup vegetable oil

Preheat Belgian waffle maker. In a mixing bowl, combine ingredients in order listed. Pour ⅔ cup of batter onto hot greased Belgian waffle maker. Bake 3 minutes.

*8 waffles*

# Blueberry Buttermilk Pancakes

| | | | |
|---|---|---|---|
| 1 | cup all-purpose flour | 2 | tablespoons vegetable oil |
| 1 | tablespoon sugar | ½ | cup blueberries, rinsed and drained (omit if preparing Blueberry Sauce) |
| 1 | tablespoon baking powder | | |
| ½ | teaspoon baking soda | | |
| ¼ | teaspoon salt | | Blueberry Sauce (see accompanying recipe) |
| 1 | egg, beaten | | |
| 1 | cup buttermilk | | |

Mix flour, sugar, baking powder, baking soda and salt. Stir egg into buttermilk and add oil. Add to flour mixture, stirring until smooth. Fold in blueberries. For each pancake, pour ¼ cup of batter onto a hot, lightly greased griddle or skillet. Turn pancakes when tops are covered with bubbles and edges are cooked. Serve with syrup or Blueberry Sauce.

*8 pancakes*

# Blueberry Sauce

*Delicious over pancakes or ice cream!*

| | | | |
|---|---|---|---|
| 3 | tablespoons butter | ⅛ | teaspoon salt, or to taste |
| 1½ | tablespoons cornstarch | | |
| ⅔ | cup sugar | ½ | cup water |
| ¼ | teaspoon ground nutmeg | 2 | cups fresh blueberries, rinsed and drained |

Combine butter and cornstarch in a saucepan. Add sugar, nutmeg, salt, water and blueberries. Cook over low heat, stirring constantly until thickened.

*2½ cups*

Use a meat baster to "squeeze" your pancake batter onto the hot griddle - perfectly shaped pancakes every time.

52

# Apricot Almond Coffee Cake

| | | | | |
|---|---|---|---|---|
| 1 | cup butter, softened | 1 | teaspoon baking powder |
| 2 | cups sugar | ¼ | teaspoon salt |
| 2 | large eggs | 1 | cup sour cream |
| 1 | teaspoon almond extract | 1 | cup sliced almonds |
| 2 | cups all-purpose flour | 1 | (10-ounce) jar apricot preserves |

Preheat oven to 350°F. With an electric mixer on medium speed, cream butter 2 minutes. Add sugar, beat 7 minutes. Add eggs one at a time, mixing well after each addition. Add almond extract. In a separate bowl, combine flour, baking powder and salt. Add to creamed mixture alternating with sour cream, beginning and ending with flour mixture. Mix on low speed until blended. Place one third of batter in a greased and floured Bundt pan. Sprinkle half of almonds on top of batter and dot with half of preserves. Pour in remaining batter. Top with remaining almonds and preserves. Bake 50 to 55 minutes. Cool in the pan 15 minutes. Remove from the pan and cool on a wire rack.

*12 to 14 servings*

A romance may begin over pancakes. E.H. worked one summer as a "hotcake" girl at Yosemite National Park, where she met her husband Bill. Now she continues to make hotcakes for Bill, their children and grandchildren.

# Sour Cream Coffee Cake

### Cake

| | | | |
|---|---|---|---|
| ½ | cup butter, softened | 1 | teaspoon baking powder |
| ½ | cup margarine, softened | ½ | teaspoon salt |
| 2 | cups plus 2 tablespoons sugar, divided | 1 | cup sour cream |
| 2 | eggs | 1 | tablespoon ground cinnamon |
| 1¾ | cups all-purpose flour | ½ | cup chopped pecans |

### Glaze

| | | | |
|---|---|---|---|
| 2 | tablespoons butter, melted | 1 | teaspoon vanilla |
| 2 | cups powdered sugar, sifted | 2-3 | tablespoons evaporated milk |

Preheat oven to 325°F. Cream butter, margarine and 2 cups sugar until light and fluffy. Add eggs, beating well. In a separate bowl, sift together flour, baking powder and salt. Add flour mixture to egg mixture alternating with sour cream. Pour half of batter into a greased and floured Bundt pan. Mix cinnamon with 2 tablespoons sugar and sprinkle half over batter in the pan. Top with pecans. Top with remaining batter and sprinkle with remaining sugar mixture. Bake 40 to 55 minutes. Cool in the pan 10 minutes. Invert onto wire rack to cool completely.

For glaze, mix butter, sugar and vanilla adding enough milk until proper consistency is achieved. Pour over cooled cake.

*12 to 14 servings*

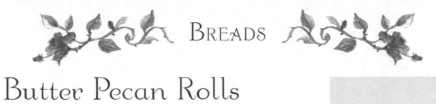
# Butter Pecan Rolls

### Dough

| | | | |
|---|---|---|---|
| 1 | (¼-ounce) package active dry yeast | ¼ | cup sugar |
| ¼ | cup warm water (105°F to 115°F) | 1 | teaspoon salt |
| | | 3¼ | cups sifted all-purpose flour, divided |
| 1 | cup milk | 1 | egg, beaten |
| ¼ | cup vegetable shortening | | |

### Filling

| | | | |
|---|---|---|---|
| 2 | tablespoons butter, melted | 2 | teaspoons ground cinnamon |
| ½ | cup sugar | | |

### Topping

| | | | |
|---|---|---|---|
| ½ | cup firmly packed brown sugar | 1 | tablespoon light corn syrup |
| ¼ | cup butter or margarine, softened or melted | ½ | cup chopped nuts |

To prepare dough, soften yeast in warm water. In a large saucepan, heat milk until bubbles form and milk is scalded. Add shortening, sugar and salt. Cool to lukewarm. Add 1 cup flour and beat well. Beat in softened yeast and egg. Gradually add remaining flour, ½ cup at a time, beating well after each addition to form a soft dough. Place dough in a lightly oiled bowl, turning once to coat. Cover and let rise in warm place until doubled, about 1½ to 2 hours. Punch down and turn out on a lightly floured surface. Divide dough in half. Roll each piece into a 12 x 8-inch rectangle.

For filling, brush each rectangle with melted butter. Combine sugar with cinnamon and sprinkle over dough. Begin with long side and roll up. Seal edge. Cut each roll into eight sections.

Combine brown sugar, butter and light corn syrup, for topping. Divide topping evenly into 2 (9-inch) cake pans. Sprinkle nuts over each pan. Place rolls in the pans. Let rise until doubled. Preheat oven to 375°F. Bake 25 minutes. Invert onto serving plate immediately.

*16 rolls*

*May be prepared ahead and frozen.*

## Canned Buttered Biscuits

**3 tablespoons butter**

**½ teaspoon celery seed**

**½ teaspoon onion or garlic salt**

**1 (10-count) can butter biscuits**

**Grated Parmesan cheese**

Preheat oven to recommended setting for canned biscuits. Melt butter and add celery seed and onion or garlic salt. Pour in the bottom of a 9-inch round cake pan. Quarter the biscuits and place in the pan. Bake according to biscuit directions. Remove from oven and sprinkle with Parmesan cheese.

*6 servings*

When summer rolls around, drive just a few miles outside of Meridian and pick the freshest, plumpest blueberries to make blueberry muffins or Blueberry Pancakes with Blueberry Sauce (see index). Johnson's Blueberry Farm is a step back to a simpler time when life's greatest stress was losing the blueberry pie-eating contest. Ah, life in the slow lane.

# Captain Lord Mansion Blueberry Muffins
*Moist and delicious*

| | | | |
|---|---|---|---|
| 2 | cups all-purpose flour | 2 | extra large eggs |
| 2 | teaspoons baking powder | 1 | teaspoon vanilla |
| ½ | teaspoon salt | ½ | cup milk |
| ½ | cup margarine, softened | 2½ | cups blueberries, rinsed, divided |
| 1 | cup sugar | | Sugar, for topping |

Preheat oven to 375°F. Mix flour, baking powder and salt. Set aside. Beat margarine with an electric mixer until fluffy. Beat in sugar until well blended. Add eggs, one at a time, beating well after each. Stir in vanilla. Stir in half of flour mixture, then half of milk. Repeat. Fold in 2 cups blueberries. Mash remaining blueberries. Fold into batter. Spoon into greased and floured muffin tins. Sprinkle tops with sugar. Bake 25 to 30 minutes. Let cool 30 minutes.

*1 dozen muffins*

# Applesauce Muffins

| | | | |
|---|---|---|---|
| 1 | cup butter, softened | 2 | teaspoons ground allspice |
| 2 | cups sugar | 4 | cups all-purpose flour |
| 2 | eggs | 2 | teaspoons baking soda |
| 2 | cups applesauce | 1 | cup chopped pecans |
| 1 | teaspoon salt | | |
| 1 | teaspoon ground cloves | | |
| 3 | teaspoons ground cinnamon | | |

Preheat oven to 350°F. Cream butter and sugar. Add eggs mixing well. Add applesauce and spices. In a separate bowl, sift together flour and baking soda. Add to applesauce mixture, mixing well. Add nuts. Spoon into greased miniature muffin tins. Bake 8 to 10 minutes.

*3 dozen miniature muffins*

# BREADS

## Cherry Mini-Muffins

| | | | |
|---|---|---|---|
| 1 | cup chopped pecans | ½ | teaspoon baking powder |
| 1 | cup sugar | 4 | tablespoons maraschino |
| 1 | cup firmly packed dark | | cherry juice |
| | brown sugar | 5 | dozen maraschino |
| ½ | cup butter, softened | | cherries |
| 4 | eggs, lightly beaten | | Powdered sugar |
| 2 | cups all-purpose flour | | |

Preheat oven to 400°F. Butter miniature muffin tins and sprinkle pecans on the bottom. Cream sugars and butter. Add eggs mixing well. Sift flour and baking powder. Stir flour mixture into creamed mixture. Stir in cherry juice. Into each muffin cup, drop 1 teaspoon batter on top of pecans. Place whole cherry in center of batter and push down. Bake 12 minutes. Let cool. Roll muffins in powdered sugar.

*5 dozen miniature muffins*

## Orange Muffins

| | | | |
|---|---|---|---|
| 1 | cup butter, softened | ½ | cup chopped pecans |
| 1 | cup sugar | | Zest of 2 oranges |
| 2 | eggs | | Juice of 2 oranges |
| 1 | teaspoon baking soda | 1 | cup firmly packed brown |
| 1 | cup buttermilk | | sugar |
| 2 | cups sifted all-purpose | | |
| | flour | | |

Preheat oven to 400°F. Cream butter and sugar. Add eggs and beat well. Dissolve baking soda in buttermilk and add to butter mixture. Add flour and mix well. Stir in pecans and zest. Fill greased muffin tins two-thirds full. Bake 20 to 25 minutes. For glaze, combine juice and brown sugar. Spoon over warm muffins. Remove muffins from tins before sauce thickens.

*3 dozen muffins*

# Sweet Potato Muffins

| | | | |
|---|---|---|---|
| ½ | cup butter, softened | ¼ | teaspoon ground nutmeg |
| 1¼ | cups sugar | ¼ | teaspoon salt |
| 1¼ | cups mashed sweet potatoes | 1 | cup milk |
| 2 | eggs | ½ | cup chopped pecans or walnuts |
| 1½ | cups all-purpose flour | ½ | cup raisins |
| 2 | tablespoons baking powder | | Cinnamon sugar |
| 1 | teaspoon ground cinnamon | | |

For cinnamon sugar, mix 2 parts sugar with 1 part ground cinnamon.

Preheat oven to 400°F. Cream butter, sugar and sweet potatoes until smooth. Add eggs, blending well. In a separate bowl, sift flour, baking powder, cinnamon, nutmeg and salt. Add flour mixture, alternating with milk to the egg mixture. Do not over mix. Fold in nuts and raisins. Fill greased muffin tins two-thirds full. Lightly sprinkle cinnamon sugar on top of each muffin. Bake 25 minutes or until done.

*2 dozen muffins*

# Sunrise Muffins

| | | | |
|---|---|---|---|
| 2 | cups all-purpose flour | ½ | cup flaked coconut |
| 1¼ | cups sugar | ½ | cup chopped pecans |
| 2 | teaspoons baking soda | 3 | eggs |
| 2 | teaspoons ground cinnamon | 1 | cup vegetable oil |
| ½ | teaspoon salt | 1 | apple, peeled, cored and shredded |
| 2 | cups grated carrot | 2 | teaspoons vanilla |
| ½ | cup raisins | | |

Preheat oven to 350°F. In a large mixing bowl, combine flour, sugar, baking soda, cinnamon and salt. Stir in carrot, raisins, coconut and pecans. In a separate bowl, combine eggs, oil, apple and vanilla. Add to flour mixture. Stir until just combined. Spoon into greased muffin tins. Bake 15 to 18 minutes.

*18 muffins*

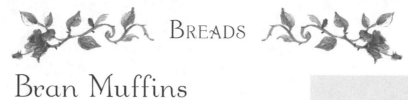

## Bran Muffins

| | | | |
|---|---|---|---|
| 1 | quart buttermilk | 1 | cup vegetable oil |
| 3 | cups sugar | 5 | cups all-purpose flour |
| 5 | teaspoons baking soda | 1 | (20-ounce) box bran |
| 1 | teaspoon salt | | flake cereal with |
| 4 | eggs | | raisins less 2 cups |

Preheat oven to 400°F. Mix all ingredients except for cereal with a mixer. Stir in cereal. Spoon into greased muffin tins. Bake 20 minutes. Let cool in the pan 10 minutes before removing.

*5 dozen muffins*

*For whole-wheat bran muffins, whole-wheat flour may be substituted for all-purpose flour.*

*For chocolate whole-wheat bran muffins, substitute 4 cups whole-wheat flour, 1 cup cocoa, and 1 (6-ounce) bag semi-sweet chocolate chips for all-purpose flour.*

*Batter will keep in refrigerator up to three weeks.*

## Banana Tea Bread

| | | | |
|---|---|---|---|
| 2¼ | cups sugar | 3 | cups cake flour |
| 1½ | cups butter, softened | 1½ | teaspoons baking soda |
| 3 | eggs, beaten | ⅛ | teaspoon salt |
| 6-7 | ripe bananas, mashed | 2-3 | cups chopped pecans |

Preheat oven to 300°F. Cream sugar, butter and eggs. Add mashed bananas. In a separate bowl, combine flour, baking soda and salt. Add creamed mixture to flour mixture a little at a time, mixing well. Add nuts. Pour batter into a well-greased and floured tube or Bundt cake pan. Bake 1½ hours or until a knife inserted in the center comes out clean.

*12 to 15 servings*

*Exceptional drizzled with Never Fail Caramel Icing (see index)*

### Pineapple Banana Bread

1 cup chopped nuts

3 cups all-purpose flour

1 teaspoon baking soda

2 cups sugar

1 teaspoon salt

½ teaspoon ground cinnamon

1½ cups vegetable oil

3 eggs, beaten

1 (8-ounce) can crushed pineapple, undrained

2 cups diced bananas

1½ teaspoons vanilla

Preheat oven to 350°F. Mix all ingredients. Bake in 2 greased and floured 9x5-inch loaf pans. Bake 1 hour or until done. Freezes well.

*2 loaves*

59

# Poppy Seed Bread

### Bread

| | | | |
|---|---|---|---|
| 3 | cups all-purpose flour | 2-4 | tablespoons poppy seeds |
| 1½ | teaspoons salt | | |
| 1½ | teaspoons baking powder | 1½ | teaspoons vanilla |
| 2¼ | cups sugar | 1½ | teaspoons almond extract |
| 3 | eggs | 1½ | teaspoons butter flavoring |
| 1½ | cups milk | | |
| 1 | cup plus 2 tablespoons vegetable oil | | |

### Glaze

| | | | |
|---|---|---|---|
| ¾ | cup powdered sugar | ¼ | teaspoon butter flavoring |
| ¼ | cup orange juice | | |
| ½ | teaspoon almond extract | ½ | teaspoon vanilla |

Preheat oven to 325°F. In a large bowl, add bread ingredients in the order listed. Beat for 2 minutes. Pour batter into 2 greased and floured 9x5-inch loaf pans. Bake 1 hour or until done. For glaze, mix ingredients until smooth. Glaze bread while hot.

*2 loaves*

# Zucchini Bread

| | | | |
|---|---|---|---|
| 3 | eggs, well beaten | 1 | tablespoon ground cinnamon |
| 1 | cup vegetable oil | | |
| 1 | tablespoon vanilla | 1 | teaspoon baking powder |
| 2 | cups sugar | | |
| 2 | cups shredded zucchini | 1 | teaspoon salt |
| 3 | cups all-purpose flour | 1 | teaspoon baking soda |

Preheat oven to 350°F. Mix together all ingredients. Pour into 2 greased and floured 9x5-loaf pans. Bake 40 minutes or until a toothpick comes out clean.

*2 loaves*

*May add 1 cup drained crushed pineapple and/or 1 cup chopped pecans.*

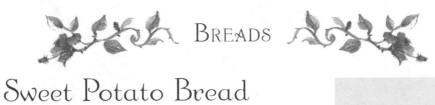

# Sweet Potato Bread

| | | | | |
|---|---|---|---|---|
| 2 | cups mashed sweet potatoes | 1 | teaspoon ground nutmeg |
| 3½ | cups sugar | 1 | teaspoon ground allspice |
| 1 | cup vegetable oil | 1 | cup chopped pecans |
| 4 | eggs | 1 | cup chopped dates or raisins |
| 3½ | cups all-purpose flour | 1 | teaspoon vanilla |
| 2 | teaspoons baking soda | | |
| 1½ | teaspoons salt | | |
| 1½ | teaspoons ground cinnamon | | |

Preheat oven to 350°F. Combine sweet potatoes, sugar and oil. Add eggs, one at a time, mixing well after each addition. In a separate bowl, sift together flour, baking soda, salt, cinnamon, nutmeg and allspice. Stir in pecans and dates or raisins. Add flour mixture to sweet potato mixture, stirring well. Add vanilla. Pour batter into 2 greased and floured 9x5-inch loaf pans. Bake 1 hour or until done.

*2 loaves*

*For pumpkin bread, substitute pumpkin for sweet potatoes.*

T.S.'s physician husband makes his famous secret recipe pumpkin bread for his friends at the hospital. Once, when he moved away, the recipe was his going-away present to them!

# Butter Crescent Rolls

## How to "Proof" Yeast

To be sure the yeast you are using is still active, "proof" it. Dissolve 1 (¼-ounce) package active dry yeast in ¼ cup of warm water (105°F to 115°F). A pinch of sugar may be added to the mixture. Set mixture aside in a warm place for five to ten minutes. If it begins to expand and bubble, the yeast is active and can leaven bread. If it does not expand and bubble, discard it and try another package.

| | | | |
|---|---|---|---|
| 2 | (¼-ounce) packages active dry yeast | 1 | cup sugar |
| 2 | cups warm water (105°F to 115°F) | 1½ | teaspoons salt |
| 2 | cups butter or margarine, melted, divided | 6 | eggs, beaten |
| | | 9 | cups all-purpose flour |

Dissolve yeast in warm water. Add 1 cup melted butter, sugar, salt and eggs. Stir well. Gradually add flour, mixing well. Cover and let rise in a warm place, free from drafts, for 4 hours. Divide dough into four equal parts. Turn each part of dough onto a lightly floured board and knead 4 or 5 times. Roll each part into a 12-inch circle. Brush with remaining cup of butter. Cut each circle into 12 wedges. Roll up each wedge, beginning at wide end. Place on lightly greased cookie sheets. Let rise 1 hour in a warm, draft free place. Preheat oven to 400°F. Bake 10 minutes or until light brown. Freezes well.

*4 dozen rolls*

*For pocketbook rolls, divide dough into 2 parts. Roll out to ¼-inch thickness. Cut with biscuit cutter. Dip half of roll into remaining butter and fold over.*

## Refrigerator Yeast Rolls

| | | | |
|---|---|---|---|
| 1 | quart whole milk | 7 | cups sifted all-purpose flour, divided |
| 1 | cup vegetable shortening | 1 | teaspoon baking soda |
| 1 | cup sugar | 1 | teaspoon salt |
| 1 | (¼-ounce) package active dry yeast | | Butter or margarine |

Combine milk, shortening and sugar in a large stockpot. Heat on top of the stove to almost boiling. Set aside and cool to lukewarm, 105°F to 115°F. Add yeast and up to 2½ cups flour for a light cake batter consistency. Cover with a towel and allow dough to rise in a warm place for 1½ to 2 hours. Add baking soda, salt and 4½ cups flour or enough to make a soft dough. Cover with a towel and let rise for approximately 3 hours. After rising, dough may be stirred and refrigerated or rolled out to ¼-inch thickness. Cut with a round biscuit cutter. Dot each roll with butter and fold in half. Place on greased cookie sheets and drizzle with melted butter. Let rise 2 hours. Preheat oven to 400°F. Bake 10 minutes or until tops are lightly browned.

*5 dozen rolls*

*The dough will keep in the refrigerator for about a week.*

*Rolls may also be frozen. Bake rolls in an aluminum pan until barely brown. Let cool and freeze. To bake, let rolls thaw 20 minutes and bake in a 400°F oven until fully cooked.*

## Easy Biscuits

| | | | |
|---|---|---|---|
| ½ | pint whipping cream | 1½ | cups self-rising flour |

Preheat oven to 450°F. Combine cream and flour. Stir until smooth. Knead on floured surface for one minute. Roll to ½-inch thickness. Fold dough in half so biscuits will split easily. Roll out again to ½-inch thickness. Cut with a biscuit cutter. Place on a greased pan. Bake 10 minutes or until lightly golden brown.

*12 biscuits*

### Angel Biscuits

2 (¼-ounce) packages active dry yeast

2 tablespoons warm water (105°F to 115°F)

4 cups all-purpose flour

1 teaspoon baking soda

1 tablespoon baking powder

4 tablespoons sugar

1 teaspoon salt

1 cup vegetable shortening

2 cups buttermilk

Margarine

Combine yeast and warm water in a large mixing bowl. Let stand until bubbly, 5 to 10 minutes. Mix flour, baking soda, baking powder, sugar and salt. Add to yeast mixture. Cut in shortening. Add buttermilk until mixed. Let stand 20 minutes. Roll out and cut into biscuits. Place on lightly greased baking sheets. Dot with margarine. Let rise at least 20 minutes. Preheat oven to 425°F. Bake 15 to 20 minutes or until golden brown.

*18 to 20 biscuits*

*Dough may be stored in refrigerator up to two days.*

## Fig Preserves

12 cups figs

2 gallons plus
1 cup water, divided

1 cup baking soda

8 cups sugar

6 lemons, sliced

6 pint-size jars, sterilized

Soak figs in 2 gallons water with baking soda 10 minutes. Rinse. In a large stockpot, cook sugar in 1 cup water. Add figs and sliced lemons. Simmer 1½ hours. Place in sterilized jars to within ½-inch of top. Cap and process in boiling water bath 10 minutes.

*6 pints*

# Currant Scones

*Serve hot with butter, preserves, whipped cream or lemon curd*

| | |
|---|---|
| ½ cup black currants | ¾ cup cold, unsalted |
| 4 cups all-purpose flour | butter, finely |
| 1 tablespoon baking | chopped |
| powder | 1½ cups whipping cream |
| ¼ cup sugar | 5 large eggs, divided |
| 1½ teaspoons salt | Sugar |

Place currants in a small bowl and fill with warm water to cover. Let sit for at least 15 minutes. Drain and set aside. Using an electric mixer on low speed, combine flour, baking powder, sugar, salt and butter until texture resembles a coarse meal. Add cream and 4 of the eggs. Mix just until blended. The dough will be slightly sticky. Fold in currants, cover with plastic wrap and refrigerate 1 hour. This may be refrigerated overnight.

Preheat oven to 400°F. On a lightly floured surface, knead dough gently 1 minute, adding flour as necessary to achieve a smooth consistency. Pat to a thickness of about ¾-inch. Cut into rounds with a 2-inch biscuit cutter and place on a greased baking sheet. Lightly beat remaining egg and brush over tops of the scones. Sprinkle with sugar. Bake about 15 minutes or until golden brown. Freezes well. To serve, thaw in refrigerator 8 hours and reheat.

*15 scones*

# Sun-Dried Tomato Bread

| | | | |
|---|---|---|---|
| 1 | clove garlic, minced | 1 | cup water, room temperature |
| 2 | tablespoons finely chopped onion | ½ | cup coarsely chopped sun-dried tomatoes, packed in oil, drained |
| 1 | tablespoon oil from sun-dried tomatoes | | |
| 1 | (¼-ounce) package active dry yeast | 3¾ | cups bread flour |
| | | 2 | teaspoons salt |
| ¼ | cup warm water (105°F to 115°F) | 1 | egg white, beaten |

Lightly sauté garlic and onion in oil. Let cool to room temperature. Stir yeast into warm water in a large mixing bowl. Let stand until foamy, about 10 minutes. Stir in sautéed mixture and water. Add tomatoes. In a separate bowl, mix flour and salt. Add flour mixture, 1 cup at a time, to yeast mixture, mixing well after each addition. Knead on a lightly floured surface until dough is soft, velvety and slightly moist, about 8 to 10 minutes. Place dough in a lightly oiled bowl, turning once to coat. Cover and let rise until doubled, about 1 hour. Punch dough down on a lightly floured surface and knead briefly. Shape dough into a ball. Place on a lightly oiled baking sheet. Cover with a towel and let rise until doubled, about 45 minutes.

Preheat oven to 425°F. Make three slashes on top of loaf. Brush top with egg white. Bake 10 minutes, spraying three separate times with water. Reduce heat to 375°F. Bake 25 to 30 minutes. Cool completely on a rack.

*1 round loaf*

# Momma Purdy's Pizza Dough

| | | | |
|---|---|---|---|
| 2 | (¼-ounce) packages active dry yeast | 1 | cup milk, scalded |
| ⅓ | cup plus 1 teaspoon sugar, divided | 5 | tablespoons margarine, softened |
| ½ | cup warm water (105°F to 115°F) | 1 | teaspoon salt |
| | | 3 | eggs |
| | | 5 | cups all-purpose flour |

Dissolve yeast and 1 teaspoon sugar in warm water, set aside. In a large mixing bowl, pour scalded milk over margarine, remaining sugar and salt. Stir to dissolve sugar. Let cool. When mixture is lukewarm, add eggs and yeast mixture. Stir to mix. Add flour, 1 cup at a time, while stirring with a wooden spoon. Dough should form a soft-ball. Add more flour, if necessary. Knead lightly on a floured surface. Add flour if dough sticks. Cover with a slightly damp cloth. Let rise in a warm place until doubled, about 1 to 2 hours, depending on room temperature.

Preheat oven to 425°F. Divide dough into thirds. Spread each section onto a cookie sheet or a pizza pan. Spread with favorite pizza sauce, cheese and toppings, as desired. Bake 10 to 15 minutes or until crust is lightly browned. Watch carefully.

*3 large pizzas*

## Hush Puppies

| | | | |
|---|---|---|---|
| 1 | cup self-rising cornmeal | ¾ | cup buttermilk |
| 3 | tablespoons self-rising flour | 1 | onion, finely minced |
| ½ | teaspoon garlic powder | 3 | tablespoons vegetable shortening, melted |
| ½ | teaspoon sugar | | Vegetable shortening, for frying |
| 1 | egg, well beaten | | |

Heat shortening to 375°F for frying. Combine cornmeal, flour, garlic powder and sugar. Add egg and buttermilk. Prior to frying, add onion and 3 tablespoons hot shortening. Drop by rounded teaspoonfuls into heated shortening. Fry until golden on each side.

*15 to 18 hush puppies*

*Dip the spoon into heated shortening after each drop and mixture will fall out easily. If mixed correctly, the "Puppies" will usually roll over themselves for easy browning. If they don't, just turn them.*

Hush Puppies allegedly got their name from cooks who would toss scraps of fried batter to hungry dogs that were begging for food and say, "Now, hush puppy!"

## Spoonbread

| | | | |
|---|---|---|---|
| 3 | cups milk, divided | 1 | teaspoon salt |
| 1¼ | cups cornmeal | 2 | teaspoons baking powder |
| 3 | eggs, beaten | | |
| 2 | tablespoons butter or margarine | | |

Preheat oven to 350°F. In a large saucepan, gently heat 2 cups milk. Slowly whisk in cornmeal. Bring to a boil while stirring. Remove from heat. Whisk in remaining milk. Slowly whisk in eggs. Whisk in remaining ingredients. Lightly grease a 1½-quart shallow baking dish. Add spoonbread mixture. Bake 25 to 35 minutes or until top is lightly browned.

*4 to 6 servings*

Spoonbread is a southern side dish that has been served since Colonial times. Thomas Jefferson loved it so much that he ate it for breakfast, lunch and dinner.

# Broccoli Cornbread

| | | | |
|---|---|---|---|
| 1 | (8½-ounce) box cornbread mix | ½ | cup margarine, melted |
| 1 | (10-ounce) package frozen chopped broccoli, thawed | 1 | onion, chopped |
| | | 1 | cup shredded mild Cheddar cheese |
| | | 3 | large eggs |

Preheat oven to 375°F. Combine all ingredients. Pour batter into a greased cast iron skillet. Bake 25 to 30 minutes or until a toothpick comes out clean.

*6 to 8 servings*

*May add ¾-cup cottage cheese and 1 (15-ounce) can cream-style corn. Pour batter into a greased 13x9-inch baking pan. Bake 45 minutes.*

*12 to 16 servings*

## Southern Cornbread

1 cup cornmeal

1 teaspoon salt

½ teaspoon baking powder

¼ teaspoon baking soda

¼ teaspoon sugar

1 cup buttermilk

1 egg

4 tablespoons bacon drippings

Preheat oven to 450°F. Combine all ingredients except bacon drippings. Heat drippings in a small cast iron skillet until hot. Pour half of drippings into batter mixture and stir. Pour batter into skillet. Bake 20 minutes or until golden brown.

*4 servings*

*May substitute 1 cup self-rising cornmeal for cornmeal, salt and baking powder.*

# Mexican Cornbread

| | | | |
|---|---|---|---|
| 1½ | cups self-rising cornmeal | ¼ | cup vegetable oil |
| ½ | teaspoon salt | ¼ | cup chopped jalapeño pepper |
| 1 | cup shredded sharp Cheddar cheese | ¾ | cup milk |
| 1 | cup chopped onion | 1 | (15-ounce) can cream style corn |
| 3 | eggs | | |

Preheat oven to 375°F. Mix all ingredients together. Pour into a greased cast iron skillet. Bake 20 to 30 minutes.

*6 to 8 servings*

*For Onion Cornbread, increase chopped onion to 2 cups and sauté in ¼ cup butter. Omit jalapeño pepper and add ¼ teaspoon dill weed.*

# Salads

# A Home Survives and Triumphs

*During the Civil War, Meridian was in the path of Union General William T. Sherman's march to the sea. His objectives were to capture and burn everything of value on his route to Georgia. Only a few houses still stood when Sherman declared, "Meridian no longer exists." One of these, a little three-room cottage, used as Confederate General Leonidas Polk's headquarters, rose above the ashes. Over a fifty-year span of time, mirroring three distinct periods of Meridian history, owners expanded the original 1858 cottage into a 20-room Italianate mansion now known as Merrehope.*

*The Meridian Restoration Foundation purchased the home in 1968. Merrehope features stately columns, exceptional woodwork, and ruby-red glass door panels. It was the first house listed in East Mississippi on the National Register of Historic Places (1971), and it was also the first house museum open to the public in East Mississippi, displaying not only the architectural elements of the home, but its museum-quality furnishings and paintings as well.*

*Its current name, Merrehope, derives from the Foundation's efforts to restore the only antebellum structure that remains in the city. "Mer" represents Meridian, "re" represents restoration, and "hope" represents the future. Befitting its name, Merrehope has emerged from conflict to become a symbol of Meridian's past prosperity and its present-day citizens' achievements.*

# Tricolor Salad with Honey Cumin Dressing

| | | | |
|---|---|---|---|
| 1 | head butter lettuce, torn into bite-size pieces | ½ | purple onion, thinly sliced |
| 1 | large bunch watercress, stems trimmed | 2 | oranges, peeled, sliced into rounds |
| 1 | large head radicchio, torn into bite-size pieces | | Honey Cumin Dressing (see accompanying recipe) |

Place salad ingredients into a large serving bowl. Toss with enough Honey Cumin Dressing to taste.

*4 to 6 servings*

## Honey Cumin Dressing

**6 tablespoons olive oil**

**3 tablespoons balsamic or red wine vinegar**

**1½ teaspoons honey**

**¾ teaspoon ground cumin**

**¾ teaspoon chili powder**

**Salt**

**Ground black pepper**

Whisk together all dressing ingredients. Season with salt and pepper.

*⅔ cup*

# Broccoli Salad

| | | | |
|---|---|---|---|
| 1 | cup mayonnaise | 1 | cup seedless red grapes, halved |
| ½ | cup sugar | | |
| 2 | tablespoons white vinegar | 3-6 | green onions, chopped |
| 2 | bunches broccoli florets, cut into bite-size pieces | 6 | slices bacon, cooked and crumbled |
| | | ¾ | cup pecan pieces |

For dressing, combine mayonnaise, sugar and vinegar. Cover and chill. In a large bowl, combine broccoli, grapes, onions, bacon and pecans. To serve, toss with dressing.

*4 to 6 servings*

*May omit grapes and pecans and add ½ cup raisins, ½ cup sunflower seeds and ½ cup cashews.*

# Autumn Salad with Nutmeg Dill Vinaigrette

*The red apples with green lettuce make a beautiful presentation at Christmas.*

## Nutmeg Dill Vinaigrette

1 tablespoon Dijon mustard

¼ cup white wine vinegar

⅛ teaspoon salt

⅛ teaspoon ground black pepper

½ teaspoon dried dill weed

½ teaspoon ground nutmeg

½ cup extra virgin olive oil

Combine mustard, vinegar, salt, pepper, dill and nutmeg. Add oil very slowly, whisking constantly. May be refrigerated for 3 days. Whisk before using.

*¾ cup*

2   large red delicious apples, unpeeled, cored and very thinly sliced

⅓   cup crumbled bleu cheese
    Nutmeg Dill Vinaigrette (see accompanying recipe)

4   tablespoons walnuts
1   head romaine lettuce, trimmed and cut
    Salt
    Cracked black pepper
    Freshly grated nutmeg

In a bowl, combine apples slices, bleu cheese, walnuts and 3 tablespoons of vinaigrette. Cover and refrigerate up to 4 hours. To serve, combine romaine and apple mixture. Toss with vinaigrette. Season to taste with salt, pepper and nutmeg.

*8 servings*

# Vegetable Tortellini Salad

## Dressing

| | | | | |
|---|---|---|---|---|
| ½ | cup finely chopped green onion | 1 | teaspoon dried dill weed | |
| ½ | cup red wine vinegar | 1 | teaspoon salt | |
| ½ | cup vegetable oil | ½ | teaspoon ground black pepper | |
| ½ | cup olive oil | ½ | teaspoon sugar | |
| 2 | tablespoons chopped fresh parsley | ½ | teaspoon dried oregano | |
| 2 | cloves garlic, minced | 1½ | teaspoons Dijon mustard | |
| 2 | teaspoons dried basil | | | |

## Salad

2 cups fresh snow peas
2 cups broccoli florets
2½ cups cherry tomato halves
2 cups sliced fresh mushrooms
1 (7¾-ounce) can whole pitted ripe olives, drained
1 (8-ounce) package cheese stuffed tortellini, prepared according to package directions, slightly cooled

8 ounces fettuccine, prepared according to package directions, slightly cooled
1 tablespoon grated Parmesan cheese
Grated Parmesan cheese, for garnish

Combine all dressing ingredients in a jar and cover tightly. Shake vigorously until well mixed. Set aside.

In a saucepan, boil snow peas 1 minute. Remove with a slotted spoon. Repeat with broccoli. In a large bowl, combine peas, broccoli, tomatoes, mushrooms and olives. Add pasta and cheese. Toss with dressing. Chill several hours before serving. Garnish with cheese.

*10 to 12 servings*

Wash and dry all produce before using.

Before prepping fresh herbs or greens, remove the leaves or fronds from the stems - the exception is cilantro, which has tender stems.

Pack fresh herbs or greens before measuring.

# Greek Salad

## Pita Croutons

2 tablespoons olive oil

1 teaspoon dried oregano

¼ teaspoon crushed garlic

⅛ teaspoon of salt,
or to taste

1 (8-inch) pita bread round,
split into 2 circles

Preheat oven to 375°F.
Combine olive oil, oregano,
garlic and salt. Brush over the
inside of each pita bread
circle. Cut each pita bread
circle into bite-size pieces.
Place on a baking sheet. Bake
5 minutes or until golden
brown. Store in a zip-top
plastic bag.

*2 cups*

### Dressing

| | | | |
|---|---|---|---|
| ¾ | cup olive oil | 1 | teaspoon dried oregano |
| ¼ | cup lemon juice | ¼ | teaspoon salt |
| ¼ | cup egg substitute | ⅛ | teaspoon ground black pepper |
| 2 | cloves garlic, minced | | |

### Salad

| | | | |
|---|---|---|---|
| 1 | head romaine lettuce, torn into bite-size pieces | ½ | cup crumbled feta cheese |
| ¾ | cup pitted kalamata olives | | Pita Croutons (see accompanying recipe) |
| 1 | small purple onion, thinly sliced | | |

In a small bowl, combine dressing ingredients stirring with a wire whisk. Cover and chill.

In a large bowl, combine lettuce, olives, onion and cheese. Gradually add enough dressing to coat leaves, tossing gently. Sprinkle with pita croutons. Serve with remaining dressing.

*6 to 8 servings*

# Mandarin Orange Salad

### Salad

| | | | | |
|---|---|---|---|---|
| 3¾ | ounces slivered almonds | 1 | head romaine lettuce, washed and torn into bite-size pieces | |
| 2 | tablespoons sugar | | | |
| 1 | (11-ounce) can Mandarin oranges, drained | ½ | cup chopped green onion | |
| | | ½ | cup chopped celery | |

### Dressing

| | | | | |
|---|---|---|---|---|
| ¼ | cup white wine vinegar | ⅛ | teaspoon salt, or to taste | |
| 1 | tablespoon sugar | | | |
| ½ | cup vegetable oil | ⅛ | teaspoon ground black pepper, or to taste | |
| 2-3 | drops Tabasco sauce | | | |

In a skillet over medium heat, combine almonds and sugar. Stir until sugar melts and coats almonds. Watch carefully so almonds do not burn. Cool. In a large bowl, combine oranges, lettuce, onion, celery and almonds. For dressing, whisk together all ingredients. To serve, toss dressing with salad.

*8 to 10 servings*

## Thousand Island Dressing

½ cup mayonnaise

¼ cup ketchup

2 teaspoons Worcestershire sauce

1 teaspoon prepared mustard

6 tablespoons piccalilli, finely puréed

Combine ingredients. Cover and refrigerate. Serve over favorite green salad.

*1 cup*

*Piccalilli is a highly seasoned pickled vegetable relish. Recipe ingredients vary and may include tomatoes, sweet peppers, onion, zucchini, cucumber, cauliflower, and beans.*

# Confetti Pasta Salad

*Wonderful for a summer cookout*

| | | | |
|---|---|---|---|
| 1 | pound vermicelli or thin spaghetti | ½ | green bell pepper, chopped |
| ½ | (3.9-ounce) bottle dry salad seasoning | ½ | orange or red bell pepper, chopped |
| 1 | (0.6-ounce) package dry Italian salad dressing mix | ½ | yellow bell pepper, chopped |
| | | 1 | small purple onion, chopped |
| 1 | (8-ounce) bottle Italian salad dressing | 1 | (4¼-ounce) can chopped ripe olives |

Break spaghetti in half and prepare according to package directions. Drain and set aside.

In a large bowl, mix salad seasoning and dressings. Add vegetables and spaghetti. Toss well.

Cover and refrigerate for two days to marinate. Toss once or twice a day while marinating.

*10 servings*

*Note: Must be made 2 days before serving.*

*May substitute shell pasta for vermicelli.*

*May add 1 (28-ounce) can diced, drained tomatoes, 2 diagonally sliced medium carrots, and ½ cup grated Parmesan cheese.*

## Honey Celery Dressing

1½ teaspoons water

¾ cup sugar

1 cup plus 2 tablespoons vegetable oil

1 cup plus 2 tablespoons honey

¾ cup fresh lemon juice

2 teaspoons paprika

1 tablespoon dry mustard

¼ teaspoon salt, or to taste

1 teaspoon celery seed

Whisk ingredients until well blended. Cover and refrigerate.

*1 quart*

# Crunchy Broccoli Salad

### Salad

| | | | |
|---|---|---|---|
| 1 | cup chopped walnuts | 1 | bunch broccoli, chopped |
| 1 | (3-ounce) package ramen noodles, uncooked and crumbled (discard flavor packet) | 1 | head romaine lettuce or red leaf lettuce, torn into bite-size pieces |
| 4 | tablespoons butter | 4 | green onions, chopped |

### Dressing

| | | | |
|---|---|---|---|
| 1 | cup oil | ⅛ | teaspoon salt, or to taste |
| 1 | cup sugar | | |
| ½ | cup red wine vinegar | ⅛ | teaspoon ground black pepper, or to taste |
| 1 | tablespoon soy sauce | | |

In a skillet, sauté walnuts and noodles in butter until light brown. Drain on paper towels. Set aside. In a large salad bowl, combine broccoli, lettuce and onions. For dressing, whisk together ingredients. To serve, sprinkle walnuts and noodles over salad. Toss with dressing.

*8 to 10 servings*

## Corn Salad

*Great with Bar-B-Que!*

2 (15¼-ounce) cans shoepeg corn, drained

1 large tomato, peeled and chopped

4-5 green onions, finely chopped

1 medium green bell pepper, chopped

2 stalks celery, chopped

½ cup mayonnaise

⅛ teaspoon salt, or to taste

⅛ teaspoon ground black pepper, or to taste

In a large bowl, combine all ingredients. May add more mayonnaise for desired consistency. Cover and refrigerate.

*8 to 10 servings*

# Spinach Pear Salad

### Salad

3-4  cups baby spinach, washed

2-3  medium ripe pears, cored, unpeeled and cut lengthwise into slices

2  tablespoons crumbled bleu cheese

### Dressing

2  tablespoons balsamic vinegar

3  tablespoons extra virgin olive oil

3  tablespoons orange juice

⅛  teaspoon salt

1  clove garlic, crushed

¼  cup chopped walnuts, toasted

In a salad bowl, place spinach, pears and cheese. Whisk dressing ingredients, except walnuts. Toss with salad. Sprinkle warm walnuts over salad.

*4 servings*

# Apple Spinach Salad

*Serve with soup on the first cool fall evening.*

2  (6-ounce) packages fresh baby spinach, washed

2  Granny Smith apples, cored and chopped

¼  cup golden raisins

½  cup salted cashews

¼  cup sugar

¼  cup vegetable oil

2  tablespoons balsamic vinegar

¼  teaspoon celery salt

In a serving bowl, combine spinach, apples, raisins and cashews. Whisk remaining ingredients until well blended. Pour over salad, tossing gently. Serve immediately.

*4 to 6 servings*

*May substitute 1 (10-ounce) package regular fresh spinach for baby spinach.*

## Marinated Tomatoes

1-2 tomatoes, sliced

⅓ cup olive oil

¼ cup red wine vinegar

1 clove garlic, minced

2 tablespoons chopped fresh parsley

1 tablespoon chopped fresh basil

2 tablespoons chopped onion

1 teaspoon salt

¼ teaspoon ground black pepper

In a non-aluminum pan, place sliced tomatoes in a single layer. Mix remaining ingredients and pour over tomatoes. Cover and refrigerate 1 to 3 hours.

*6 to 8 servings*

## Spinach Salad with Hot Citrus Dressing

| | | | |
|---|---|---|---|
| 2 | pounds fresh spinach, washed and trimmed | 3 | ounces chèvre cheese, crumbled |
| 2 | (11-ounce) cans Mandarin oranges, drained | ½ | cup chopped pecans, toasted |
| 1 | large purple onion, thinly sliced and separated into rings | | Hot Citrus Dressing (see accompanying recipe) |

Dry spinach leaves and arrange on salad plates. Top with oranges, onion, cheese and pecans. Drizzle with Hot Citrus Dressing.

*May use 4 oranges, peeled and sectioned in place of Mandarin oranges*

*8 to 10 servings*

## Black Bean and Mango Salad

| | | | |
|---|---|---|---|
| 1 | (0.6-ounce) package dry Italian salad dressing mix | 1 | cup chopped ripe mango |
| | | ½ | cup chopped red bell pepper |
| 1 | (16-ounce) can black beans, drained and rinsed | ⅓ | cup chopped purple onion |
| | | ⅓ | cup chopped fresh cilantro |
| 1 | (10-ounce) package frozen corn, thawed | ¼ | cup fresh lime juice |

Combine all ingredients and refrigerate.

*12 servings*

*Great as a dip with corn chips!*

### Hot Citrus Dressing

1 (6-ounce) can frozen orange juice concentrate, thawed

1 small onion, diced

⅓ cup red wine vinegar

1 cup firmly packed light brown sugar

1 tablespoon orange zest

1 teaspoon dry mustard

1 teaspoon salt

1 teaspoon hot pepper sauce

1 cup peanut oil

Process juice, onion and vinegar in a blender until smooth. Add brown sugar, orange zest, mustard, salt and hot pepper sauce. Blend until smooth. With blender on high speed, add oil slowly in a thin stream. Place mixture in a non-aluminum saucepan and bring to a boil. Cook over medium heat 10 minutes. Drizzle hot dressing over salad.

*2½ cups*

# Korean Salad

**Dressing**

| | | | | |
|---|---|---|---|---|
| 1 | cup oil | 1 | medium onion, grated |
| ¼ | cup vinegar | ⅛ | teaspoon salt, or to taste |
| ⅓ | cup ketchup | | |
| ⅓ | cup sugar | | |

**Salad**

| | | | | |
|---|---|---|---|---|
| 1 | pound fresh spinach, washed, trimmed and torn into bite-size pieces | 1 | (5-ounce) can water chestnuts, drained and sliced |
| 1 | (1-pound) can bean sprouts, drained and rinsed | 2 | hard-boiled eggs, chopped |
| | | 6-8 | slices bacon, cooked and crumbled |

In a small bowl, combine dressing ingredients. Refrigerate for a few hours. In a serving bowl, combine spinach, bean sprouts and water chestnuts. Toss with dressing. Sprinkle with egg and bacon.

*6 to 8 servings*

## Garlic Sauce

*Fabulous sauce for shrimp, crab, or just for a green salad!*

1 quart mayonnaise

1 tablespoon prepared mustard

1 teaspoon dry mustard

3-4 cloves garlic, finely minced

1 medium onion, finely grated

2 tablespoons finely chopped green onion tops

2 tablespoons soy sauce

2½ ounces prepared horseradish

1 teaspoon paprika

4 teaspoons sugar

1 teaspoon dried basil

2 teaspoons Worcestershire sauce

10 drops Tabasco sauce

1 teaspoon Accent

2 tablespoons ketchup

Juice of 1 lemon

¼ teaspoon cayenne pepper

¼ teaspoon ground black pepper

¼ teaspoon salt

Combine ingredients. Allow flavors to blend at least 1 hour. Correct seasonings to taste.

*1½ quarts*

# Marinated Green Bean Salad

| | | | | |
|---|---|---|---|---|
| 4 | (14-ounce) cans whole green beans, drained | | Salt |
| 1 | (14-ounce) can sliced mushrooms, drained | | Ground black pepper |
| 1 | large white onion, sliced | 1 | (8-ounce) bottle Italian salad dressing |

In a salad bowl, layer half of the green beans, mushrooms and onion. Repeat layers. Sprinkle with salt and pepper to taste. Pour dressing over layers. Refrigerate 24 hours.

*10 to 12 servings*

*Note: Must marinate for 24 hours prior to serving.*

# Layered Spinach Salad

| | | | |
|---|---|---|---|
| 1 | pound fresh spinach, washed, trimmed and torn into bite-size pieces | 1 | (10-ounce) package frozen green peas, thawed |
| 2 | hard-boiled eggs, chopped | 1 | (8-ounce) carton sour cream |
| 5 | green onions, finely chopped | 1 | cup mayonnaise |
| 10 | slices bacon, cooked and crumbled | ¼ | teaspoon lemon pepper |
| | | ⅛ | teaspoon garlic powder |
| | | ½ | cup freshly grated Romano cheese (optional) |

In a deep serving bowl, layer spinach, eggs, onions, bacon and peas. Combine sour cream, mayonnaise, lemon pepper and garlic powder, stirring well. Evenly spoon over peas, sealing to edge of bowl. Sprinkle with cheese. Cover tightly, and chill 8 hours. Toss gently before serving.

*Note: Must chill for 8 hours prior to serving.*

*8 servings*

# Market Salad

| | | | |
|---|---|---|---|
| ½ | cup white vinegar | 2 | medium carrots, peeled and juilenned |
| ½ | cup vegetable oil | | |
| 1 | teaspoon dried oregano | 1 | (16-ounce) can kidney beans, drained |
| 2 | cloves garlic, minced | | |
| ½ | teaspoon salt | 2 | cups shredded mozzarella cheese |
| 2 | cups cauliflower florets | | |
| 2 | cups broccoli florets | | |

In a large bowl, whisk vinegar, oil, oregano, garlic and salt. Add vegetables. Toss thoroughly to blend. Add cheese and toss lightly. Cover and chill 2 to 3 hours, stirring occasionally.

*8 servings*

## Kumback Sauce

*Great on salads, shrimp, saltine crackers... a beach week staple!!!*

2 cloves garlic

1 cup mayonnaise

¼ cup chili sauce

¼ cup ketchup

1 teaspoon Worcestershire sauce

1 teaspoon ground black pepper

¼ cup vegetable oil

⅛ teaspoon Tabasco sauce, or to taste

⅛ teaspoon paprika, or to taste

½ teaspoon bottled onion juice

2 tablespoons water

1 teaspoon prepared mustard

In a food processor with blade running, drop garlic through feed tube and chop. Stop processor and remove top. Add remaining ingredients. Replace top and process until blended. Cover and refrigerate.

*1 pint*

# Marinated Vegetables
*A colorful appetizer, too!*

### Lemon Thyme Salad Dressing

2 cups vegetable oil

2 tablespoons lemon zest

1 cup fresh lemon juice

1 cup chopped fresh parsley

4 small cloves garlic, minced

5 tablespoons sugar

3 tablespoons fresh thyme

2 tablespoons salt, or to taste

½ teaspoon ground black pepper

Combine all ingredients and blend thoroughly. Chill. Serve over mixed greens.

*3½ cups*

*For best flavor, prepare a day or two ahead.*

### Vegetables

| | | | |
|---|---|---|---|
| 1 | (12-ounce) bag fresh broccoli florets | 1 | (12-ounce) package whole mushrooms |
| 1 | (12-ounce) bag fresh cauliflower florets | 1 | (1-pint) carton cherry tomatoes |
| 1 | (16-ounce) bag peeled baby carrots | | |

### Marinade

| | | | |
|---|---|---|---|
| 1 | cup white vinegar | 1 | tablespoon ground black pepper |
| ½ | cup vegetable oil | | |
| 1 | tablespoon dill weed | 1 | tablespoon sugar |
| 1 | tablespoon salt | 1 | tablespoon Accent |
| 1 | tablespoon garlic salt | | |

In a large bowl, combine vegetables. For marinade, mix ingredients. Pour over vegetables. Refrigerate 3 hours before serving.

*20 servings*

*Vegetables may be cut into bite-size pieces.*

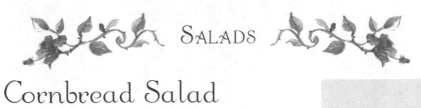

# Cornbread Salad

### Salad

| | | | | |
|---|---|---|---|---|
| 1 | (8½-ounce) box cornbread mix, prepared according to package directions | 1 | medium onion, chopped |
| | | ½ | cup chopped sweet pickles |
| 4 | medium tomatoes, chopped | 9 | slices bacon, cooked and crumbled |
| 1 | green bell pepper, chopped | 2 | cups shredded Cheddar cheese |

### Dressing

| | | | |
|---|---|---|---|
| 1 | cup mayonnaise | ¼ | cup sweet pickle juice |

Cool cornbread and cut into cubes. Combine tomatoes, bell pepper, onion, pickles and bacon. In a serving bowl, layer cornbread, ⅓ cheese, tomato mixture, ⅓ cheese and dressing. Top with remaining cheese. Cover and chill 8 hours.

*8 servings*

*Note: Must chill 8 hours prior to serving.*

*Great during the summer, using homegrown tomatoes and Vidalia onions.*

One of the most vital elements to the Meridian community, the Naval Air Station, is located 15 miles northeast of downtown Meridian on over twelve thousand acres of land. The facility provides training to Navy and Marine Corps jet pilots as well as technical training in the aviation field. Military personnel stationed in Meridian add depth and interest to the community, and many Navy wives have taught at Lamar and other Meridian schools, adding their knowledge of far away people and places to the educational environment of our community.

# Tangy Bean Salad

### Dressing

| | | | | |
|---|---|---|---|---|
| 1 | cup sugar | 1 | teaspoon salt |
| ½ | cup oil | 1 | teaspoon ground black pepper |
| ¾ | cup white vinegar | | |

### Salad

| | | | | |
|---|---|---|---|---|
| 1 | (15-ounce) can small English peas, drained | 1 | (4-ounce) jar chopped pimiento, drained |
| 1 | (14½-ounce) can French style green beans, drained | 4 | stalks celery, chopped |
| | | 1 | medium purple onion, chopped |
| 1 | (15¼-ounce) can shoepeg corn, drained | 1 | medium green bell pepper, chopped |

In a saucepan, combine all dressing ingredients and bring to a boil. Cool. For salad, combine all ingredients in a large bowl. Toss salad with dressing. Refrigerate 12 hours before serving.

*8 to 10 servings*

*Note: Must be refrigerated at least 12 hours prior to serving.*

# West Indies Salad

| | | | | |
|---|---|---|---|---|
| 1 | medium onion, finely chopped | | Salt |
| | | | Ground black pepper |
| 1 | pound fresh lump crabmeat, picked over for shells | ½ | cup vegetable oil |
| | | ⅓ | cup apple cider vinegar |
| | | ½ | cup ice water |

Spread ½ onion over the bottom of a large mixing bowl. Top with crabmeat. Add layer of remaining onion. Sprinkle with salt and pepper. In order, pour oil, vinegar and ice water over salad. Cover and refrigerate 2 to 12 hours. When ready to serve, toss lightly.

*4 servings*

# Layered Chicken Pasta Salad

### Dressing

| | |
|---|---|
| 1 | cup sour cream |
| ½ | cup ricotta cheese |
| 2-3 | tablespoons white wine vinegar |
| 2 | cloves garlic, minced |

| | |
|---|---|
| 1 | cup coarsely chopped fresh basil |
| 2½ | teaspoons sugar |
| ½ | teaspoon salt |

### Salad

| | |
|---|---|
| 12 | ounces bowtie pasta, prepared according to package directions |
| 2 | tablespoons olive oil |
| 2 | bunches fresh spinach, washed and trimmed |
| 3 | cups cooked, cubed chicken breast |

| | |
|---|---|
| 1 | pound broccoli or asparagus, steamed and cut into bite-size pieces |
| 4 | tomatoes, peeled, seeded and chopped |

In a non-aluminum bowl, combine all dressing ingredients. Mix well and chill.

Toss pasta with oil and refrigerate. In a trifle bowl, layer half of spinach, chicken, pasta, broccoli and tomatoes. Ladle half of dressing over tomatoes. Repeat layers, ending with remaining dressing. Chill.

*12 servings*

# Cold Shrimp Pasta Salad

| | |
|---|---|
| 12 | ounces rotini pasta, cooked, drained and cooled |
| 1 | pound shrimp, cooked and peeled |
| 12 | cherry tomatoes, halved |
| 1 | (6-ounce) can whole pitted ripe olives, drained |

| | |
|---|---|
| 1 | (3-ounce) jar real bacon bits or 8 slices bacon, cooked and crumbled |
| 6 | ounces Caesar or Italian salad dressing |

In a bowl, mix all ingredients together. Chill 1 hour before serving.

*6 servings*

## Shrimp and Wild Rice Salad

1 (10-ounce) package herb flavored Rice-A-Roni, prepared according to package directions and chilled

8 ounces shrimp, cooked, peeled and deveined

¼ cup finely chopped green onion

1 (2¼-ounce) can sliced ripe olives

⅓ cup sliced almonds

⅓ cup Italian dressing

In a bowl, combine ingredients. Cover and chill until serving.

*4 cups*

# Cold Rainbow Tuna Salad

1 (12-ounce) package rainbow rotini pasta, prepared according to package directions

2 (6-ounce) cans solid white albacore tuna in spring water, drained

1 (2¼-ounce) can sliced ripe olives, drained

1 (5-ounce) can water chestnuts, drained

1 (0.7-ounce) envelope dry Italian salad dressing mix

1 medium tomato, chopped

1 small cucumber, sliced

1-1½ cups mayonnaise

Grated Parmesan cheese, for topping

Chow mein noodles, for topping

Let pasta cool 20 minutes. Add remaining ingredients. Mix well. Chill 2 hours before serving. To serve, top with cheese and noodles.

*6 servings*

# Classic Chicken Salad

4 cups diced cooked chicken breast, still warm

9 hard-boiled eggs, chopped, still warm

1 cup chicken broth

2 teaspoons prepared mustard

2 tablespoons mayonnaise-mustard sauce

2 tablespoons sugar

½-1 cup mayonnaise

¼ cup fresh lemon juice

3 cups diced celery

¾ cup sweet pickle relish

In a large bowl, combine chicken and eggs. Add broth, stirring well. Cover and chill 30 to 60 minutes. In a separate bowl, combine mustards, sugar, mayonnaise and lemon juice. To chicken, add celery and relish. Gradually stir in dressing mixture. Cover and chill until serving.

*10 to 12 servings*

## Rémoulade Sauce

*Serve over a bed of lettuce, fried green tomatoes and shrimp.*

1 cup mayonnaise

2 tablespoons Creole mustard

2 tablespoons ketchup

½ cup finely chopped green onion

2 tablespoons finely chopped fresh parsley

1½ teaspoons minced garlic

2 tablespoons finely minced celery

1 teaspoon paprika

1 teaspoon Tabasco sauce

¼ teaspoon salt, or to taste

¼ teaspoon freshly ground black pepper, or to taste

Mix, cover and chill 2 hours.

*2 cups*

*May substitute ⅛ teaspoon celery salt for 2 tablespoons minced celery.*

# Fruit and Chicken Salad

| | | | | |
|---|---|---|---|---|
| 4 | cups diced cooked chicken breast | 1 | (16-ounce) can pineapple chunks, drained |
| 1 | (5-ounce) can sliced water chestnuts, drained | ½ | cup slivered almonds |
| ¾ | cup finely chopped celery | 1 | cup mayonnaise |
| 1 | pound whole fresh seedless grapes, halved | 1 | tablespoon soy sauce |
| | | 1½ | tablespoons fresh lemon juice |
| | | ½ | teaspoon curry powder |

In a large bowl, combine chicken, water chestnuts, celery, grapes, pineapple chunks and almonds. In a small bowl, mix mayonnaise, soy sauce, lemon juice and curry powder. Gently toss mayonnaise mixture with chicken. Mix thoroughly. Chill 3 hours before serving.

*9 cups*

# Layered Fruit Salad with Citrus Sauce

| | | | | |
|---|---|---|---|---|
| 2 | cups diced fresh pineapple | 2 | oranges, sectioned |
| 3 | medium bananas, sliced | 2 | kiwis, peeled and sliced |
| 2 | pints fresh strawberries, sliced | 1 | cup seedless red grapes |
| | | | Citrus Sauce (see accompanying recipe) |

In a clear glass bowl, layer fruit. Pour Citrus Sauce over fruit. Chill.

*12 to 15 servings*

## Citrus Sauce

½ teaspoon orange zest

½ teaspoon lemon zest

⅔ cup fresh orange juice

⅓ cup fresh lemon juice

⅓ cup firmly packed brown sugar

1 cinnamon stick

In a medium saucepan, combine all ingredients. Heat to boiling. Reduce heat and simmer 5 minutes. Cool. Remove cinnamon stick. Chill.

*1 cup*

## Poppy Seed Dressing

1 cup vegetable oil

¾ cup sugar

⅓ cup white vinegar

2 tablespoons minced onion

1 teaspoon salt

½ teaspoon dry mustard

1½ teaspoons poppy seeds

In an electric blender, combine all ingredients except poppy seeds. Process on low speed 30 seconds. Stir in poppy seeds. Cover and chill. Stir immediately before serving.

*1½ cups*

# Fresh Fruit Salad with Poppy Seed Dressing

| | | | |
|---|---|---|---|
| 3 | bananas, sliced | 2 | cups cantaloupe balls |
| 1½ | teaspoons fresh lemon juice | 2 | cups honeydew melon balls |
| 1 | small head romaine lettuce | 2 | kiwis, peeled and sliced |
| 2 | cups pineapple chunks | | Poppy Seed Dressing (see accompanying recipe) |
| 2 | cups strawberry halves | | |

Sprinkle banana slices with lemon juice. Line a bowl or serving platter with lettuce. Arrange fruit on lettuce. Serve with Poppy Seed Dressing.

*6 servings*

# Frozen Pink Salad

| | | | |
|---|---|---|---|
| 2 | (3-ounce) packages cream cheese, softened | 1 | (8¼-ounce) can crushed pineapple, drained |
| 2 | tablespoons mayonnaise | ½ | cup chopped nuts |
| 2 | tablespoons sugar | 1 | cup whipping cream, whipped |
| 1 | (16-ounce) can whole berry cranberry sauce | | |

Blend cream cheese, mayonnaise and sugar until smooth. Add cranberry sauce, pineapple and nuts. Mix well. Fold in whipped cream. Pour into a 9x5-inch loaf pan and freeze. To serve, let stand at room temperature 5 minutes and slice.

*8 to 10 servings*

# Orange Trilby Cream

| | | | |
|---|---|---|---|
| 12 | small or 8 large oranges, peeled and sectioned | 1 | (6¼-ounce) package miniature marshmallows |
| 1 | (20-ounce) can crushed pineapple | 1 | cup chopped nuts |
| 1 | cup sugar | ½ | pint whipping cream |

In a deep serving bowl, layer ½ of each ingredient except cream. Repeat layers and refrigerate. When ready to serve, whip and fold in cream.

*10 to 12 servings*

# Fruit Salad Ice

| | | | |
|---|---|---|---|
| 1 | (17-ounce) can apricots, drained, reserve juice, and chopped | 3 | (10-ounce) packages frozen strawberries |
| 1 | (17-ounce) can crushed pineapple, drained and reserve juice | 1 | (6-ounce) can frozen orange juice concentrate |
| ½ | cup sugar | 2 | tablespoons fresh lemon juice |
| | | 3 | bananas, chopped |
| | | ¼ | cup sour cream |
| | | ¼ | cup mayonnaise |

If necessary, add water to reserved juices to make 1 cup. In a saucepan, heat juice and sugar until sugar dissolves. Add apricots, pineapple, strawberries, orange juice, lemon juice and bananas. Continue heating until well combined. Place cupcake papers in muffin tins. Fill with salad mixture. Freeze until solid. May remove from tins and store in zip-top plastic bags. Remove from freezer 10 to 20 minutes before serving. Combine sour cream and mayonnaise. Place a teaspoonful on each serving.

*36 servings*

## Fast Fruit Salad

1 (16-ounce) can sliced peaches, drained and chopped

1 (16-ounce) can sliced pears, drained and chopped

1 (16-ounce) can chunk pineapple, drained and chopped

1 cup chopped pecans

4 bananas, chopped

1 (10-ounce) package frozen sliced strawberries, thawed

1 (20-ounce) can peach pie filling

In a large bowl, combine ingredients. Cover and refrigerate until serving.

*12 to 15 servings*

# Blueberry Congealed Salad

### Salad

| | | | |
|---|---|---|---|
| 1 | (3-ounce) package black raspberry flavored gelatin | 1 | (15-ounce) can blueberries, drained, reserve juice |
| 1 | (3-ounce) package lemon flavored gelatin | 1 | (8-ounce) can crushed pineapple, drained, reserve juice |
| 2 | cups boiling water | 1 | (8-ounce) package cream cheese, softened |

### Topping

| | | | |
|---|---|---|---|
| ½ | cup sour cream | ½ | teaspoon vanilla |
| ½ | cup sugar | ½ | cup chopped nuts |

Dissolve flavored gelatin in boiling water. Combine reserved juices to make 1 cup. Add juice to flavored gelatin mixture. Stir in fruit. Pour into a 2-quart mold. Chill until set. For topping, combine cream cheese, sour cream, sugar and vanilla. Spread over flavored gelatin. Sprinkle with nuts.

*10 to 12 servings*

*May substitute 1 (6-ounce) package black raspberry flavored gelatin for both (3-ounce) packages flavored gelatin.*

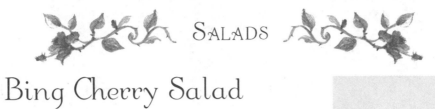
# Bing Cherry Salad

| | | | |
|---|---|---|---|
| 1 | (20-ounce) can Bing cherries, drained and reserve juice | 2 | (3-ounce) packages cherry flavored gelatin |
| 1 | cup crushed pineapple, drained and reserve juice | 1 | (12-ounce) can cola-flavored carbonated beverage |
| | | 1 | cup chopped nuts |

If necessary, add water to reserved juices to make 2 cups. Bring to a boil. In a large bowl, dissolve flavored gelatin with juice. Let cool and add cola. Chill until partially congealed. Add cherries, pineapple and nuts. Pour into a 2-quart mold or individual molds. Refrigerate until firm.

*12 servings*

# Strawberry Congealed Salad

| | | | |
|---|---|---|---|
| 2 | (3-ounce) packages cherry flavored gelatin | 1 | (10-ounce) package frozen strawberries, thawed |
| 2 | cups boiling water | 1 | (8-ounce) package cream cheese, softened |
| 3 | bananas, mashed | 1 | cup mayonnaise |
| 1 | (20-ounce) can crushed pineapple, undrained | 1-2 | tablespoons milk (optional) |

Dissolve flavored gelatin in boiling water. Cool slightly. Add bananas, pineapple and strawberries. Into a 2-quart mold or baking dish, pour half of fruit mixture. Refrigerate 1 hour or until partially congealed. In a separate bowl, combine cream cheese and mayonnaise until creamy. If necessary, add milk for creamy consistency. Spread over partially congealed fruit mixture. Top with remaining fruit mixture. Refrigerate until congealed.

*10 to 12 servings*

# Holiday Cranberry Salad

*A special Thanksgiving or Christmas Salad*

| | | | |
|---|---|---|---|
| 1 | quart fresh cranberries | 2 | (3-ounce) packages raspberry flavored gelatin |
| | Zest of 1 orange | | |
| 2 | oranges, peeled and sectioned | | |
| 1½ | cups sugar | 1 | cup boiling water |
| 1 | tablespoon unflavored gelatin | 1 | (8-ounce) can crushed pineapple, drained |
| 2 | cups cold water, divided | 1 | cup chopped pecans |

In a food processor, grind cranberries, zest and oranges. Add sugar and let stand. Soften unflavored gelatin in ¼ cup cold water. Set aside. Dissolve raspberry gelatin in 1 cup boiling water. Stir in 1¾ cups cold water. Combine gelatins, cranberry mixture, pineapple and pecans. Pour into a 13x9-inch glass dish or large glass serving bowl. Chill until firm.

*12 to 15 servings*

## Sour Cream and Dill Potato Salad

3 pounds unpeeled new potatoes

⅔ cup mayonnaise

1 cup sour cream

1 tablespoon chopped fresh dill

2 teaspoons chopped fresh parsley

Boil potatoes until tender. Cut into bite-size pieces, leaving skins on. Combine remaining ingredients. Toss with hot potatoes. Refrigerate 8 hours.

*8 to 10 servings*

*Note: Must be refrigerated 8 hours.*

# Lemon Potato Salad

*A refreshing and light potato salad that's also healthy.*

## Salad

| | | | |
|---|---|---|---|
| 6 | medium potatoes | 2 | cups thinly sliced fresh spinach |
| 2 | medium cucumbers, peeled and chopped | | |

## Dressing

| | | | |
|---|---|---|---|
| | Zest of 2 lemons | 2 | tablespoons finely chopped fresh basil |
| | Juice of 2 lemons | | |
| 3 | tablespoons olive oil | 2 | teaspoons sugar |
| 1 | tablespoon Dijon mustard | ½ | teaspoon salt |

Boil potatoes until tender. Let cool. Peel, if desired, and cut into cubes. Combine with cucumbers and spinach. Combine dressing ingredients, mixing well. Pour over vegetables. Toss to cover evenly. Chill before serving.

*12 to 14 servings*

# Southern Tomato Aspic

| | | | |
|---|---|---|---|
| 2 | (¼-ounce) envelopes unflavored gelatin | 2 | stalks celery, finely chopped |
| ½ | cup hot water | 1 | teaspoon salt |
| 3¼ | cups tomato juice | ½ | teaspoon ground black pepper |
| 1 | tablespoon fresh lemon juice | 1 | (3-ounce) package cream cheese, softened |
| 2 | teaspoons Worcestershire sauce | | Lettuce leaves |
| ½ | teaspoon Tabasco sauce, or to taste | | Mayonnaise |
| 1 | small onion, finely chopped | | |

Dissolve gelatin in hot water. Add tomato juice, lemon juice, Worcestershire, Tabasco, onion, celery, salt and pepper. Mix well. Place 1 teaspoon cream cheese in ten 4 or 5 ounce individual molds. Fill molds with tomato mixture. Chill until firm. To serve, unmold and place on a lettuce leaf. Top with a dollop of mayonnaise.

*10 servings*

## Sauerkraut Salad

1 quart sauerkraut, drained

1 cup chopped onion

1 cup chopped green bell pepper

1 cup chopped celery

1 (4-ounce) jar chopped pimiento

1½ cups sugar

½ cup white vinegar

½ cup oil

Combine ingredients. Refrigerate 8 hours before serving.

*8 servings*

*Note: Must be refrigerated 8 hours.*

# Crunchy Slaw

| | | | |
|---|---|---|---|
| 1 | (3-ounce) package beef flavored ramen noodles, crumble noodles | ⅓ | cup apple cider vinegar |
| | | ½ | cup oil |
| | | 1 | (10-ounce) package angel hair slaw mix |
| 1 | seasoning packet, reserved from ramen noodles package | 3 | green onions, chopped |
| | | 1 | (2.25-ounce) package sliced almonds |
| ¼ | cup sugar | 1 | cup sunflower seeds |

In a saucepan, boil sugar, seasoning packet, vinegar and oil until sugar is dissolved. Set aside and let cool. In a large bowl, combine slaw mix, onions, almonds, sunflower seeds and crumbled noodles. Just before serving, toss slaw with dressing.

*10 to 12 servings*

Watch out for
salmonella in raw eggs

If you plan to serve a
food containing raw
eggs to the very young
or to the elderly,
please don't.
If you plan to serve a
food containing raw
eggs to anyone with a
health problem,
think twice.
If you plan to serve a
food containing raw
eggs to an attorney,
whose face appears on
television or on
highway billboards,
forget it.
If you enjoy eating
foods containing raw
eggs, buy the eggs from
a reputable store. Keep
them refrigerated, don't
use them after the
expiration date and
don't forget about all
the times you sampled
raw cookie dough
and survived!

# Coleslaw with
# Celery Seed Dressing

| | | | |
|---|---|---|---|
| 1 | large head cabbage, shredded | ¼ | cup sugar |
| 1 | carrot, peeled and shredded | 2 | tablespoons apple cider vinegar |
| 1 | small onion, finely chopped | ½ | teaspoon celery seed |
| 1½ | tablespoons oil | 1½ | tablespoons prepared mustard |
| ¾ | cup mayonnaise | ¼ | teaspoon salt |

In a large bowl, combine cabbage, carrot and onion. In a medium bowl, whisk oil, mayonnaise, sugar, vinegar, celery seed, mustard and salt. Toss slaw with dressing. Chill 1 hour.

*10 to 12 servings*

*To prepare ahead of time, omit oil from dressing. Toss slaw with oil. Cover and refrigerate. One hour before serving, toss slaw with dressing.*

# Homemade Mayonnaise

| | | | |
|---|---|---|---|
| 1 | egg | 1 | teaspoon vinegar |
| 1 | egg yolk | 2 | cups oil |
| 1 | teaspoon salt | 4 | tablespoons fresh lemon juice |
| ½ | teaspoon ground white pepper | | |

In a food processor with the chopping blade, combine egg, egg yolk, salt, pepper and vinegar. Continue processing and slowly add oil in a very small stream through the feed tube. When mixture is thick, add lemon juice and blend. Cover and refrigerate.

*2½ cups*

# Soups & Sandwiches

 # A Park
with Promise

*Owned by the City of Meridian, 3,300-acre Bonita Lakes Park includes two lakes and several recreational areas. Park visitors enjoy hiking, bike-riding, and horse-riding trails. On the lakes, they can fish, ride paddleboats, or launch their own boats. The park hosts several athletic and community events, too.*

*These activities and the many picnic facilities make Bonita Lakes Park a popular year-round family destination. Further, with its convenient location and undeveloped acreage, it holds much promise for future tourist attractions.*

# Roasted Shallot and Bacon Soup with Crabmeat

| | | | | |
|---|---|---|---|---|
| ¾ | pound hickory smoked unsliced slab bacon | 6 | cups chicken stock | |
| 1 | pound shallots | 7 | tablespoons unsalted butter | |
| ¼ | cup olive oil | ¾ | cup all-purpose flour | |
| | Salt | ¼ | cup whipping cream | |
| | Ground black pepper | ½ | pound lump crabmeat, picked over for shells | |
| 2 | stalks celery, chopped | | | |
| 1 | medium onion, chopped | | | |

*After puréeing, mixture may be cooled completely and refrigerated 3 days. To reheat, bring to a simmer. Adjust consistency with chicken stock, if necessary. Add bacon and slivered shallots and continue with recipe instructions.*

Preheat oven to 325°F. Trim rind and excess fat from bacon. Dice into ⅜-inch pieces. In a 15x10-inch roasting pan, bake bacon 30 minutes or until well browned, stirring twice. With a slotted spoon, transfer bacon onto paper towels to drain. Reserve 2 tablespoons bacon fat and discard the rest. Lower oven temperature to 300°F. Quarter whole shallots, do not peel. Place in the roasting pan. Sprinkle with olive oil, salt and pepper. Roast 20 minutes, stirring once. Remove and cool. Trim and peel shallots. Cut half of shallots into thin slivers. In a 3-quart saucepan over medium heat, heat reserved bacon fat. Sauté quartered shallots, celery and onion 5 minutes. Add chicken stock and bring to a boil.

In a separate 3-quart saucepan over low heat, melt butter and stir in flour to make a roux. Continue cooking and stirring 6 to 8 minutes or until mixture bubbles and turns a light brown color. Stir constantly to prevent browning and scorching. Strain 4 cups of chicken stock into roux, reserving vegetables. Whisk vigorously until smooth. Add remaining stock and vegetables. Whisk until well combined. Bring to a boil. Lower heat and simmer 15 minutes. Remove from heat.

In a food processor fitted with a metal blade, purée ¼ of stock mixture at a time or in a blender, purée ½ at a time. Return to the saucepan. Over medium heat, bring to a simmer. Stir in bacon and slivered shallots. Season with salt and pepper.

In a separate saucepan, warm cream. Fold in crabmeat. Gently stir crabmeat mixture into soup. Serve immediately.

*6 to 8 servings*

# Mushroom Feta Soup

| | | | | |
|---|---|---|---|---|
| 1-2 | cloves garlic, crushed | | ½ | cup grated Parmesan cheese |
| 1 | cup unsalted butter or margarine, divided | | 1 | teaspoon fresh thyme |
| 1 | onion, diced | | 1 | teaspoon chopped fresh basil |
| 2 | tablespoons chopped green onion | | 1 | tablespoon Worcestershire sauce |
| ¾ | pound fresh mushrooms, sliced | | ¼ | teaspoon salt, or to taste |
| ½ | cup all-purpose flour | | ⅛ | teaspoon freshly ground black pepper, or to taste |
| 1 | (12-ounce) can beer | | | |
| 2 | cups chicken broth | | | |
| 1 | cup milk | | ⅛ | teaspoon cayenne pepper, or to taste |
| 1 | (12-ounce) can evaporated milk | | | |
| ½ | pound feta cheese, crumbled, divided | | | Chopped fresh basil, for garnish |

In a medium skillet, sauté garlic in 2 tablespoons butter. Add onion, green onion and mushrooms and cook until soft. Set aside.

In a large stockpot, melt remaining butter and stir in flour. Cook over low heat 5 to 8 minutes or until golden brown. Whisk in beer. Cook until thick and smooth. Combine chicken broth and milks. Slowly pour into the stockpot. Cook until thick and smooth. Add vegetable mixture, ½ of feta cheese and remaining ingredients. Simmer 10 to 15 minutes. Serve topped with remaining feta cheese and garnished with basil.

*6 to 8 servings*

# Cream of Brie Soup

| | | | | |
|---|---|---|---|---|
| 1 | bunch green onions, chopped | | 1 | quart milk |
| 2-3 | ounces mushrooms, chopped | | ½ | cup half-and-half |
| ½ | cup butter, divided | | ⅛ | teaspoon salt, or to taste |
| 12 | tablespoons all-purpose flour, divided | | ⅛ | teaspoon ground white pepper, or to taste |
| 1 | quart chicken broth, divided (see accompanying recipe) | | 4 | ounces Brie cheese |

In a skillet, sauté onions and mushrooms in 2 tablespoons butter until onion bottoms are clear but not browned. Remove from the skillet. In the same skillet, melt remaining butter and stir in 6 tablespoons flour. Blend well but do not brown. Transfer to a large stockpot. Stir in ½ of broth and blend well. Add remaining broth, milk and vegetables. Mix remaining flour with a little of broth mixture and add to soup. Stir in half-and-half and heat thoroughly. Season with salt and white pepper. When hot, add cheese. Allow cheese to melt. Blend and serve.

*8 to 10 servings*

## Chicken Broth

1 (¾ to 1-pound) chicken

Water

1 small stalk celery, cut into pieces

1 small carrot, cut into pieces

Salt

Ground black pepper

In a stockpot, cover chicken with water. Add celery, carrot, salt and pepper. Boil until chicken is very tender. Cool slightly, remove chicken and strain broth. Water may be added to make 1-quart of broth. Refrigerate. Skim fat from chilled broth.

*1 quart*

# Artichoke and Oyster Soup

| | | | |
|---|---|---|---|
| 2 | (14-ounce) cans artichoke hearts, undrained | 1 | clove garlic, minced (optional) |
| 4 | tablespoons butter | ¼ | cup chopped fresh parsley |
| 4 | tablespoons all-purpose flour | ⅛ | teaspoon dried thyme |
| 1 | (12-ounce) jar oysters, drained, reserve liquid | ⅛ | teaspoon salt, or to taste |
| | | ⅛ | teaspoon ground black pepper, or to taste |
| 1 | cup milk | 1 | cup whipping cream |
| 3 | green onions, chopped | | |

Quarter or halve 4 artichoke hearts. Set aside for garnish. In a blender, purée remaining artichoke hearts with their liquid. In a skillet, prepare a roux with butter and flour, blend well without browning. Stir in artichoke purée, oyster liquid and milk. Add green onions, garlic, parsley, thyme, salt and pepper. Simmer 10 minutes or until flavors are well blended. Add oysters and cream. Heat until oysters plump and curl around the edges. Immediately serve in deep bowls. Garnish with reserved artichoke hearts. May be frozen.

*6 to 8 servings*

# Cream of Artichoke Soup

| | | | |
|---|---|---|---|
| ½ | cup butter, divided | 1 | clove garlic, minced |
| 6 | fresh artichoke bottoms, uncooked and sliced | 1 | large baking potato, peeled and diced |
| ⅔ | cup finely chopped white onion | 1 | quart water |
| | | 2¼ | teaspoons salt |
| 1½ | stalks celery, finely chopped | ¼ | teaspoon ground white pepper |
| 1 | leek, white part only, cleaned and diced | 1 | cup whipping cream |
| | | 2 | tablespoons French brandy |

In a 3-quart saucepan, melt 6 tablespoons butter. Sauté artichoke bottoms, onion, celery, leek and garlic 7 to 10 minutes. Add potato, water, salt and pepper. Cover and simmer 20 minutes or until potatoes are very soft. Stir in cream, remaining butter and brandy. Ladle into a blender and purée. Return soup to saucepan. Reheat and serve.

*6 to 8 servings*

# Crawfish Stew

| | | | |
|---|---|---|---|
| 1 | medium onion, chopped | ¼ | teaspoon dried oregano |
| 1 | medium green bell pepper, chopped | ¼ | teaspoon cayenne pepper |
| ½ | cup butter | ¼ | teaspoon ground white pepper |
| 2 | (10¾-ounce) cans cream of mushroom soup | ¼ | teaspoon ground black pepper |
| 1 | (10-ounce) can diced tomatoes with green chiles | 1 | pound peeled crawfish tails |
| ¼ | teaspoon dried basil | | Cooked rice |

In a saucepan, simmer onion and bell pepper in butter 2 to 3 minutes. Add soup, tomatoes with green chiles and all seasonings. Bring to a boil. Add crawfish and simmer 30 minutes, stirring occasionally. Serve over rice.

*4 to 6 servings*

# Louisiana Style Chicken and Sausage Gumbo

| | | | |
|---|---|---|---|
| 2 | (3½ to 4-pound) chickens | 1 | tablespoon ground black pepper |
| | Salt | ½-1½ | tablespoons cayenne pepper, to taste |
| | Ground black pepper | | |
| 2½ | cups oil | 2-3 | pounds smoked sausage, cut into bite-size pieces |
| 2½ | cups all-purpose flour | | |
| 2 | large onions, chopped | | |
| 1 | cup celery, chopped | 4 | chicken bouillon cubes |
| 2 | (10-ounce) packages frozen chopped okra (optional) | | Parsley |
| | | | Green onions, tops only, chopped |
| 2½ | tablespoons salt | | Cooked rice |
| | | | Gumbo filé (optional) |

Place chickens in a large roaster. Fill the pan half full of water seasoned with salt and pepper. Bring to a boil. Cover and simmer 1 hour or until chickens are tender. Remove chickens. Strain broth and reserve. Debone and chop chickens. In a heavy black iron skillet on medium high heat, make a roux by heating oil for 3 minutes. Slowly stir in flour. Stir constantly until brown. Reduce heat to low, add onions and celery. Cook until soft. Transfer roux mixture to a large roaster or gumbo pot. Add enough water to reserved broth to make 1½ gallons. Stir broth into roux mixture. Bring to a boil. Add okra, salt, black pepper, cayenne pepper, sausage and bouillon cubes. Simmer 1 hour. Skim fat off the top. Add chicken. Simmer 30 minutes. Add parsley and onion tops. Simmer 5 minutes. Serve over rice. May sprinkle ½ teaspoon gumbo filé on each serving.

*16 to 18 servings*

*Leftover turkey, smoked turkey or smoked ducks may be substituted for chicken.*

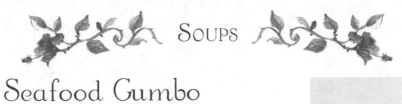

# Seafood Gumbo

| | | | | |
|---|---|---|---|---|
| 5-8 | tablespoons oil, divided | 1 | teaspoon salt | |
| 1 | pound smoked pork sausage, diced | 1 | cup fresh parsley, chopped | |
| 2 | pounds okra, chopped | 1 | (8-ounce) can tomato sauce | |
| | Water | 1 | (10-ounce) can diced tomatoes with green chiles (optional) | |
| ½ | cup butter or margarine | | | |
| 6 | tablespoons self-rising flour | 1-2 | pounds fresh shrimp, peeled and deveined | |
| 1 | large onion, chopped | | | |
| 1-2 | cloves garlic, chopped | 1-2 | pounds crabmeat, picked over for shells | |
| 1 | small bunch green onions, chopped | 1 | pound crab claws (optional) | |
| 1 | teaspoon garlic powder | | | |
| 1 | teaspoon liquid crab boil | 8 | ounces small fresh oysters (optional) | |
| 1 | teaspoon dried thyme | | Cooked rice | |
| ½ | teaspoon gumbo filé | | | |
| 2-4 | bay leaves | | | |

In a large stockpot, heat 2 to 3 tablespoons oil and brown sausage. Reduce heat. Add okra and simmer 20 minutes or until tender. Stir in 2½ cups water and cover. Simmer over low heat while continuing with recipe.

In a large skillet over medium to medium high, melt 4 to 5 tablespoons oil with butter. Stir in flour to make a roux. Cook 15 to 20 minutes until roux is very brown. Be very careful to stir constantly to prevent burning. When browned, stir in onion, garlic, green onions, garlic powder, crab boil, thyme and gumbo filé. Stir constantly 4 to 5 minutes or until onions are tender, being careful not to scorch mixture.

Combine roux mixture with okra mixture and blend well. Add water until the mixture is covered and simmer on low heat for 20 minutes. Add remaining ingredients, except seafood and rice. If necessary, add more water. Cover and simmer over low heat 30 minutes, stirring 3 times. Increase heat to high, add seafood and simmer 5 minutes, stirring constantly. Remove from heat. Let sit 30 minutes to 1 hour covered. Discard bay leaves. Serve in individual bowls over cooked rice.

*10 to 15 servings*

## Gumbo Filé

Louisiana's Choctaw Indians are believed to be the first to use gumbo filé to thicken dishes. Filé is made from dried sassafras leaves which have been ground. It thickens and flavors gumbos and other Creole dishes.

# Catfish Gumbo

*Quick, easy and delicious*

| | | | |
|---|---|---|---|
| ½ | cup chopped green bell pepper | 1 | (10-ounce) package frozen sliced okra |
| ½ | cup chopped celery | 2 | teaspoons salt |
| ½ | cup chopped onion | ¼ | teaspoon dried thyme |
| 1 | clove garlic, finely chopped | ¼ | teaspoon ground black pepper |
| ¼ | cup oil | 1 | whole bay leaf |
| 2 | beef bouillon cubes | 1 | pound catfish fillets, cut into 1-inch pieces |
| 2 | cups boiling water | 1½ | cups hot cooked rice |
| 1 | (14½-ounce) can tomatoes | | |

In a stockpot, sauté bell pepper, celery, onion and garlic in oil until tender. Dissolve bouillon cubes in boiling water. Add to sautéed mixture. Stir in tomatoes, okra, salt, thyme, pepper and bay leaf. Cover and simmer 30 minutes. Add catfish. Cover and simmer 15 minutes or until catfish flakes easily when tested with a fork. Discard bay leaf. Place ¼ cup of rice in each of six soup bowls and fill with gumbo.

*6 servings*

# Shrimp Confetti Soup

*A colorful presentation*

| | | | | |
|---|---|---|---|---|
| 2 | tablespoons olive oil | 1 | tablespoon chopped fresh thyme |
| 1 | cup chopped yellow onion | ½ | tablespoon chopped fresh sage |
| ½ | cup chopped green bell pepper | 2 | tablespoons chopped fresh parsley |
| ¼ | cup chopped red bell pepper | 1 | pound medium shrimp, peeled and deveined |
| ¼ | cup chopped celery | 12 | ounces crab claws, reserve 6 to 8 for garnish |
| 2 | tablespoons chopped garlic | | |
| 2 | cups chicken broth | ½ | cup diagonally cut green onion, for garnish |
| 1 | quart whipping cream | | |
| 1 | cup cream style corn | | |
| 1 | cup whole kernel corn, drained | 1 | cup shredded mozzarella cheese, for garnish |
| 1 | (10-ounce) can diced tomatoes with green chiles, drained | | |

In a heavy stockpot over high heat, heat olive oil. Sauté onion, bell peppers, celery and garlic 5 minutes. Stir in broth, cream, corns, tomatoes, thyme, sage and parsley. Reduce heat to low and simmer 20 minutes, stirring occasionally. Add shrimp and crab claws. Simmer until shrimp turn pink. Ladle into soup bowls. Sprinkle each serving with green onion and cheese. Add a crab claw to each bowl.

*6 to 8 servings*

# Spicy Vegetable Soup
*A vegetable soup kids love!*

| | | | |
|---|---|---|---|
| 1 | pound ground beef | 1 | cup chopped celery |
| 1 | cup chopped onion | 1 | teaspoon sugar |
| ¼ | teaspoon garlic powder or 2 cloves garlic, pressed | 1 | teaspoon salt |
| | | ½ | teaspoon ground black pepper |
| 1 | (30-ounce) jar meatless spaghetti sauce | 1 | (10-ounce) can diced tomatoes with green chiles |
| 1 | (14½-ounce) can beef broth, undiluted | 1 | (15-ounce) can mixed vegetables |
| 2 | cups water | | |

In a large Dutch oven over medium heat, brown ground beef, onion and garlic, stirring to crumble. Drain. Add sauce, broth, water, celery, sugar, salt and pepper. Bring to a boil and cover. Reduce heat and simmer 20 minutes, stirring occasionally. Stir in tomatoes and vegetables. Return to a boil. Cover and simmer 10 to 12 minutes.

*12 servings*

*Recipe may be doubled, but do not double the diced tomatoes with green chiles.*

*Ground venison may be substituted for ground beef. Also, any leftover cooked vegetables may be substituted for mixed vegetables.*

## Brunswick Stew

2 (8-ounce) cans barbequed beef or pork

2 (4½-ounce) cans chunk chicken

1 small onion, chopped

1 (14¾-ounce) can cream style corn

1 (15¼-ounce) can lima beans

1 (14½-ounce) can diced tomatoes

2 tablespoons Worcestershire sauce

⅛ teaspoon salt, or to taste

⅛ teaspoon ground black pepper, or to taste

In a crockpot, combine all ingredients. Cook on high 1 to 2 hours or on low 4 to 6 hours, stirring occasionally.

*6 to 8 servings*

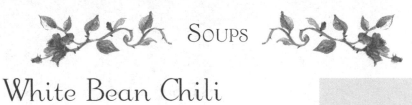
# White Bean Chili

| | |
|---|---|
| 2-3 | boneless, skinless chicken breast halves, sliced into strips |
| 2 | tablespoons oil |
| 1 | medium onion, chopped |
| ¼ | cup chopped celery |
| 1 | clove garlic, minced |
| 2 | (14½-ounce) cans chicken broth |
| 2 | (14½-ounce) cans diced tomatoes, undrained (optional) |
| 2 | (4½-ounce) cans chopped green chiles |
| ¼ | cup fresh lime juice |
| ½ | teaspoon ground cumin |
| 1 | teaspoon dried oregano |
| 1 | teaspoon dried cilantro |
| ⅛ | teaspoon cayenne pepper |
| 2 | (15.8-ounce) cans great Northern beans, undrained |
| 1½ | cups frozen white shoepeg corn |
| | Shredded Monterey Jack cheese, for garnish |
| | Sour cream, for garnish |
| | Chopped green onions, for garnish |
| | Salsa, for garnish |
| | Fresh cilantro, for garnish |

In a skillet, sauté chicken strips in oil until lightly browned. Let cool and cut into small chunks. In the same skillet, sauté onion, celery and garlic until soft. Transfer sautéed vegetables to a stockpot. Stir in chicken broth, tomatoes, green chiles, lime juice, cumin, oregano, cilantro, cayenne pepper, beans and corn. Bring to a boil and add chicken. Reduce heat to low, simmer until ready to serve. Top with your choice of garnishes.

*8 to 10 servings*

## Cowboy Bean Stew

*Great crockpot recipe - serves a crowd!*

1½ pounds ground beef

1 small onion, chopped

1 tablespoon chopped garlic

1 cup firmly packed brown sugar

1 cup ketchup

1½ teaspoons dry mustard

1 cup Worcestershire sauce

2 (15¼-ounce) cans lima beans, drained

2 (15½-ounce) cans hot chili beans

2 (15-ounce) cans pork and beans

In a skillet, brown meat, onion and garlic. Drain well. Transfer to a crockpot. Stir in remaining ingredients. Simmer on low for 6 to 8 hours.

*10 to 12 servings*

*Note: Must simmer 6 to 8 hours.*

103

# Baked Potato Soup

## Crockpot Chili

1½ pounds ground beef

1 cup chopped celery

1 cup chopped onion

1 green bell pepper, chopped

1 (8-ounce) can tomato sauce

1 (1-ounce) package chili seasoning

2 tablespoons sugar

1 teaspoon garlic powder

1 (15-ounce) can kidney beans

1 (15.8-ounce) can great Northern beans

1 (14½-ounce) can diced tomatoes

⅛ teaspoon salt, or to taste

⅛ teaspoon ground black pepper, or to taste

In a large skillet, brown meat. Drain well. Add celery, onion, and bell pepper and sauté until vegetables are soft. Drain and transfer to a crockpot. Stir in remaining ingredients. Cook 3 to 4 hours on low heat.

*10 to 12 servings*

| | | | |
|---|---|---|---|
| 4 | medium baking potatoes, unpeeled and cut into fourths | 1 | teaspoon dried parsley flakes |
| ¼ | cup butter or margarine | 1 | teaspoon dried chives |
| 5 | tablespoons all-purpose flour | ½ | teaspoon salt |
| 2 | (14½-ounce) cans chicken broth | ¼ | teaspoon ground black pepper |
| 2 | cups half-and-half or evaporated skimmed milk | | Chopped onion, for garnish |
| | | | Shredded Cheddar cheese, for garnish |
| | | | Cooked crumbled bacon, for garnish |

Preheat oven to 350°F. Bake potatoes until partially cooked but still firm. Dice potatoes and set aside. In a heavy saucepan over low heat, melt butter. Stir in flour until smooth. Increase heat to medium and add broth. Continue stirring and heat until thickened. Stir in cream and cook until thickened. Add potatoes, parsley, chives, salt and pepper. Simmer 10 minutes. Reduce heat and simmer 20 minutes, stirring occasionally until mixture reaches desired consistency. Ladle into individual serving bowls. Garnish with onion, cheese and bacon.

*8 to 10 servings*

# Spicy Squash Soup

| | | | | |
|---|---|---|---|---|
| 1 | winter squash, such as butternut | 1 | tablespoon whole cumin seed |
| 1 | tablespoon butter | ⅛ | teaspoon salt, or to taste |
| 2 | small yellow onions, diced | ⅛ | teaspoon ground black pepper, or to taste |
| 1 | mild chili pepper, cored, seeded and diced | | Lightly whipped cream, for garnish |
| 1 | quart chicken stock or canned broth | | Toasted pine nuts, for garnish |

Preheat oven to 375°F. Cut squash in half and scrape out all pulp and seeds. Place squash face down in a baking pan with enough water to cover the bottom of the pan. Bake until soft, about 45 minutes. Peel off and discard skin, mash squash, reserve juices and set aside. In a large saucepan over low heat, melt butter and sauté onions and chili pepper. Add cooked squash and pan juices to sautéed mixture. Stir in stock and bring to a simmer. In a hot, dry saucepan over medium high heat, toast cumin seeds until golden brown. Using a mortar and pestle, grind cumin to a fine powder. Add to soup. Season with salt and pepper. Garnish individual servings with a dollop of cream and toasted pine nuts.

*8 servings*

The "Singing Brakeman" Jimmy Rodgers, former brakeman for the New Orleans and Northeastern Railroad, brought a unique mixture of German, English, Irish and African-American music to the nation's attention. His "blues-yodels" style of music, popularized in the late 1920's and early 1930's, earned him fame as the "Father of Country Music." The "Singing Brakeman," as Rodgers came to be called, was inducted into the Country Music Hall of Fame, the Bluegrass Hall of Fame and the Rock 'N Roll Hall of Fame for his contributions to the world of music. The Jimmy Rodgers Memorial Festival, held each year in Meridian, features concerts by top country music artists and attracts visitors from as far away as England and Australia.

# Corn and Shrimp Chowder

| | | | |
|---|---|---|---|
| ½ | pound sliced bacon | 2 | tablespoons all-purpose flour |
| 2 | cups finely chopped onion | 2 | (10¾-ounce) cans cream of shrimp soup |
| 1 | cup finely chopped celery | 1 | (10¾-ounce) can cream of celery soup |
| ½ | cup finely chopped green bell pepper | 1 | quart half-and-half |
| ½ | cup grated carrots | 1 | (14¾-ounce) can cream style corn |
| 2 | bay leaves | 1 | (15¼-ounce) can whole kernel corn |
| 2 | cups diced potatoes | 2 | pounds shrimp, peeled and deveined |
| ¼ | cup water | | |
| 1 | tablespoon salt | | |
| 1 | teaspoon ground black pepper | | |

Cook bacon until crisp. Remove bacon and drain, reserving 3 tablespoons bacon grease. In a saucepan, sauté onion, celery, bell pepper and carrots in reserved bacon grease. Add bay leaves, potatoes, water, salt and pepper. Sprinkle in flour. Stir in soups and half-and-half. Bring to a boil. Add corn. Simmer over low heat 30 to 45 minutes or until potatoes are done. Add shrimp. Cook until shrimp turn pink. Adjust consistency with milk. Discard bay leaves. Ladle into serving bowls. Garnish with crumbled bacon.

*12 to 15 servings*

## Asparagus Spinach Soup

1 onion, chopped

6 tablespoons margarine

8 cups chicken stock or broth

2 potatoes, peeled and grated

2 carrots, thinly sliced

¼ cup long grain white rice

2 cups powdered coffee creamer

1 (10-ounce) package frozen chopped spinach, thawed

1 (14½-ounce) can cut asparagus, undrained

Chicken bouillon

Salt

Ground black pepper

In a stockpot, sauté onion in margarine until transparent. Add chicken stock, potatoes, carrots and rice. Simmer 30 minutes. Add creamer, spinach and asparagus. Simmer an additional 30 minutes. Season with bouillon, salt and pepper.

*12 servings*

Asparagus Spinach Soup was a specialty of Marcia Via's Square Plate Restaurant which operated during the 1980's in downtown Meridian.

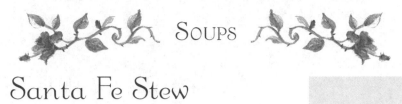

# SOUPS

## Santa Fe Stew

| | | | |
|---|---|---|---|
| 2 | pounds ground beef | 1 | (16-ounce) can kidney or red beans, undrained |
| ½ | medium onion, diced (optional) | 1 | (15½-ounce) can black-eyed peas, undrained |
| 1 | (1¼-ounce) package taco seasoning mix | 2 | (14½-ounce) cans stewed tomatoes, undrained |
| 1 | (1-ounce) package ranch party dip mix | 1 | (15¼-ounce) can whole kernel corn, undrained |
| 2 | (15-ounce) cans ranch style beans, undrained | | |

In a skillet, brown ground beef and onion. Drain well. Transfer to a stockpot. Add taco mix and ranch party dip, mix well. Stir in beans, peas, tomatoes and corn. Simmer over medium low heat until thoroughly heated.

*6 to 8 servings*

*Santa Fe Stew is also an excellent dip. Serve with tortilla chips.*

## Tortilla Soup

1 large onion, chopped

4-6 cloves garlic, minced

2 tablespoons chopped fresh cilantro

2 tablespoons olive oil

2 cups chopped cooked chicken

2 quarts chicken broth

1 (10-ounce) can diced tomatoes with green chiles

1 tablespoon ground cumin

1 bay leaf

1 (11-ounce) can white shoepeg corn

½ teaspoon ground black pepper

Shredded Monterey Jack cheese, for garnish

Avocado slices, for garnish

Crumbled tortilla chips, for garnish

In a saucepan, sauté onion, garlic and cilantro in olive oil. Add chicken, broth, tomatoes, cumin, bay leaf, corn and pepper. Bring to a boil and reduce heat. Simmer 30 minutes. Discard bay leaf. Serve topped with cheese, avocado and tortilla chips.

*6 to 8 servings*

# Hearty Braised Beef Stew

May use a
small amount of
quick-cooking oats,
grated potato or instant
potato flakes to
thicken stews.

1-1½ pounds cubed stewing beef
All-purpose flour
Salt
Ground black pepper
3-4 tablespoons olive oil
1 medium onion, chopped
3 cloves garlic, minced

1 cup sliced carrot or whole baby carrots
1 (14½-ounce) can diced tomatoes
1 cup canned beef broth
¼ teaspoon dried thyme
¼ teaspoon dried oregano
Cooked noodles

Dredge meat in a mixture of flour, salt and pepper. In a braiser or a skillet with a tight fitting lid, brown meat in olive oil. When evenly browned on all sides, add onion and garlic. Sauté 4 to 5 minutes. Add carrot and tomatoes. Stir in broth, thyme and oregano. Bring to a boil. Cover and simmer 3 hours. Check every 30 minutes to be sure liquid has not evaporated. Add more broth if needed. Serve over noodles.

*6 servings*

*Variation: Before simmering, add ¼ cup red wine. One hour before finishing, may also add sliced small potatoes and quartered fresh mushrooms.*

# Stromboli

| | | | |
|---|---|---|---|
| 1 | (16-ounce) loaf frozen bread dough, thawed according to package directions | ½ | teaspoon dried oregano, divided |
| ¼ | pound thinly sliced ham | 3 | ounces sliced Provolone cheese |
| ¼ | pound sliced hard salami | 1 | cup shredded mozzarella cheese |
| ½ | teaspoon dried basil, divided | 2 | tablespoons butter, melted and divided |
| | | 1 | teaspoon cornmeal |

Preheat oven to 375°F. Place bread dough on a lightly greased baking sheet. Pat into a 15x10-inch rectangle. Arrange ham slices lengthwise down center. Place salami on top. Sprinkle with ¼ teaspoon basil and ¼ teaspoon oregano. Arrange Provolone cheese over herbs and top with mozzarella cheese. Sprinkle with remaining herbs. Moisten all edges of dough with water. Bring both long edges of dough to center. Securely press edges together to seal. Seal ends. Brush dough with 1 tablespoon of butter. Sprinkle with cornmeal and carefully invert. Brush top with remaining butter. Bake 20 to 22 minutes.

*4 servings*

# Mexican Beef Heros

| | | | |
|---|---|---|---|
| 1 | pound ground beef | ½ | teaspoon salt |
| ½ | cup chopped onion | ½ | teaspoon chili powder |
| ½ | cup sliced ripe olives | 6 | hero buns |
| 1 | (4½-ounce) can chopped green chiles | 6 | slices Colby cheese |
| | | 6 | slices cooked bacon |
| ¼ | cup ketchup | 6 | slices Muenster cheese |

Preheat oven to 375°F. In a skillet, brown beef and onion. Drain well. Return to skillet. Stir in olives, green chiles, ketchup, salt and chili powder. On bottom of each bun, layer Colby cheese, meat mixture, bacon, Muenster cheese and bun top. Wrap in foil. Bake 15 minutes.

*6 servings*

## Easy French Dip Sandwiches

1 (3-pound) beef brisket

1 (1.3-ounce) package dry onion soup mix

1 (14½-ounce) can beef broth

8 mini baguettes or sandwich buns

Place beef in a crockpot on low heat. In a small bowl, combine dry soup mix and beef broth. Pour over beef. Cover and cook 8 to 10 hours or until beef is tender. Skim fat from liquid. Remove beef and slice thinly across the grain. Fill baguettes or buns with beef. Serve with broth for dipping.

*8 servings*

*Note: Must cook 8 to 10 hours.*

# Grilled Portobello Mushroom Sandwiches

*Serve open-faced with Roasted Pepper Mayonnaise*

| | | | |
|---|---|---|---|
| 4 | large portobello mushroom caps | | Roasted Pepper Mayonnaise (see accompanying recipe) |
| 4 | slices purple onion | | |
| | Olive oil | | |
| | Salt | 2 | tablespoons balsamic vinegar |
| | Ground black pepper | | |
| 4 | (½-inch) thick crusty country bread slices | 4 | cups baby spinach, washed |

Prepare grill. Brush mushroom caps and onion with oil. Sprinkle with salt and pepper. Grill mushrooms and onion 12 minutes and bread 5 minutes, turning often. Vegetables should be tender and bread should be golden. In a bowl, whisk 2 tablespoons Roasted Pepper Mayonnaise with vinegar. Toss with spinach. Divide among 4 plates. On spinach, layer bread slice, mushroom cap and onion slice. Top with 2 tablespoons Roasted Pepper Mayonnaise.

*4 servings*

*May served mushroom caps topped with spinach on whole-wheat hamburger buns.*

## Roasted Pepper Mayonnaise

½ cup chopped roasted red peppers, drained well

¼ cup low-fat mayonnaise

1 clove garlic, chopped

⅛ teaspoon cayenne pepper

Salt

Ground black pepper

In a food processor, blend red peppers, mayonnaise, garlic and cayenne pepper until smooth. Season with salt and black pepper. Refrigerate until ready to serve.

*½ cup*

# Cheesy Roast Beef and Ham Sandwiches

| | | | |
|---|---|---|---|
| 1 | (16-ounce) loaf unsliced Italian bread | ⅓ | cup chopped green onion |
| 2 | (8-ounce) packages cream cheese, softened | ¼ | cup mayonnaise |
| | | 1 | pound thinly sliced cooked ham |
| 1 | cup shredded Cheddar cheese | ½ | pound thinly sliced cooked roast beef |
| | | 12-14 | thinly sliced hamburger dill pickles |

Cut bread in half lengthwise. Hollow out top and bottom of loaves, leaving a ½-inch shell. Discard removed bread. In a small bowl, combine cheeses, onion and mayonnaise. Spread on both sides of cut bread. Layer ham and roast beef on bottom of bread. Layer pickles over meats. Replace bread top and gently press halves together. Wrap in foil. Refrigerate 1 day. To serve, cut into 1½-inch slices.

*12 to 14 servings*

*Note: Must be made 1 day in advance.*

## Miss Sadie's Air Sandwiches

During the summer many Meridian children spent happy hours in the imaginative world of Miss Sadie. She told stories with puppets and created magic out of thin air. Holding a piece of Sunbeam bread in one hand and an imaginary can of air in the other, Miss Sadie would spray the air onto the bread, saying "Pssst." Folding the air-filled bread in half, she offered the children an "air sandwich" and a slice of fantasy.

# Super Bowl Sandwich

Al and Fred Key made aviation history in 1935 when they broke all records for sustained flight. The brothers, owners of a small flight school and managers of the Meridian Airport, remained airborne for more than 27 days.

A unique mid-air refueling technique was developed by the Keys and mechanical expert Anthony Davis Hunter. The plane used by the Key brothers was a Curtis Robbin powered by a 175 horsepower Wright Whirlwind engine. This plane, christened the "Ole Miss," flew to Washington, D.C. in 1955 to become a permanent exhibit for the Smithsonian Institution.

| | | | |
|---|---|---|---|
| 1 | (16-ounce) loaf unsliced French bread | ¼ | cup chopped fresh parsley |
| ½ | pound ground beef | 1 | teaspoon Dijon mustard |
| ½ | pound bulk pork sausage | ½ | teaspoon fennel seeds |
| 1 | medium onion, chopped | ¼ | teaspoon salt |
| 1 | cup shredded mozzarella cheese | ¼ | teaspoon ground black pepper |
| 2 | eggs, beaten | 2 | tablespoons butter or margarine, melted |
| | | | Garlic salt |

Preheat oven to 400°F. Cut off ends of bread loaf and discard. Hollow out center of loaf with a long serrated knife, leaving ½-inch shell. In a food processor, grind bread from inside of loaf. Set aside. In a skillet, brown beef, sausage and onion. Drain well. Add 1 cup bread crumbs, cheese, eggs and parsley. Simmer on low until eggs are cooked and cheese is melted. Add mustard, fennel, salt and pepper. Mix well. Place all ingredients inside bread shell. Brush melted butter over bread. Sprinkle with garlic salt. Wrap in foil. Bake 20 minutes.

*4 to 6 servings*

# Entrées

# A Grand Tradition Returns

*First opened in 1890 by the Marks-Rothenberg family, Meridian's elegant Grand Opera House attracted America's premier musical and dramatic performances on tour between New York and New Orleans. Performers included Sarah Bernhardt, Lillian Russell, Lon Chaney, Helen Hayes, and John Philip Sousa. George Gershwin signed a dressing room wall to attest that he performed there, too.*

*The Grand Opera House, so named because it adhered to strict theatrical standards, is the only remaining second-story access McAlfatrick Theater in the world. To enter the auditorium, guests ascended a marble staircase leading to the second-floor parquet, dress circle, and plush private boxes. A massive unique gas sunburner illuminated the plush interiors decorated in cream, blue, gold, and rose.*

*The Grand Opera House eventually closed, but recent efforts to restore and revitalize the beautiful building hold great promise for restoring Meridian's place as a leader in Mississippi's great tradition of cultural arts.*

# Chicken with Raspberry Basil Sauce

*Elegant, healthy and delicious!*

| | | | |
|---|---|---|---|
| 8 | boneless, skinless chicken breast halves | ½ | teaspoon curry powder |
| 5 | ounces raspberry spreadable fruit | ½ | teaspoon garlic powder |
| | | ¾ | cup fresh raspberries, reserve some for garnish |
| ½ | cup pineapple juice | | |
| ¼ | cup soy sauce | ¾ | cup fresh basil leaves, reserve some for garnish |
| 2 | tablespoons rice wine vinegar | | |
| ½ | teaspoon chili powder | | |

Place chicken in a 13x9-inch baking dish. Blend remaining ingredients together. Pour over chicken. Cover, refrigerate and marinate for several hours. Preheat oven to 350°F. Bake 45 minutes to 1 hour or until done. Garnish with reserved raspberries and basil.

*8 servings*

Sela Ward, actress

# Chicken Breasts Royale

| | | | |
|---|---|---|---|
| 4 | boneless, skinless chicken breast halves | 3 | tablespoons margarine |
| 8 | ounces cream cheese with chives | 6 | ounces fresh mushrooms, sliced |
| 3 | tablespoons grated Parmesan cheese | ½ | cup sherry |

Flatten chicken between sheets of wax paper. Spread cream cheese over chicken. Sprinkle with Parmesan cheese. Roll up each breast and secure with 1 or 2 toothpicks. In a skillet, heat margarine. Add chicken, cover and sauté over low heat about 10 minutes, turning once. Add mushrooms and sherry. Cook 5 minutes.

*4 servings*

# Chicken Piccata
*Specialty of Calla Grill*

## Calla Grill

*Formerly Gigi's Bakery and Restaurant*

Gigi's began in 1998 when a grandmother named "Gigi" began selling cakes which were so delicious that many of Meridian's other grandmothers stopped baking altogether. Working or bridge-playing grandmas simply neglected to reveal to their families which grandmother had baked that marvelous Italian cream cake. In 1999, Gigi sold her business to Terry Clark who has continued her baking tradition. Terry's desserts and lunches have won Gigi's two People's Choice Awards, and have been responsible for the expansion of the business to include fine dining on the weekends in the Calla Grill.

| | | | |
|---|---|---|---|
| 1 | cup all-purpose flour | 1 | cup butter |
| 2 | teaspoons seasoning salt | 5 | tablespoons fresh lemon juice |
| 4 | teaspoons garlic powder, divided | 3 | tablespoons capers, drained well |
| 2 | teaspoons ground black pepper | 8 | ounces vermicelli or angel hair pasta, prepared according to package directions |
| 4 | boneless, skinless chicken breast halves | | |
| 2 | egg whites, beaten | | |

In a bowl, combine flour, salt, 2 teaspoons garlic powder and pepper. Dip chicken in egg whites. Roll in seasoned flour. In a skillet, heat butter and remaining garlic powder until very hot, but being careful not to burn. Place chicken in the skillet. Cover and cook 5 minutes. Reduce heat and turn chicken over. Add lemon juice and capers. Cover and cook 5 minutes or until done. Serve over cooked pasta. Spoon caper sauce over chicken.

*4 servings*

Terry Clark, owner and chef, Calla Grill, Meridian, MS

# Herbed Chicken with Sun-Dried Tomatoes

| | | | |
|---|---|---|---|
| 4 | boneless, skinless chicken breast halves | 3 | ounces oil-packed sun-dried tomatoes, drained, cut into thin strips |
| 1 | bunch green onions, chopped | 2 | teaspoons dried dill weed |
| ¼ | red bell pepper, chopped | ½ | pint whipping cream |
| ½ | cup olive oil | 1 | (8-ounce) carton sour cream |
| ½ | cup butter or margarine | | Pasta, cooked according to package directions |
| ¼ | teaspoon dried basil | | |
| ¼ | teaspoon dried tarragon | | |
| ¼ | teaspoon ground black pepper | | |
| ½ | teaspoon salt | | |

Cut chicken into thin slices. In a skillet, sauté green onions and red pepper in oil and butter. Remove vegetables with a slotted spoon to a bowl. Add chicken to the skillet and sauté until cooked through, drain. Stir in basil, tarragon, pepper, salt, tomatoes, dill weed and sautéed vegetables. Add cream and sour cream. Mix well. Cook over low heat until thoroughly heated, stirring constantly. Serve over pasta.

*4 servings*

For less calories, substitute evaporated skimmed milk for whipping cream and light sour cream for sour cream.

# Sicilian Skillet Chicken

| | | | |
|---|---|---|---|
| 4 | boneless, skinless chicken breast halves | 3 | tablespoons olive oil |
| 6 | tablespoons grated Parmesan cheese, divided | 1 | cup sliced fresh mushrooms |
| 3 | tablespoons all-purpose flour | ½ | onion, finely sliced |
| ⅛ | teaspoon salt, or to taste | 1 | teaspoon dried rosemary |
| ⅛ | teaspoon ground black pepper, or to taste | 1 | (14½-ounce) can Italian style stewed tomatoes |
| | | 8 | ounces pasta, cooked and drained |

Flatten chicken between sheets of wax paper. Coat with 4 tablespoons of Parmesan. Mix flour, salt and pepper. Roll chicken in flour mixture. In a skillet, cook chicken in oil over medium-high heat until done. Remove to a serving dish and keep warm. In the same skillet, sauté mushrooms, onion and rosemary until soft. Add tomatoes, cooking uncovered over medium-high heat until thickened. Spoon over chicken. Top with remaining cheese. Serve over hot pasta.

*4 servings*

## Cranberry Orange Relish

2 oranges

1½ (12-ounce) bags cranberries, fresh or frozen

2 medium to large apples, unpeeled, cored and quartered

2 cups sugar

¼ cup orange liqueur, or to taste

Slice top and bottoms off oranges. Quarter and remove seeds. In a food processor, chop oranges, cranberries and apples. Once processed, place in a large bowl. Stir in sugar and liqueur by hand. Cover and chill in refrigerator for several hours before serving. May be frozen; thaw before serving.

*6 cups*

*This is an excellent accompaniment served with baked chicken or turkey.*

# Chicken Pot Pie

| | | | |
|---|---|---|---|
| 1 | (10¾-ounce) can cream of potato soup | 2 | cups diced cooked chicken |
| 1 | (10¾-ounce) can cream of chicken soup | ½ | cup milk |
| 2 | cups frozen mixed vegetables | 2 | (9-inch) pie crusts |
| | | 1 | egg, lightly beaten (optional) |

Preheat oven to 375°F. Combine soups, vegetables, chicken and milk. Spoon into 1 pie crust. Cover with remaining crust, crimping edges to seal. Slit top crust and brush with egg, if desired. Bake 40 minutes. Cool 10 minutes.

*6 servings*

# Chicken Scallopini

*Heart healthy recipe*

| | | | |
|---|---|---|---|
| 4 | boneless, skinless chicken breast halves | ¼ | teaspoon dried marjoram |
| | Salt substitute | ¼ | teaspoon dried thyme |
| 4 | egg whites, lightly beaten | 1 | tablespoon fresh lemon juice |
| 3 | tablespoons bread crumbs | ¼ | cup Butter Buds |
| | Garlic powder | ¾ | cup white wine |
| | | ½ | cup sherry |

Flatten chicken slightly between sheets of wax paper. Salt lightly. Dip pieces into egg whites, then dredge through bread crumbs. Season with garlic powder. In a large skillet, combine marjoram, thyme, lemon juice and Butter Buds. Add chicken and brown. Add white wine and cook over low heat 30 minutes or until tender. Add sherry just before serving.

*4 servings*

# Baked Chicken with Mushrooms and Sherry

| | | | |
|---|---|---|---|
| 8 | boneless, skinless chicken breast halves | 1 | (8-ounce) carton sour cream |
| | Salt | 1 | (4-ounce) can sliced mushrooms, drained or 1 cup fresh sliced mushrooms |
| ½ | cup sherry | | |
| ½ | cup margarine, melted | | |
| 1 | (10¾-ounce) can cream of mushroom soup | | |

Preheat oven to 350°F. Salt chicken breasts and place in a lightly greased 13x9-inch baking dish. Combine remaining ingredients in a mixing bowl and blend well. Pour over chicken and bake 1 hour to 1 hour 30 minutes.

*8 servings*

Cooking sherry is a salt-laden inferior sherry, which would not be consumed by itself. It is best not to use wines in cooking which would normally not be served at the table. The added salt can also interfere with the flavor of the dish.

# Baked Chicken Supreme

| | | | |
|---|---|---|---|
| 1 | (8-ounce) carton sour cream | ½ | teaspoon salt |
| 2 | tablespoons fresh lemon juice | ¼ | teaspoon ground black pepper |
| 2 | teaspoons Worcestershire sauce | 6 | boneless, skinless chicken breast halves |
| 2 | cloves garlic, minced | 1 | cup bread crumbs |
| | | ½ | cup butter |

Combine sour cream, lemon juice, Worcestershire, garlic, salt and pepper. Add chicken, coating each piece. Cover and refrigerate overnight. Preheat oven to 350°F. Roll chicken in crumbs and arrange in single layer in a 13x9-inch baking dish. Melt butter and spoon half over chicken. Bake uncovered 45 minutes. Spoon remaining butter over chicken and bake 10 to 15 minutes.

*6 servings*

*Note: Must be refrigerated overnight before cooking.*

# Easy Chicken and Dumplings
### Comfort food that kids love

| | | | |
|---|---|---|---|
| 1 | large fryer, cut up or 4 chicken breast halves | 6 | eggs, hard-boiled, peeled and chopped |
| 1 | large yellow onion, finely chopped | ⅛ | teaspoon salt, or to taste |
| ½ | cup margarine | ⅛ | teaspoon ground black pepper, or to taste |
| 1 | (10¾-ounce) can cream of chicken soup | 1 | (8.5-ounce) package 7-inch flour tortillas, cut into 1-inch pieces |
| 1 | (10¾-ounce) can cream of celery soup | | |

Place chicken in a large Dutch oven and cover with water. Add onion and boil until tender. Remove from liquid and cool. Strain and reserve broth. Debone chicken and discard skin, bones and fat. Shred meat and return to broth. Add margarine, soups and eggs. Bring to a slow boil, stirring occasionally. Add salt and pepper to taste. One at a time, drop half of tortillas into broth. Stir. Add remaining tortillas one at a time. Cover and simmer 10 to 15 minutes. Stir as little as possible.

*4 to 6 servings*

---

## Bar-B-Que Sauce for Chicken

2 cups cider vinegar

1 cup vegetable oil

1 teaspoon Tabasco sauce

½ teaspoon ground black pepper

1 teaspoon crushed red pepper

1 tablespoon onion powder

¼ teaspoon liquid garlic

4 tablespoons salt

In a saucepan, combine all ingredients. Grill chicken 20 minutes. Baste with sauce. Continue basting every 5 to 10 minutes until chicken is done.

*3 cups, enough for 8 to 10 chicken breast halves*

Everyone claims this bar-b-que sauce to be "our secret family recipe," but it was really developed by the Mississippi Department of Agriculture and Commissioner Jim Buck Ross in their effort to promote Mississippi's poultry industry.

# Chicken and Wild Rice

| | | | |
|---|---|---|---|
| 2 | cups carrots, cut into 1-inch julienne strips | ½ | cup sherry |
| 4 | tablespoons butter, divided | ½ | teaspoon salt |
| 1 | (6-ounce) package long grain and wild rice, prepared according to package directions | 6 | boneless, skinless chicken breast halves, cooked and torn into pieces |
| 10 | medium mushrooms, sliced | 2 | (14-ounce) cans artichoke hearts, drained and quartered |
| 10 | green onions, chopped | 10 | slices thick bacon, fried and crumbled |
| 2 | (10¾-ounce) cans cream of chicken soup | 3 | cups shredded mozzarella cheese |
| ½ | cup whipping cream | | Grated Parmesan cheese |

Preheat oven to 350°F. Blanch carrots 5 minutes. Rinse with cold water and drain well. Grease a 13x9-inch baking dish with 2 tablespoons butter and spread cooked rice over bottom. In a skillet, sauté mushrooms and green onions in remaining butter. Add soup, cream, sherry and salt. Mix well. In a very large bowl, combine mushroom mixture, chicken, artichoke hearts, bacon, carrots and mozzarella cheese. Mix well. Spread over rice and sprinkle with Parmesan. Bake covered 30 minutes. Uncover and bake 15 minutes.

*8 to 10 servings*

## No Longer "Chicken Feed"

Mississippians have always valued the chicken. Years ago, a housewife's family recipe for fried chicken was guarded more carefully than Grandma's silver. In addition to its value as dinner, the chicken also provided pest control. One expert, who wishes to remain anonymous, reports that the termite is a "chicken's chocolate." Sadly, the average Mississippian no longer maintains an individual relationship with the chicken. Poultry production is now agribusiness. Huge facilities process vast amounts of poultry. The estimated impact of the poultry industry on Mississippi's economy is greater than 8 billion dollars annually. That's not "chicken feed."

# Mexican Chicken

P.S.'s favorite Lamar memory is a cheerleader squad supper hosted by M.B. Mexican Chicken was the featured entrée and received "#1" reviews from all! Maybe it should be named #1 Raider Casserole! Go Raiders!

| | | | |
|---|---|---|---|
| 1 | (13½-ounce) bag tortilla chips | 3 | cups shredded Cheddar cheese, divided |
| 1 | (4½-ounce) can chopped green chiles | 5-6 | chicken breast halves, cooked, skinned, deboned and chopped |
| 1 | (10¾-ounce) can chicken and rice soup | | |
| 1 | (10¾-ounce) can cream of chicken soup | 1 | head lettuce, chopped |
| | | 2 | tomatoes, chopped |
| 1 | (8-ounce) carton sour cream | 1 | (6-ounce) can sliced ripe olives |
| | | 1 | (8-ounce) jar picante sauce |

Preheat oven to 350°F. Crush tortilla chips. Place ¾ of chips in the bottom of a greased 13x9-inch baking dish. Mix green chiles, soups, sour cream and 2 cups shredded cheese with chicken. Pour over chips. Top with remaining chips. Bake 30 minutes. Remove from oven and top with lettuce, tomatoes and olives. Garnish with remaining cheese and picante sauce.

*8 servings*

# Chicken and Artichoke Casserole

| | | | |
|---|---|---|---|
| 2 | (14-ounce) cans artichoke hearts or bottoms | 1 | cup mayonnaise |
| | | 1 | teaspoon lemon juice |
| 8 | chicken breast halves, cooked, skinned, deboned and chopped | 1 | teaspoon curry powder |
| | | 1¼ | cups shredded Cheddar cheese |
| | | 1¼ | cups croutons or 1 roll buttery crackers, crumbled |
| 2 | (10¾-ounce) cans cream of chicken soup | 2 | tablespoons butter, melted |

Preheat oven to 350°F. Arrange artichoke hearts or bottoms in a greased 13x9-inch baking dish. Top with chicken. Combine soup, mayonnaise, lemon juice and curry powder. Pour over chicken. Sprinkle with cheese. Toss croutons or crumbs with butter and place on top. Bake 25 to 30 minutes.

*6 to 8 servings*

*May substitute 1 bunch fresh broccoli, cut into spears and cooked, for artichoke hearts.*

# Chicken and Asparagus Casserole Olé

*Chi O Casserole*

This was served at the dinner party for early arrivals at Chi Omega State Day in Meridian sometime in the 1980's. When I gave the recipe to one of my Kappa Delta friends for a dinner party, it became known as "Chi O Casserole" - and the rest is history!

| | | | |
|---|---|---|---|
| 1 | medium onion, chopped | ½ | teaspoon ground black pepper |
| ½ | cup butter or margarine | 1 | teaspoon salt |
| 1 | (8-ounce) can mushrooms, drained | 1 | teaspoon Accent |
| 1 | (10¾-ounce) can cream of chicken soup | 2 | tablespoons chopped pimiento, drained |
| 1 | (5-ounce) can evaporated milk | 12 | chicken breast halves, cooked, skinned, deboned and cut into bite-size pieces |
| 8 | ounces shredded sharp Cheddar cheese | 2 | (15-ounce) cans green asparagus spears, drained |
| ¼ | teaspoon Tabasco sauce | ½ | cup slivered almonds |
| 2 | teaspoons soy sauce | | |

Preheat oven to 350°F. In a skillet, sauté onion in butter or margarine. Add remaining ingredients except chicken, asparagus and almonds. In a lightly greased 13x9-inch baking dish, layer half of chicken, 1 can asparagus and half of sauce. Repeat layers, ending with sauce. Top with almonds. Bake 30 minutes or until bubbly. Do not add liquid, even if it looks dry. Freezes well.

*12 servings*

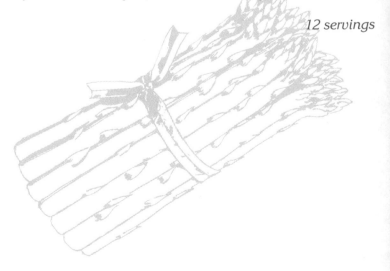

122

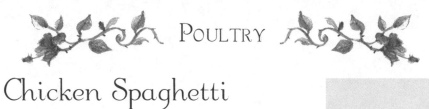

# Chicken Spaghetti

| | | | |
|---|---|---|---|
| 5 | chicken breast halves, cooked, skinned, deboned and chopped, reserve broth | 1 | (10¾-ounce) can cream of mushroom soup |
| 1 | (12-ounce) package vermicelli | 1 | (10¾ ounce) can cream of chicken soup |
| 1 | onion, chopped | 1 | (12-ounce) loaf processed cheese, cubed or melted |
| ½ | green bell pepper, chopped | 1½ | cups sour cream |
| 3 | tablespoons butter | ⅛ | teaspoon salt, or to taste |
| 1 | (10-ounce) can diced tomatoes with green chiles | ⅛ | teaspoon ground black pepper |

Preheat oven to 350°F. Cook vermicelli in reserved broth. Drain. Sauté onion and bell pepper in butter 5 minutes or until tender. Combine all ingredients in a large bowl. Mix well. Pour into a lightly greased 13x9-inch baking dish. Bake 20 minutes or until bubbly and hot.

*6 to 8 servings*

## Chicken Jambalaya

1 large onion, chopped

1 large green bell pepper, chopped

3 stalks celery, chopped

4 cloves garlic, chopped

2 tablespoons canola oil

1 (16-ounce) package kielbasa smoked sausage, sliced

4 chicken breast halves, cooked, skinned, deboned and diced

2 (14½-ounce) cans diced tomatoes

1¼ cups uncooked long grain rice

2½ cups chicken broth

½ teaspoon ground black pepper

½ teaspoon salt

½ teaspoon cayenne pepper

½ teaspoon dried thyme

½ teaspoon Old Bay Seasoning

Preheat oven to 350°F. Sauté onion, bell pepper, celery and garlic in hot oil in a Dutch oven. Stir in meats and cook 5 to 10 minutes. Add all remaining ingredients, stirring until mixed well. Transfer into a lightly greased 13x9-inch baking dish. Cover dish and bake 45 minutes or until rice is done.

*8 to10 servings*

**2 cups water**

**½ teaspoon garlic powder**

**1 stalk celery, chopped or
1 tablespoon celery seed**

**½ teaspoon paprika**

**3 tablespoons
Worcestershire sauce**

**½ cup lemon juice or
½ cup vinegar**

**½ teaspoon onion powder**

**½ teaspoon thyme**

**1 bay leaf**

**1 tablespoon salt**

In a saucepan,
combine all ingredients.
Simmer 10 minutes.

*3 cups*

# No More Burnt Bar-B-Qued Chicken

*With this recipe, you'll never
eat another piece of grilled burnt chicken.*

**Chicken pieces with
skins or without
Basting Sauce
for Chicken
(see accompanying
recipe)**

**Finishing Sauce
for Chicken
(see accompanying
recipe)**

Prepare grill. Simmer chicken with skins in water 10 minutes. Cool and skin. If using skinless chicken, simmer with ½ cup butter added to water. Baste skinned chicken with Basting Sauce and allow to dry before placing on the grill. Close cover on grill. Keep grill temperature below 200°F. Grill 2½ hours, basting every 20 to 30 minutes. Test for doneness - 165°F at thickest part of chicken. When done, baste with Finishing Sauce diluted with any remaining basting sauce. Do not allow the Finishing Sauce to burn. After 10 to 15 minutes, remove and serve with Finishing Sauce.

# Barbequed Chicken

| | | | |
|---|---|---|---|
| 1 | whole chicken, cut into pieces | 2 | tablespoons Worcestershire sauce |
| ¾ | cup ketchup | 1 | teaspoon salt |
| ¾ | cup water | 1 | teaspoon chili powder |
| 1 | medium onion, diced | ½ | teaspoon ground black pepper |
| 3 | tablespoons vinegar | | |

Preheat oven to 325°F. Place chicken in a lightly greased 13x9-inch baking dish. Bake 30 minutes. Remove from oven and drain juices from pan. Combine remaining ingredients in a saucepan and boil 5 minutes. Pour sauce over chicken and cook covered 1 hour 15 minutes. Remove cover and bake 15 minutes.

*6 to 8 servings*

# Glazed Cornish Hens with Cajun Spices

| | | | |
|---|---|---|---|
| 1½ | cups butter, divided | ¾ | cup white Zinfandel wine |
| 1 | medium white onion, chopped | 1 | (6.2-ounce) box instant long grain white and wild rice, prepared according to package directions |
| 2 | stalks celery, chopped | | |
| 1 | green bell pepper, chopped | | |
| 8 | large fresh mushrooms, sliced | 4 | Cornish hens |
| | Cavender's Greek Seasoning | | Worcestershire sauce |
| | | | Garlic salt |
| 2 | tablespoons minced garlic | | Cracked black pepper |
| | | 1 | cup bourbon |
| | Lemon pepper | 1 | (8-ounce) jar muscadine jelly |
| | Cayenne pepper | | |
| | Tabasco sauce | | |

Preheat oven to 425°F. In a 10-inch or larger skillet, melt ½ cup butter. Sauté onion, celery, bell pepper and mushrooms until soft. While sautéing, season with Cavender's, garlic, lemon pepper, cayenne pepper, Tabasco and wine. When vegetables are soft, add rice to mixture and remove from heat.

Season hens with Worcestershire, Cavender's, lemon pepper, Tabasco, garlic salt and cayenne pepper. Stuff hens' cavities with skillet mixture. Place hens breast side up in a 13x9-inch baking dish. Melt ½ cup butter. Pour over hens and season with freshly cracked pepper. Place hens in oven 20 minutes. In a small saucepan, melt ½ cup butter and mix with bourbon. During this 20 minutes, baste hens three times with mixture.

Reduce heat to 350°F. Bake 30 minutes. Add muscadine jelly to butter and bourbon mixture and melt. During this 30 minutes, baste hens three or four times with mixture. Turn hens breast side down and bake 15 minutes. Remove from oven. Cut hens in half and serve.

*4 servings*

## Finishing Sauce for Chicken

1 cup water

½ cup vinegar

4 tablespoons brown sugar

Juice of 2 lemons

1 tablespoon salt

1 cup ketchup

½ cup butter

2 tablespoons mustard

1 tablespoon ground black pepper

4 tablespoons Worcestershire sauce

2 tablespoons hot sauce, or to taste

In a saucepan, combine all ingredients except Worcestershire and hot sauce. Simmer 10 minutes. Stir in Worcestershire and hot sauce.

*3½ cups*

## Tropical Fruit Salsa

1 small fresh pineapple, peeled, cored and chopped

1 mango, peeled and chopped

1 (11-ounce) can Mandarin oranges, drained and chopped

3 kiwis, peeled and chopped

Juice of 1 lime

1 tablespoon chopped fresh cilantro

2 tablespoons finely diced purple onion (optional)

1-2 tablespoons raspberry preserves

1 teaspoon water

Combine fruits, lime juice, cilantro and onion. Microwave preserves with water 5 seconds or until liquid. Add to fruit mixture. Spoon over grilled fish.

*4 cups*

# Pumpkin Seed Encrusted Yellowfin Tuna

*Simplicity at its best - melts in your mouth!*

| | | | |
|---|---|---|---|
| 1½ | cups pumpkin seeds | 1 | teaspoon salt |
| 1 | tablespoon chili powder | 4 | (6 to 8-ounce) tuna |
| 1 | teaspoon ground | | steaks |
| | oregano | 1-2 | tablespoons olive oil |
| 1 | teaspoon ground cumin | | |

In a food processor, grind pumpkin seeds. Sift through a colander. Add chili powder, oregano, cumin and salt. Press mixture onto all sides of tuna steak. In a skillet, heat oil and sear tuna 1 minute on each side or until desired doneness.

*4 servings*

# Grilled Mahi Mahi with Tropical Fruit Salsa

| | | |
|---|---|---|
| 6 | mahi mahi fillets | Tropical Fruit Salsa |
| ⅓ | cup cilantro flavored or | (see accompanying |
| | regular olive oil | recipe) |

Prepare grill. Brush fish with oil on both sides. Grill 10 minutes per side or until fish flakes. Serve with Tropical Fruit Salsa.

*6 servings*

# Catfish with Crawfish Topping

| | | | |
|---|---|---|---|
| 6-8 | catfish fillets | 1 | cup chopped green onion |
| | Salt | 1 | (8-ounce) package reduced fat cream cheese |
| | Ground black pepper | | |
| ½ | cup butter | | |
| 1 | pound peeled crawfish tails | | Tabasco sauce, to taste |

Preheat oven to 500°F. Salt and pepper catfish. Place on a greased foil covered pan. Bake 6 to 8 minutes or until golden brown.

In a separate pan, melt butter. Sauté crawfish and green onion 10 minutes. Add cream cheese and cook until melted. Add Tabasco. To serve, top each catfish fillet with crawfish mixture.

*6 to 8 servings*

# Catfish Provençal

| | | | |
|---|---|---|---|
| 1 | onion, sliced | ¼ | teaspoon salt, or to taste |
| 2 | tomatoes, cut into thin wedges | ⅛ | teaspoon ground black pepper, or to taste |
| 4 | tablespoons butter, divided | | Tabasco sauce |
| 4 | catfish fillets | | Worcestershire sauce |
| 1 | teaspoon chopped fresh oregano | | |

Preheat oven to 350°F. Lightly sauté onion and tomatoes in 1 tablespoon butter. Set aside. Place fillets in a lightly greased 13x9-inch baking dish. Do not overlap fish. Sprinkle with oregano, salt and pepper. Dot fish with remaining butter. Spoon sautéed mixture over fish. Bake 15 minutes or until fillets flake with a fork. Just prior to serving, sprinkle with dashes of Tabasco and Worcestershire.

*4 servings*

The Honorable Thad Cochran, United States Senate, Mississippi

## Fresh Fruit Fish Marinade

2 tablespoons fresh lime juice

½ cup fresh grapefruit juice

1 teaspoon crushed garlic

1 tablespoon raspberry preserves

⅛ teaspoon salt, or to taste

⅛ teaspoon ground black pepper, or to taste

Combine all ingredients. Pour over any type fish. Let stand at room temperature 30 minutes. Cook fish as desired. Serve with Tropical Fruit Salsa (see index).

*¾ cup*

# Catfish Casserole

| | | | |
|---|---|---|---|
| 1 | (10-ounce) package frozen chopped spinach, thawed and well drained | ¼ | pound sliced fresh mushrooms |
| ⅛ | teaspoon salt, or to taste | 1 | small onion, chopped |
| ⅛ | teaspoon ground black pepper, or to taste | 2 | tablespoons all-purpose flour |
| 6 | small catfish fillets | 1 | cup milk |
| 4 | tablespoons butter, divided | ¼ | cup white wine (optional) |
| | | ¼ | cup grated Parmesan cheese |

Preheat oven to 375°F. In a buttered 13x9-inch baking dish, spread spinach. Sprinkle with salt and pepper. Top with fillets. In a skillet, heat 1 tablespoon butter. Sauté mushrooms and onion. Pour over fillets. In a saucepan, melt 3 tablespoons butter. Stir in flour. Slowly add milk and wine. Continue stirring until thick. Add Parmesan cheese. Pour over sautéed mixture. Bake 20 to 25 minutes or until bubbly.

*6 servings*

*May substitute flounder or sole fillets for catfish.*

The Honorable Trent Lott, United States Senate, Mississippi

Dear Trent and Thad,

Y'all may not remember me. We met once in the "Grove" at Ole Miss. Mississippi has a problem. Our catfish farmers overdid it. Their grain-fed catfish look too good! Those Yankees will eat every last one.
We had our hubcaps stolen looking for a catfish dinner up North. Now, they'll be serving our fish at the Waldorf-Astoria! The "Grove" is full of Yankees. My football parking spot has a fancy table and flowers. An N.B.C. reporter sat in my lawn chair. It's too late for the "Grove," but please, Thad and Trent, keep our catfish a secret!

Your friend,
Bubba

# Cajun Sautéed Redfish

| | | | |
|---|---|---|---|
| 4 | (6 to 8-ounce) redfish fillets | ½ | cup all-purpose flour |
| 2 | tablespoons Seafood Rub, divided (see accompanying recipe) | 1 | egg, beaten |
| | | ¼ | cup water |
| | | ⅓ | cup vegetable oil |

Season fillets with 1 tablespoon rub. In a shallow bowl, combine flour with 2 teaspoons rub. In another bowl, mix egg, water and remaining rub. Dredge fillets in seasoned flour, then in egg mixture, then again in flour, shaking off any excess. In a large nonstick skillet over medium heat, heat oil. Pan fry fillets 4 to 5 minutes on each side. Drain on paper towels. Serve immediately.

*4 servings*

*May substitute red snapper, trout or grouper fillets for redfish fillets.*

## Seafood Rub

5 tablespoons ground black pepper

6 tablespoons garlic powder

3 tablespoons onion powder

6 tablespoons salt

2½ tablespoons dried oregano

2½ tablespoons dried thyme

1-3 tablespoons cayenne pepper

Combine all ingredients. Blend well. May store in an airtight container 3 months.

*1½ cups*

# Salmon Teriyaki

| | | | |
|---|---|---|---|
| 4 | tablespoons frozen orange juice concentrate | | Ground black pepper |
| 4 | cloves garlic, minced | 4 | (6-ounce) salmon steaks or fillets |
| 1 | teaspoon ground ginger | 4 | green onions, chopped |
| ¼ | cup soy sauce | ¼ | cup toasted sesame seeds |
| | Salt | | |

In a bowl, combine orange juice concentrate, garlic, ginger and soy sauce. Set aside. Salt and pepper salmon. Place in a lightly greased 8x8-inch baking dish. Pour sauce over salmon. Cover and refrigerate 1 hour. Preheat oven to 350°F. Bake salmon uncovered 20 minutes or until fish flakes easily with a fork. Top with green onions and sesame seeds.

*4 servings*

# Baked Grouper with Cheesy Herb Sauce

| | | | |
|---|---|---|---|
| 2 | tablespoons chopped onion | ⅛ | teaspoon salt |
| 2 | tablespoons chopped red bell pepper | ⅛ | teaspoon ground black pepper |
| 2 | tablespoons chopped celery | ⅛ | teaspoon dried tarragon |
| 8 | fresh mushrooms, sliced | ¾ | cup milk |
| 2 | tablespoons butter | ½ | cup shredded Monterey Jack cheese |
| 2 | tablespoons all-purpose flour | 4 | (8-ounce) grouper fillets |

Preheat oven to 425°F. In a skillet over medium heat, sauté onion, bell pepper, celery and mushrooms in butter until tender. Stir in flour, salt, pepper and tarragon. Cook 1 minute, stirring constantly. Reduce heat to low. Gradually add milk, stirring constantly until thickened. Add cheese and stir until melted. Remove from heat and set aside. In a lightly greased baking dish, place fillets. Spoon sauce evenly over fish. Bake 8 to 10 minutes or until fish flakes easily with a fork.

*4 servings*

# Trout Amandine

| | | | |
|---|---|---|---|
| 4 | trout fillets | | Salt |
| ½-¾ | cup butter | | Ground black pepper |
| ¾ | cup all-purpose flour | 1 | cup slivered almonds |
| | Juice of 1 lemon | | |

Pat trout dry with paper towels. In a large skillet over medium heat, melt butter. Dredge trout in flour. Sprinkle with lemon juice, salt and pepper. Pan fry 5 minutes per side until crisp. Remove and keep warm. Add almonds to butter and sauté 1 to 2 minutes. Pour over trout before serving.

*4 servings*

---

## Ginger Shallot Cream Sauce

½ cup dry white wine

½ cup rice wine vinegar

3 tablespoons minced shallots

1 (2-inch) piece fresh gingerroot, peeled and thinly sliced

½ cup whipping cream

3-5 tablespoons cold butter, cut into pieces

In a heavy saucepan over medium high heat, combine wine, vinegar, shallots and ginger. Bring to a boil. Cook 15 minutes or until reduced by half. Stir in cream. Cook 10 minutes or until reduced by half. Strain into a clean saucepan. May be prepared to this point up to 3 hours in advance and chilled. Return to low heat. Whisk in butter, 1 piece at a time. Serve immediately over grilled salmon or tuna.

*¾ cup*

## Trout Florentine

| | | | |
|---|---|---|---|
| 6 | whole trout, deboned if possible | 1¼ | teaspoon salt, divided |
| ¼ | cup grated onion | ⅛ | teaspoon ground black pepper, or to taste |
| ¼ | cup plus 3 tablespoons butter, divided | 1 | egg |
| 1 | (10-ounce) package frozen chopped spinach, thawed and drained well | ¼ | cup milk or half-and-half |
| | | ¾ | cup bread crumbs |
| | | ½ | cup shredded Swiss cheese |

Preheat oven to 450°F. Wash and pat fish dry. Do not omit this step. Sauté onion in 1 tablespoon butter. Add ¼ cup butter and spinach. Season with ¼ teaspoon salt and pepper. Heat until butter is melted and flavors are blended. Cool and stuff into fish cavities. In a separate bowl, combine egg, milk and 1 teaspoon salt. In another dish, combine bread crumbs and cheese. Dip fish into milk mixture and roll in bread crumb mixture. Place fish into a lightly greased 13x9-inch baking dish. Sprinkle with remaining bread crumb mixture. Dot with 2 tablespoons butter. Bake 15 to 20 minutes or until fish is tender and brown.

*6 servings*

Pretty Presentations Catering, Newton, MS

## Parmesan Crusted Fish

| | | | |
|---|---|---|---|
| ½ | cup grated Parmesan cheese | 2 | tablespoons chopped green onion |
| ½ | teaspoon Cajun seasoned salt | | Dash paprika |
| ½ | cup light mayonnaise | 4 | fish fillets |
| | | 2-3 | tablespoons butter, thinly sliced |

Preheat oven to 375°F. To prepare sauce, combine Parmesan, salt, mayonnaise, onion and paprika. Set aside. Rinse fish and pat dry. Place fish in a shallow greased baking dish. Dot with butter. Bake 10 minutes. Cover with sauce. Bake 10 to 15 minutes or until fish flakes with a fork and is lightly browned on top.

*4 servings*

### Papaya Corn Salsa

1 cup fresh or frozen corn, blanched 2 minutes and well drained

1 ripe papaya, peeled, seeded and diced

⅓ cup finely diced purple onion

2 Roma tomatoes, seeded and diced

1½ teaspoons finely minced garlic

1 tablespoon lime zest

¼ cup fresh lime juice

2 tablespoons chopped fresh cilantro

In a glass bowl, combine all ingredients except cilantro. Cover and chill 2 hours. Just before serving, add cilantro and toss. Serve with grilled or broiled fish, chicken or turkey.

*4 cups*

*May be prepared up to 8 hours in advance, but add papaya no more than 2 hours before serving.*

## Brandy Fried Shrimp

1 pound large shrimp

¼ cup plus 1 teaspoon brandy, divided

Oil for frying

1 cup all-purpose flour

1 teaspoon baking powder

¼ teaspoon salt

⅔ cup milk

2 eggs

1 teaspoon oil

Peel shrimp leaving tails intact. Butterfly and devein. In a glass dish, place shrimp in a single layer. Sprinkle brandy over shrimp. Cover and refrigerate 1 hour. Prepare oil for deep frying. In a mixing bowl, combine all remaining ingredients. Add 1 teaspoon brandy. Dip shrimp in batter and deep fry until golden brown. Drain on paper towels. Serve immediately.

*4 servings*

*Batter may also be used for onion rings.*

# Italian Shrimp and Pasta
*A fabulous alternative to spaghetti*

| | | | |
|---|---|---|---|
| 5 | green onions, sliced | ½ | teaspoon fresh rosemary, minced |
| 3 | cloves garlic, minced | ¼ | teaspoon salt |
| 2 | tablespoons olive oil | ¼ | teaspoon ground black pepper |
| 1 | (12-ounce) jar marinated artichoke hearts, undrained | 1 | pound medium shrimp, peeled and deveined |
| 6 | plum tomatoes, chopped | 1 | (8-ounce) package vermicelli pasta, prepared according to package directions |
| 1 | cup sliced fresh mushrooms | | |
| ¼ | cup dry white wine | ⅓ | cup freshly grated Parmesan cheese |
| 2 | teaspoons dry Italian seasoning | 1 | cup sliced ripe olives |

In a large skillet over medium high heat, sauté onions and garlic in hot oil until tender. Stir in artichoke hearts, tomatoes, mushrooms, wine and seasonings. Bring to a boil. Reduce heat and simmer 5 minutes. Add shrimp. Simmer 4 minutes or until shrimp turn pink, stirring occasionally. Serve over vermicelli. Sprinkle with cheese and olives.

*4 servings*

# Shrimp and Artichoke Vermicelli

| | | | |
|---|---|---|---|
| 1 | (8-ounce) package vermicelli pasta, prepared according to package directions | ½ | pint whipping cream |
| | | ½ | cup milk |
| | | 1 | teaspoon salt |
| | | ½ | teaspoon ground white pepper |
| 1 | (14-ounce) can artichoke hearts, drained and quartered | ¼ | cup dry sherry |
| | | 1 | tablespoon Worcestershire sauce |
| 1½ | pounds large shrimp, boiled, peeled and deveined | ¼ | cup freshly grated Parmesan cheese |
| ½ | cup butter, divided | ¼ | teaspoon paprika |
| 8 | ounces large fresh mushrooms, sliced | | Toasted pine nuts, for garnish |
| 3 | tablespoons all-purpose flour | | Fresh rosemary, for garnish |

Preheat oven to 350°F. Place pasta in the bottom of a well greased 1½-quart baking dish. Layer artichoke hearts over pasta. Cover with shrimp. In a skillet, melt 3½ tablespoons butter and sauté mushrooms 6 to 8 minutes. Drain and layer over shrimp. In a medium saucepan over low heat, melt remaining butter. Stir in flour. Cook 3 to 5 minutes, stirring constantly. Gradually add cream and milk. Cook until thick enough to heavily coat a spoon. Add salt, pepper, sherry and Worcestershire. Stir until smooth. Pour over casserole. Top with cheese and sprinkle with paprika. Bake uncovered 25 minutes or until light brown and bubbly. Garnish with pine nuts and rosemary before serving.

*6 servings*

## Crab Imperial

1 pound lump crabmeat, picked over for shells

1 cup butter, melted

½ cup finely chopped green bell pepper

5 tablespoons mayonnaise

1 egg, lightly beaten

1 teaspoon dry mustard

1 teaspoon ground white pepper

½ teaspoon salt

½ cup bread crumbs

Preheat oven to 350°F. In a bowl, combine all ingredients except bread crumbs. Pour into a shallow 2-quart baking dish. Top with bread crumbs. Bake 30 minutes.

*6 to 8 servings*

# Velvet Shrimp

| | | | | |
|---|---|---|---|---|
| 1 | tablespoon butter | | 1 | pound shrimp, peeled and deveined |
| ½ | cup chopped green onion | | ½ | teaspoon minced garlic |
| 1 | tablespoon Cajun seafood seasoning mix, divided | | 1 | cup whipping cream |
| | | | ½ | cup shredded Muenster cheese |
| | | | | Cooked rice or pasta |

Heat a 10-inch skillet over high heat 1 minute. Add butter. Stir in onion and 2 teaspoons seasoning mix. Sauté 1 minute. Add shrimp and garlic. Cook, stirring occasionally, 2 minutes. Stir in cream and remaining seasoning mix. Cook 1 minute. Remove shrimp with a slotted spoon. Return cream to a boil, whisking constantly 2 minutes. Stir in cheese and shrimp. Serve over hot cooked rice or pasta.

*4 servings*

# Crawfish Étouffée

| | | | | |
|---|---|---|---|---|
| ½ | cup butter | | 1 | pound peeled crawfish tails |
| 2 | medium onions, chopped | | ¼ | teaspoon salt |
| 1 | green bell pepper, chopped | | ⅛ | teaspoon cayenne pepper |
| 3 | stalks celery, chopped | | 3 | green onions, chopped (optional) |
| 2-3 | cloves garlic, chopped | | | Cooked rice |

In a large skillet, melt butter. Sauté 2 medium onions, bell pepper, celery and garlic until tender. Reduce heat to low, add crawfish tails. Simmer 15 minutes. Add salt, cayenne and green onions. Simmer 3 to 5 minutes. Serve over rice.

*4 to 6 servings*

*May substitute shrimp for crawfish tails.*

---

## Seafood Substitutions

The following seafood are grouped according to similar flavor or texture. Fish and shellfish in each group may be prepared the same way. Substitute fish for fish and shellfish for shellfish.

### Delicate Texture

*Mild Flavor:*
*cod, flounder, crab, scallops*

*Moderate Flavor:*
*lake perch, whitefish*

*Full Flavor:*
*mussels, oysters*

### Moderate Texture

*Mild Flavor:*
*orange roughy, pike, tilapia, crawfish, lobster, shrimp*

*Moderate Flavor:*
*ocean perch, trout*

*Full Flavor:*
*bluefish, mackerel*

# Shrimp and Chicken Creole

| | | | | |
|---|---|---|---|---|
| 1 | pound medium shrimp, peeled and deveined | ½ | cup cooking sherry | |
| 4 | boneless, skinless chicken breast halves, cut into bite-size pieces | 1 | tablespoon Worcestershire sauce | |
| | | 1½ | teaspoons salt | |
| | | ¼ | teaspoon ground black pepper | |
| 3 | tablespoons olive oil | ¼ | teaspoon dried thyme | |
| 3 | tablespoons butter | 2 | tablespoons chopped fresh parsley | |
| ½ | cup chopped green bell pepper | 1 | cup half-and-half | |
| 4 | green onions, chopped | | Cooked rice | |
| 1 | (10-ounce) can diced tomatoes with green chiles | | | |

Preheat oven to 350°F. In a skillet, sauté shrimp in olive oil and butter until pink. Remove with a slotted spoon and set aside. In the same skillet, sauté chicken until firm but not brown. Remove with a slotted spoon and set aside. Add bell pepper and onions. Sauté until tender. Add tomatoes, sherry, Worcestershire, salt, pepper, thyme, parsley and chicken. Pour chicken mixture into a greased 2-quart baking dish. May be prepared to this point and refrigerated. Bake, uncovered, 40 minutes. Remove from oven. Stir in shrimp and half-and-half. Return to oven. Bake 5 minutes or until thoroughly heated. Serve in bowls over rice.

*4 to 6 servings*

## Firm Texture

*Mild Flavor:*
*grouper, halibut, monkfish, sea bass, snapper*

*Moderate Flavor:*
*amberjack, catfish, mahi mahi, pompano, shark*

*Full Flavor:*
*marlin, salmon, swordfish, tuna, clams*

# Shrimp, Rice and Artichoke Casserole

| | | | |
|---|---|---|---|
| ½ | cup chopped celery | ¾ | teaspoon cayenne pepper |
| 1 | tablespoon minced garlic | ¼ | teaspoon salt, or to taste |
| 1 | cup chopped green bell pepper | 4 | cups cooked long grain and wild rice |
| 1 | cup chopped onion | 2 | (14-ounce) cans artichoke hearts, drained and chopped |
| 4 | tablespoons butter | | |
| 3 | pounds steamed shrimp, peeled | 1½ | cups shredded Swiss cheese |
| 1 | cup whipping cream | | |

Preheat oven to 350°F. In a skillet, sauté celery, garlic, bell pepper and onion in butter. Stir in shrimp. Add cream, cayenne and salt. Set aside. Spread cooked rice in the bottom of a greased 13x9-inch baking dish. Spread shrimp mixture over rice. Layer artichoke hearts over shrimp. Bake 20 minutes. Remove from oven. Sprinkle with cheese. Bake until cheese is melted.

*8 servings*

Pretty Presentations Catering, Newton, MS

## Grilling Tips

Choose fish steaks, pan-dressed or fillets that are at least ¾-inch thick.

Coat the grill rack with nonstick cooking spray before grilling to keep fish from sticking.

Use a fish basket when grilling very tender, delicate fish. Spray basket with nonstick cooking spray.

Baste fish often with marinade or other sauce while grilling to keep it moist and tender.

Fish is done when it flakes easily when pricked with a fork.

# Sunday Shrimp

| | | | |
|---|---|---|---|
| 1 | medium onion, chopped | 1½ | teaspoons dried marjoram |
| 1 | green bell pepper, chopped | 4 | tablespoons Worcestershire sauce |
| 4 | stalks celery, chopped | 1½-2 | cups shredded sharp Cheddar cheese |
| 8 | ounces fresh mushrooms, sliced | 1 | pint half-and-half |
| ¾ | cup butter or margarine | 3 | pounds shrimp, cooked and peeled |
| 5 | tablespoons all-purpose flour | 2 | tablespoons chopped fresh parsley |
| ½ | teaspoon dried thyme | | Cooked rice or patty shells |
| ½ | teaspoon dry mustard | | |
| 4-5 | drops Tabasco sauce | | |

In a large skillet or Dutch oven, sauté onion, bell pepper, celery and mushrooms in butter until tender. Stir in flour until combined. Add thyme, mustard, Tabasco, marjoram, Worcestershire, cheese and half-and-half. Simmer until thick and creamy. Stir in shrimp and parsley. Simmer until thoroughly heated. Serve over rice or in patty shells.

*6 to 8 servings*

A Southern gentleman was grilling shrimp alongside his boat in the Bahamas. K.R. and her husband were walking along the dock admiring his vessel and enjoying the aroma of his dinner. Being a Southerner, he offered them a sample of the shrimp and his outstanding recipe. K.R. says that it tastes even better with a good Jimmy Buffett song playing in the background!

## Bahama Shrimp

Wrap peeled shrimp with bacon and skewer. Brush with a sweet and tangy barbeque sauce and grill.

# Crawfish and Sun-Dried Tomatoes with Pasta

*A delightfully new way to serve crawfish*

| | | | |
|---|---|---|---|
| 3 | tablespoons olive oil | ½ | red bell pepper, julienned |
| 2 | cloves garlic, minced | 1 | Roma tomato, chopped |
| 2 | tablespoons chopped fresh basil | ¼ | cup white wine |
| 1 | pound peeled crawfish tails | 1 | cup half-and-half |
| 1 | (3-ounce) package dry packed sun-dried tomatoes, chopped | ¾ | cup freshly grated Parmesan cheese, divided |
| 2 | green onions, chopped | 1 | pound penne pasta, cooked al dente |
| ½ | green bell pepper, julienned | | Salt |
| | | | Cracked black pepper |

In a sauté pan over high heat, heat oil. Sauté garlic, basil, crawfish and sun-dried tomatoes 7 minutes. Stir in onions, bell peppers and Roma tomato. Cook 2 minutes. Add wine, half-and-half and ¼ cup Parmesan cheese. Cook 3 to 5 minutes or until thickened. Stir in remaining Parmesan cheese. Toss in hot pasta. Season with salt and pepper.

*4 to 6 servings*

This simple salmon recipe was collected in southern France by a group of Lamar School students and their chaperones. The French language students broadened their knowledge of the country's cuisine and history. They climbed the ruins of an ancient fortress, watched a fencing exhibition and walked along the pebble beaches of the French Riviera.

## Simple, Elegant Salmon

Sear salmon steak in olive oil and minced garlic until done. Top with slivered almonds which have been sautéed in butter.

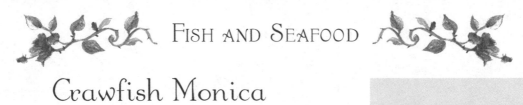

## Crawfish Monica

| | | | |
|---|---|---|---|
| 1 | pound unsalted butter | ½ | (2-ounce) bottle Paul Prudhomme's Seafood Magic Seasoning |
| 2 | pounds peeled crawfish tails | | |
| 1½ | bunches green onions, finely chopped | 1 | pint half-and-half |
| ½ | bunch parsley, finely chopped | | Tabasco sauce, to taste |
| | | 1½ | pounds egg noodles, prepared according to package directions |

In a skillet, melt butter. Sauté crawfish, onions, parsley and seasoning. Be careful not to overcook crawfish. Bring to a slow boil. Reduce heat to low. Slowly add half-and-half. Simmer 10 minutes, stirring frequently. Add Tabasco. Serve over hot egg noodles.

*4 to 6 servings*

## Seafood Newburg

| | | | |
|---|---|---|---|
| 3 | tablespoons butter | 1 | cup half-and-half |
| 2 | tablespoons all-purpose flour | 2 | egg yolks, lightly beaten |
| ½ | teaspoon salt | 2 | tablespoons cream sherry |
| ¼ | teaspoon ground black pepper | 1 | pound shrimp, cooked, peeled and deveined |
| | Dash cayenne pepper | 1 | pound crabmeat, picked over for shells |
| ¼-½ | teaspoon ground nutmeg | | Cooked rice |
| 1 | cup milk | | |

In a saucepan over medium heat, melt butter. Stir in flour and seasonings. Slowly stir in milk and half-and-half, stirring constantly. Add a little warmed milk mixture to yolks. Pour yolks into milk mixture, stirring rapidly. Cook until thickened. Add cream sherry, shrimp and crabmeat. Heat thoroughly. Serve over rice.

*8 servings*

# Low Fat Crawfish Enchiladas

## Three Citrus Marinade

*A fresh change
for shellfish or fish*

¼ cup fresh lime juice

¼ cup fresh lemon juice

1 cup fresh orange juice

½ cup olive oil

2 teaspoons minced garlic

2 teaspoons coarsely ground
black pepper

3 bay leaves, crushed

2 tablespoons chopped
fresh cilantro

⅛ teaspoon salt, or to taste

In a glass bowl, combine all ingredients. Let stand at room temperature 30 minutes. Divide marinade into thirds. Using ⅓ marinade, allow shellfish to marinate 10 to 15 minutes and fish 30 to 60 minutes. Grill brushing frequently with another ⅓ marinade. Drizzle with remaining ⅓ fresh marinade and serve.

*2 cups*

| | | |
|---|---|---|
| 3 | tablespoons reduced calorie margarine | |
| 1 | cup finely chopped onion | |
| ⅓ | cup chopped green bell pepper | |
| 1½ | cups evaporated skim milk | |
| ½ | cup reduced calorie cream cheese spread | |
| ⅔ | cup low-fat cottage cheese | |
| ½ | teaspoon ground oregano | |
| ¼ | teaspoon salt, or to taste | |
| ¼ | teaspoon ground white pepper | |
| 1 | pound peeled crawfish tails | |
| 2 | tablespoons finely chopped green onion | |
| 2 | tablespoons minced fresh jalapeño pepper | |
| ½ | cup shredded part-skim mozzarella cheese, divided | |
| 4 | corn tortillas or fat-free flour tortillas | |

In a medium skillet over medium heat, melt margarine. Sauté 1 cup onion and bell pepper 5 minutes. Stir in milk, cream cheese and cottage cheese. Cook 5 minutes, stirring constantly. Reduce heat and add oregano, salt and white pepper. Simmer 5 minutes, stirring often to prevent burning. Add crawfish, green onion and jalapeño. Simmer 3 to 4 minutes. Stir in ¼ cup mozzarella cheese. Cook 1 minute. Set aside.

In a small cast iron skillet over medium heat, brown tortillas 1 minute on each side. Place each tortilla on a serving plate. Divide crawfish filling into 4 equal portions. For each serving, spoon ½ crawfish filling onto middle of each tortilla. Fold in tortilla edges across filling and turn seam side down. Top with remaining filling. Sprinkle with remaining cheese. Serve immediately.

*4 servings*

# Caribbean Grilled Scallops in Lime Marinade

| | | | |
|---|---|---|---|
| | Zest of 1 lime | ⅛ | teaspoon crushed red pepper |
| ½ | cup fresh lime juice | | |
| 1 | teaspoon salt | ¼ | teaspoon chopped fresh parsley |
| 1 | tablespoon soy sauce | | |
| ½ | teaspoon dried oregano | 3 | pounds fresh sea scallops |
| 1 | teaspoon ground black pepper | | |
| | | ½ | pound thinly sliced bacon |
| 6-8 | peppercorns | | |

Combine all ingredients except scallops and bacon. Add scallops. Marinate in refrigerator 1 hour. Reserve marinade.

Prepare grill or heat oven to broil. Weave bacon around scallops while threading onto skewers. Leave room between scallops so bacon will crisp. Grill over medium coals or broil in oven. Turn often and baste with marinade during cooking. Cook 5 to 6 minutes or until scallops are springy to the touch.

*8 servings*

Pretty Presentations Catering, Newton, MS

If using metal skewers, spray with nonstick cooking spray prior to skewering food. If using bamboo skewers, soak in water 15 minutes before using. For a creative skewer, use fresh rosemary stalks that have been soaked in water. The rosemary flavor will be infused into your food.

# Crab Remic

| | | | |
|---|---|---|---|
| 1 | pound lump crabmeat, picked over for shells | ½ | cup chili sauce |
| | | 1½ | cups mayonnaise |
| 3 | tablespoons butter, cut into 6 pieces | ½ | teaspoon celery salt |
| | | ½ | teaspoon Tabasco sauce |
| 6-9 | slices bacon, cooked | | |
| 1 | teaspoon dry mustard | 1 | teaspoon tarragon vinegar |
| ½ | teaspoon paprika | | |

Preheat oven to 350°F. Divide crabmeat among 6 individual ramekins or shells. Place butter on top of each. Crumble bacon over top. Mix remaining ingredients to make sauce. Pour over crabmeat. Bake 10 minutes or until bubbly.

*6 servings*

# Crab and Artichoke Cakes with Rémoulade Sauce

## Rémoulade Sauce

1 cup mayonnaise

3 tablespoons Dijon mustard

2 tablespoons white wine vinegar, or to taste

1 tablespoon paprika

2 tablespoons prepared horseradish

1 teaspoon finely chopped garlic

⅓ cup finely chopped green onion

⅓ cup finely chopped celery

2 tablespoons finely chopped fresh parsley

2 tablespoons ketchup

¼ teaspoon salt, or to taste

⅛ teaspoon ground black pepper, or to taste

In a bowl, stir together all ingredients. Mix well. Cover and refrigerate until serving time. Serve over crab cakes.

*2 cups*

| | |
|---|---|
| 6 | tablespoons unsalted butter, divided |
| 6 | green onions, include 2 inches of top, finely chopped |
| ¾ | cup celery, chopped |
| 1 | cup finely crushed saltine crackers |
| 1 | tablespoon dry mustard |
| ½ | teaspoon Tabasco sauce |
| 2 | teaspoons Worcestershire sauce |
| 2 | eggs, well beaten |
| ¼ | cup mayonnaise |
| 3 | tablespoons finely chopped fresh parsley |
| ½ | pound fresh crabmeat, picked over for shells |
| ½ | (14-ounce) can artichoke hearts, chopped |
| ⅛ | teaspoon salt, or to taste |
| ⅛ | teaspoon ground black pepper, or to taste |
| 2 | cups fresh bread crumbs, divided |
| | Rémoulade Sauce (see accompanying recipe) |

In a large frying pan over low heat, melt 2 tablespoons butter. Add green onions and celery. Cover and cook, stirring occasionally, 10 minutes or until soft. Using a slotted spoon, transfer to a bowl and cool. Add all remaining ingredients except remaining butter and bread crumbs. Mix well. If crab mixture seems too wet to hold its shape, add up to ½ cup bread crumbs to absorb moisture. Shape mixture into 6 cakes. Place remaining bread crumbs in a shallow bowl. Dredge cakes lightly in crumbs.

In a frying pan over medium heat, melt 2 tablespoons butter. Sauté three crab cakes 3 minutes on each side or until golden brown. Using a slotted spatula, transfer to paper towels to drain. Keep warm. Using remaining butter, sauté remaining crab cakes. Serve crab cakes immediately with Rémoulade Sauce.

*6 servings*

*May use 1 pound crabmeat and omit artichoke hearts.*

# Oysters Rockefeller

| | | | |
|---|---|---|---|
| 2 | bunches green onions, chopped | 2 | tablespoons Tabasco sauce |
| 1 | bunch parsley, minced | 2 | tablespoons prepared horseradish |
| ½ | cup butter | | |
| 4 | (10-ounce) packages frozen chopped spinach, cooked, drained well and puréed | 2 | teaspoons dried basil |
| | | 1 | teaspoon dried marjoram |
| | | 2 | tablespoons vodka |
| | | 1 | tablespoon bitters |
| 1 | tablespoon celery salt | ⅛ | teaspoon salt, or to taste |
| ¾ | tablespoon anchovy paste | | |
| | | 5 | dozen oysters, shucked and drained |
| 2 | tablespoons Worcestershire sauce | | |

Preheat oven to 450°F. In a large Dutch oven, sauté onions and parsley in butter 20 minutes. Cool. Remove and purée until smooth. Return to pan. Add spinach and seasonings. Bring to a full boil. Remove from heat. Add vodka and bitters. May refrigerate or freeze at this point. Lightly grease 12 individual ramekins. Place 6 to 8 oysters in each ramekin. Bake 10 minutes or until edges of oysters curl. Remove from oven. Pour off excess liquid and top oysters with sauce. Bake 5 to 10 minutes or until slightly brown and bubbly on top. Serve immediately.

*12 servings*

# Flank Steak Florentine with Chianti Rosemary Sauce

## Chianti Rosemary Sauce

*Enjoy the wonderful aroma*

**2 cups chicken stock**

**½ cup Chianti wine**

**1 tablespoon fresh rosemary**

**⅛ teaspoon salt**

**Freshly ground black pepper**

**6 tablespoons butter, cut into 6 pieces**

In a saucepan, combine all ingredients except butter and bring to a boil. Cook over high heat 30 minutes or until reduced to ⅓ cup. Remove from heat. Whisk in butter, 1 tablespoon at a time until thickened.

*1 cup*

The home cook may easily tenderize meat by simple mechanical or chemical methods. Pounding the meat with a meat mallet mechanically tenderizes the meat. The pounding breaks down the meat's tough fibers. Chemically tenderizing meat refers to softening the meat fibers by long, slow cooking, using an acid-based marinade, or using a commercial meat tenderizing powder.

| | | | |
|---|---|---|---|
| 1 | (1½ to 2-pound) flank steak | ½ | medium onion, diced |
| | Salt | 6-8 | cups fresh spinach, cleaned and trimmed |
| | Freshly ground black pepper | | Freshly ground nutmeg |
| 2 | tablespoons unsalted butter, divided | | Chianti Rosemary Sauce (see accompanying recipe) |
| 2 | large shallots, minced | | |

Preheat oven to 450°F. Trim membrane from steak and butterfly. Tenderize with a mallet. Season generously with salt and pepper. In a large skillet, heat 1 tablespoon butter. Add shallots, onion and spinach. Cook until shallots are tender and moisture from spinach has evaporated. Spread spinach mixture over steak, covering entire surface. Sprinkle with nutmeg. Roll up, across the grain. Tie with cotton kitchen twine. Melt remaining butter. Brush over rolled meat. Generously sprinkle with pepper, rolling so pepper sticks to meat. Place seam side down on a rack in a roasting pan. Place in oven, immediately lower heat to 275°F. Bake 1 hour 15 minutes to 1 hour 30 minutes, depending on desired doneness. Remove from pan and remove twine. Slice thinly. Serve hot with Chianti Rosemary Sauce. May also be served cold.

*6 servings*

*Two (10-ounce) packages frozen spinach, thawed and squeezed dry, may be substituted for fresh spinach.*

# Fabulous Flank Steak

| | | | |
|---|---|---|---|
| 1 | (1-pound) flank steak | ½ | teaspoon ground |
| 2 | tablespoons sugar | | cinnamon |
| 1 | teaspoon salt | 2 | tablespoons soy sauce |
| | | 3 | tablespoons sherry |

Place flank steak in a shallow pan. Combine remaining ingredients and pour over steak. Cover and marinate in refrigerator for 6 to 8 hours, turning once. Grill over medium coals to desired degree of doneness, about 4 minutes per side for medium. Let stand 5 minutes. Slice on the diagonal and serve.

*4 servings*

*Note: Must marinate 6 to 8 hours.*

# Beef Tenderloin

| | | | |
|---|---|---|---|
| 1 | (3½ to 5-pound) beef | ½ | cup water |
| | tenderloin | ½ | cup red wine |
| | Kitchen Bouquet | | Minced fresh parsley |
| | Garlic powder | | (optional) |
| | Salt | | Sliced mushrooms |
| | Cracked black pepper | | (optional) |

Coat tenderloin with Kitchen Bouquet. Season with garlic powder, salt and pepper. Allow tenderloin to reach room temperature, about 1 hour. Preheat oven to 450°F. Bake 20 minutes. Remove tenderloin from the pan and cover lightly with foil to keep warm. To pan juices, add water, wine, parsley and mushrooms. Simmer and serve as a sauce.

*8 to 10 servings*

## Rump Roast

2 tablespoons
all-purpose flour

1 (17x15-inch) foil
cooking bag

1 (3-pound) boneless
rump roast

1 (1.3-ounce) package
onion soup mix

2½ cups water

Preheat oven to 350°F. Shake flour into oven bag. Place roast and soup mix in the bag. Pour in water and close. Place bag in a baking dish. Cut several slits in top of bag. Bake 1 hour. Remove from bag, slice roast. Serve with gravy.

*8 to 10 servings*

# Tenderloin St. Joe

## Oven Dried Beef Jerky

1½-2 pounds lean beef

½ cup soy sauce

1 tablespoon Worcestershire sauce

¼ teaspoon ground black pepper

¼ teaspoon garlic powder

½ teaspoon onion powder

1 tablespoon hickory smoke flavored salt

Trim all fat from meat. Cut meat into strips ¼-inch thick, 1½-inches wide and any length preferred. In a zip-top plastic bag, combine remaining ingredients. Add strips, thoroughly coating each piece. Marinate 1 hour. Preheat oven to 150°F. Position the oven racks in center of the oven. Line the lower rack with aluminum foil. Lay meat on the upper rack in a single layer. Bake 8 hours.

*20 (4-inch long) pieces*

*Note: Must bake for 8 hours.*

### Tenderloin Steak

| | | |
|---|---|---|
| 4 | (1½-inch thick) beef tenderloin steaks | Cavender's Greek Seasoning |
| | Worcestershire sauce | Garlic salt |
| | Tabasco sauce | Cracked black pepper |
| | | Squeeze butter |

### Crawfish Sauce

| | | | | |
|---|---|---|---|---|
| 1 | pound crawfish tails | 1 | cup unpeeled julienne zucchini, 2-inches long |
| | Cavender's Greek seasoning | | |
| | Tabasco sauce | ½ | teaspoon ground white pepper |
| | Lemon pepper | | |
| ¼ | cup butter | 1 | teaspoon cayenne pepper |
| 1 | cup julienne onion, 2-inches long | 1 | tablespoon fresh lemon juice |
| 1 | cup unpeeled julienne yellow squash, 2-inches long | ½ | pint whipping cream |
| | | ½ | cup grated Parmesan cheese |
| | | ½ | teaspoon salt |

Prepare grill. Season steaks on each side with condiments and sauces. Grill steaks 4 minutes per side, basting with squeeze butter.

Season crawfish tails with Cavender's, Tabasco and lemon pepper. In a saucepan, melt butter over high heat. Add vegetables and sauté until soft. Add peppers and cook 1 minute. Add seasoned crawfish tails and lemon juice. Cook 1 minute. Stir in cream and cheese. Cook until hot. Remove from heat and stir in salt. Pour in 4 equal portions over steaks.

*4 servings*

*This crawfish sauce is also wonderful served over angel hair pasta.*

# Marinated Eye of Round with Horseradish Cream Sauce

| | | | |
|---|---|---|---|
| 1 | (4-pound) eye of round roast | 4 | cloves garlic, crushed |
| 1 | cup soy sauce | | Horseradish Cream Sauce |
| ¼-½ | cup gin | | (see accompanying recipe) |
| ½ | cup vegetable oil | | |

Place roast in a large zip-top plastic bag. In a small bowl, combine remaining ingredients and mix well. Pour marinade over roast. Refrigerate 48 hours, turning several times. Preheat oven to 350°F. Remove roast from marinade. Pat roast dry. Bake 1 hour or until meat thermometer registers medium rare. Serve with Horseradish Sauce.

*8 to 10 servings*

*Note: Roast must marinate 48 hours.*

# Foolproof Rib Roast of Beef

| | | |
|---|---|---|
| 1 | (5 to 10-pound) rib roast of beef | Garlic powder (optional) |
| | Salt | Morton's Nature's Seasons seasoning blend |
| | Freshly ground black pepper | |

Allow roast to reach room temperature, 2 to 3 hours. Preheat oven to 500°F. Place roast in a shallow pan, fat side up. Sprinkle with seasonings. Bake 5 minutes per pound. Turn oven off, do not open oven. Leave roast in oven 2 to 4 hours.

*8 to 10 servings*

*Eye of round roast may be substituted for rib roast of beef. Pierce roast with a fork and sprinkle with meat tenderizer. Let stand at least 45 minutes. Sprinkle with seasonings and bake. If roast is 2 pounds or less, leave in oven 30 minutes. If over 2 pounds, leave 2 hours.*

## Horseradish Cream Sauce

1 cup whipping cream

1 cup mayonnaise

⅛ teaspoon salt

¼ cup prepared horseradish, well drained

Whip cream until soft peaks form. Beat in mayonnaise and salt. Fold in horseradish.

*3 cups*

147

## Escalopes de Veau à la Normande

| | | | | |
|---|---|---|---|---|
| 12 | veal scallops | 1½ | cups whipping cream |
| 4 | tablespoons butter, divided | ½ | tablespoon cornstarch |
| | | 1 | tablespoon water |
| 2 | tablespoons oil, divided | | Salt |
| 3 | tablespoons green onion, minced | | Ground black pepper |
| | | ½ | pound sliced mushrooms |
| ⅓ | cup dry vermouth | | |
| ⅔ | cup beef bouillon | | |

In a skillet, sauté veal on both sides in 2 tablespoons butter and 1 tablespoon oil. Remove veal from skillet. In the same skillet, sauté onion slowly 1 minute. Deglaze skillet with vermouth and bouillon. Boil liquid down rapidly to ½ cup. Add cream to skillet. Combine cornstarch with water and stir into cream. Simmer a few minutes. Season with salt and pepper. In another skillet, sauté mushrooms in remaining butter and oil until lightly browned. Salt and pepper mushrooms and veal. Add to cream sauce. Baste veal with sauce. Heat through.

*4 to 6 servings*

## Barbecued Sloppy Joes

| | | | | |
|---|---|---|---|---|
| 2 | pounds ground beef | ¼ | cup firmly packed brown sugar |
| 2 | tablespoons butter | | |
| ⅓ | cup white vinegar | 2 | cups finely chopped onion |
| ½ | cup water | | |
| 2 | cups ketchup | 3 | cups finely chopped celery |
| 1 | tablespoon dry mustard | 25 | hamburger buns |

In a large saucepan, brown ground beef. Drain well. Add butter, vinegar, water, ketchup, dry mustard and brown sugar. Stir and bring mixture to a boil. Add onion and celery. Heat thoroughly, keeping vegetables crunchy. Serve on buns.

*25 sandwiches*

Holey Burgers!

Tired of burgers with shriveled or burnt edges and raw centers? Try Holey Burgers! Make any size patty flattened to ½-inch thickness. Using your finger or an apple corer, make a hole in the center. The hole should be 1 inch in diameter for an 8-ounce patty and ½-inch, for a 4-ounce patty. Grill 7 to 10 minutes for medium or 11 to 12 minutes for well done, turning only once. Your Holey Burgers will be cooked to perfection!

# Southwestern Enchiladas

| | | | |
|---|---|---|---|
| 1 | pound ground beef | 1 | (13.5-ounce) package |
| ¾ | teaspoon salt | | 8-inch corn tortillas |
| ½ | teaspoon ground black | 4 | green onions, chopped |
| | pepper | 1 | cup shredded Cheddar |
| 1 | tablespoon chili powder | | cheese, divided |
| 1 | (8-ounce) can tomato | | Shredded lettuce, for |
| | sauce | | topping |
| 1 | (10-ounce) can | | |
| | enchilada sauce | | |

Preheat oven 350°F. In a skillet, brown ground beef with salt, pepper and chili powder. Drain well. In a separate skillet, combine and heat sauces. Dip each tortilla in sauce. Fill each tortilla with meat, onion and ¾ cup cheese. Roll and place in a greased 13x9-inch baking dish. Top with remaining sauce and sprinkle with remaining cheese. Bake 20 minutes or until heated thoroughly. Top each serving with lettuce.

*6 servings*

*May be prepared, covered and refrigerated until ready to bake.*

# Popeye's Burgers

| | | | |
|---|---|---|---|
| ½ | cup cooked, chopped | 1 | tablespoon finely |
| | spinach, well drained | | chopped onion |
| 1 | (3-ounce) package | ½ | teaspoon hot pepper |
| | cream cheese, | | sauce |
| | softened | 1 | pound ground beef |
| 2 | tablespoons grated | | Salt |
| | Parmesan cheese | | Ground black pepper |

In a small bowl, combine spinach, cheeses, onion and pepper sauce. Mix well. Shape meat into 8 flat, thin patties. Spoon spinach mixture over 4 patties, spreading within ½-inch of edges. Top with remaining patties. Press edges together to seal. Sprinkle with salt and pepper. Grill over medium coals 5 minutes per side.

*4 servings*

## Firecracker Enchilada Casserole

2 pounds ground beef

1 large onion, chopped

2 tablespoons chili powder

1 teaspoon ground cumin

1 teaspoon salt

1 (15-ounce) can
ranch style beans

6 (8-inch) corn tortillas

1½ cups shredded
Monterey Jack cheese

1½ cups shredded
Cheddar cheese

1 (10-ounce) can diced
tomatoes with green chiles

1 (10¾-ounce) can cream
of mushroom soup

In a skillet, cook beef and onion until meat is brown and onion is tender. Drain well. Add chili powder, cumin and salt. Stir well. Cook over low heat 10 minutes. Spoon meat mixture into a greased 13x9-inch baking dish. Over meat mixture, layer beans, tortillas, cheeses and tomatoes. Top with soup. Cover and refrigerate overnight.

Preheat oven to 350°F. Bake, uncovered, 1 hour. Let stand 10 to 15 minutes before serving.

*8 to 10 servings*

*Note: Casserole must be refrigerated overnight.*

# BEEF

## Baked Meatballs

| | | | | |
|---|---|---|---|---|
| 1½ | pounds ground round | ¼ | teaspoon salt |
| ½ | cup bread crumbs | ¼ | teaspoon crushed red pepper |
| ⅓ | cup chopped fresh parsley | ¾ | teaspoon Italian seasoning |
| ¼ | cup grated Parmesan cheese | | Meatball Sauce (see accompanying recipe) |
| ¼ | cup tomato sauce | | |
| 1 | teaspoon dry mustard | | |
| 2 | cloves garlic, crushed | | |

Preheat oven to 350°F. In a bowl, combine all ingredients and mix well. Shape into 1-inch balls. Place in a 13x9-inch baking pan. Pour Meatball Sauce over meatballs. Bake 45 minutes.

*6 servings*

### Meatball Sauce

4 tablespoons Worcestershire sauce

2 tablespoons Dale's Steak Seasoning

2 cups ketchup

6 tablespoons brown sugar

1 cup water

Combine all ingredients. Stir well.

*3½ cups*

## Family Favorite Casserole

*A thumbs up rating from kids!*

| | | | | |
|---|---|---|---|---|
| 1 | pound ground beef | ¼ | teaspoon ground black pepper |
| ⅓ | cup chopped green onion | 4 | cups uncooked medium egg noodles |
| ½ | cup chopped onion | 1 | (8-ounce) package cream cheese, softened |
| ¼ | cup chopped green bell pepper | | |
| 2 | (8-ounce) cans tomato sauce | 1 | cup small curd cottage cheese |
| 1 | teaspoon sugar | 1 | cup sour cream |
| ¾ | teaspoon salt | | |

Preheat oven to 350°F. In a skillet, brown ground beef with onions and bell pepper. Drain liquid. Stir in tomato sauce, sugar, salt and pepper. Remove from heat. Prepare noodles according to package directions and drain. In a separate bowl, combine cheeses and sour cream. Add noodles to cheese mixture. In a greased 11x7-inch baking dish, spread half of noodle mixture. Top with half of meat sauce. Repeat layers. Bake 30 minutes. Do not freeze.

*8 to 10 servings*

# Médaillons de Porc au Camembert

*Pork Medallions with Camembert Cheese*

| | | | |
|---|---|---|---|
| 1 | pound pork tenderloin | 1 | teaspoon chopped fresh thyme |
| ⅛ | teaspoon freshly ground black pepper, or to taste | 1 | teaspoon chopped fresh sage |
| 1 | tablespoon butter | 1½ | teaspoons Dijon mustard |
| 3 | tablespoons dry white wine | 4 | ounces Camembert cheese, rind removed and sliced |
| ¼-½ | cup whipping cream | | Fresh parsley, for garnish |
| 1 | teaspoon chopped fresh marjoram | | |

Slice pork tenderloin into 1-inch thick steaks. Place between wax paper and pound to flatten to ¼-inch thickness. Sprinkle with pepper. In a heavy skillet, over medium high heat, melt butter until it begins to brown. Add pork and cook about 5 minutes or until cooked through, turning once. Transfer to a serving dish and keep warm. To the skillet, add wine. Bring to a boil, scraping the base of the skillet. Stir in cream and herbs. Return to a boil. Add mustard and any accumulated juice from pork. Add cheese and adjust seasonings. To serve, pour sauce over pork. Garnish with parsley.

*4 servings*

Dried herbs may be substituted for fresh herbs using a 1:3 ratio. For example, 1 teaspoon dried herbs equals 3 teaspoons fresh herbs. Mix dried herbs with an equal amount of fresh parsley for a fresher taste.

# PORK

## Cajun Grilled Pork Tenderloin

| | | | |
|---|---|---|---|
| 4 | tablespoons Tabasco sauce | 1 | package (2 per package) pork tenderloins |
| 4 | tablespoons teriyaki sauce | | Horseradish Mustard Sauce (see accompanying recipe) |
| 2 | tablespoons Worcestershire sauce | | |
| 1 | tablespoon Creole seasoning | | |

Combine Tabasco, teriyaki, Worcestershire and Creole seasoning in a zip-top plastic bag. Add tenderloin and marinate at room temperature for 90 minutes only. Grill tenderloins 8 to 10 minutes on each side or until internal temperature reaches 165°F. Let stand 5 minutes before slicing. Serve warm or at room temperature with Horseradish Mustard Sauce.

*10 servings*

## Honey Roasted Pork Tenderloin

*Great for tailgating*

| | | | |
|---|---|---|---|
| 1 | package (2 per package) pork tenderloins | | Worcestershire sauce |
| | Olive oil | | Soy sauce |
| | Greek seasoning | | Pickapeppa sauce |
| | | | Honey |
| | | ½ | cup beer |

Preheat oven to 350°F. Rub tenderloins with olive oil and sprinkle with Greek seasoning. Place tenderloins in a baking pan with sides touching. Drizzle Worcestershire, soy sauce, Pickapeppa and honey over each tenderloin. Add beer to bottom of pan for moisture. Bake uncovered 45 minutes to 1 hour.

*10 servings*

### Horseradish Mustard Sauce

1 cup whipping cream

¼ cup Dijon mustard

¼ cup horseradish, well drained

Juice of ½ lemon

Whip cream until stiff. Fold in mustard, horseradish and lemon juice. Keep refrigerated until ready to serve.

*2½ cups*

# Roasted Pork Tenderloin with Cranberry Stuffing and Autumn Sauce

| | | | |
|---|---|---|---|
| 1 | cup water | | Salt |
| ¾ | cup sweetened dried cranberries | | Freshly ground black pepper |
| 2 | tablespoons toasted pine nuts | ½ | cup all-purpose flour |
| 1 | teaspoon ground cinnamon | 2 | tablespoons vegetable oil |
| 1 | tablespoon brown sugar | | Autumn Sauce (see accompanying recipe) |
| 1 | teaspoon chili powder | | |
| 1 | (1½ to 2-pound) pork tenderloin, butterflied | | |

In a small saucepan, bring water to a boil and add cranberries. Remove from heat and let sit 1 hour. Drain, reserving 3 tablespoons of liquid. Preheat oven to 400°F. In a food processor, coarsely chop cranberries, pine nuts, cinnamon, brown sugar, chili powder and reserved liquid. Season tenderloin with salt and pepper. Put cranberry mixture in center of tenderloin and tie together with butcher string. Dredge lightly in flour. In a skillet, heat oil and brown tenderloin on all sides. Place in a baking dish. Bake 30 to 45 minutes. Remove and let rest 10 minutes. Slice tenderloin. Serve with Autumn Sauce.

*8 to 10 servings*

## Autumn Sauce

2 tablespoons olive oil

1 small onion, finely chopped

1 carrot, finely diced

1 stalk celery, finely chopped

2 cloves garlic, minced

4 cups chicken stock

½ cup apple juice

1 teaspoon crushed chipotle chili pepper

1 teaspoon black peppercorns

1 tablespoon butter

Salt

Pepper

In a saucepan, heat oil and sauté onion, carrot and celery 8 to 10 minutes. Add garlic and sauté 2 minutes. Stir in stock, juice, chili pepper and peppercorns. Increase heat to high and cook sauce until reduced to 2 cups. Strain sauce. Return to saucepan. Simmer and whisk in butter. Season with salt and pepper. Pour over sliced pork.

*2 cups*

## Southwestern Stir Fry

| | | | |
|---|---|---|---|
| 2 | tablespoons dry sherry | 1 | green bell pepper, cut into thin strips |
| 2 | teaspoons cornstarch | | |
| 1 | teaspoon ground cumin | 1 | medium onion, thinly sliced |
| 1 | clove garlic, minced | | |
| ½ | teaspoon salt | 12 | cherry tomatoes, halved |
| 1 | pound pork tenderloin, sliced into ½-inch steaks | | Cooked rice (optional) |
| 1 | tablespoon vegetable oil | | Green salsa or picante sauce |

In a medium bowl, combine sherry, cornstarch, cumin, garlic and salt. Add pork slices and stir to coat. In a skillet over high heat, heat oil and stir-fry seasoned pork slices 3 to 4 minutes. Add bell pepper and onion. Simmer 3 to 4 minutes. Stir in tomatoes. Serve over rice with green salsa or picante sauce.

*4 servings*

### Marinating Sauce for Bar-B-Que

¼ cup margarine

½ cup vinegar

½ cup water

1 lemon, cut into wedges

1 onion, chopped

¼ (4-ounce) bottle liquid smoke

3-4 drops Tabasco sauce

In a saucepan, combine all ingredients and bring to a boil. Pour over meat and marinate overnight in refrigerator.

*2 cups*

*Note: Must marinate meat overnight.*

## Grilled Marinated Pork Chops

| | | | |
|---|---|---|---|
| 6 | (¾-inch thick) pork chops | 1 | tablespoon Allegro Hot and Spicy Marinade |
| ⅓ | cup zesty Italian dressing | | Juice of 1 lemon |
| ¼ | cup Dale's Steak Seasoning | | Morton's Nature's Seasons seasoning blend |

Rinse chops under cold water and place in a flat glass dish. Combine dressing, Dale's, Allegro and lemon juice. Pour over chops. Sprinkle with seasoning blend. Place in refrigerator for 1 hour. Preheat grill. Grill over hot coals with lid closed 4 to 5 minutes. Turn chops, baste with marinade and grill 5 minutes.

*6 servings*

# Teriyaki Pork Chops with Calypso Salsa

| | | | |
|---|---|---|---|
| ⅔ | cup soy sauce | 1 | (2-inch) piece fresh |
| ⅓ | cup firmly packed | | gingerroot, peeled |
| | brown sugar | | and finely chopped |
| ⅓ | cup water | 6 | (1½-inch) pork chops |
| ¼ | cup rice wine vinegar | | Mint leaves |
| 1½ | teaspoons finely | | Calypso Salsa |
| | chopped garlic | | (see accompanying |
| | | | recipe) |

In a medium saucepan, combine soy sauce, brown sugar, water, vinegar, garlic and ginger. Heat to boiling, stirring until sugar is dissolved. Remove from heat and cool to room temperature. Place pork chops in a shallow baking dish or a zip-top plastic bag. Add cooled soy sauce mixture. Marinate in refrigerator overnight, turning occasionally. Pour marinade from pork chops into saucepan. Heat to boiling and boil 5 minutes. Oil grill surface and preheat to medium high. Grill chops 7 to 9 minutes per side, or until thoroughly cooked. Baste with heated marinade during last 5 minutes of grilling. Garnish with mint leaves and serve with Calypso Salsa.

*6 servings*

*Note: Must marinate overnight.*

*Pork tenderloins may be substituted for pork chops.*

## Calypso Salsa

2 cups finely diced fresh pineapple

1 cup finely diced papaya

¾ cup finely diced red bell pepper

½ cup finely diced onion

½ teaspoon minced garlic

1 small fresh serrano pepper, cored, seeded, and minced

3 tablespoons shredded mint leaves

⅛ teaspoon salt, or to taste

In a medium bowl, combine all ingredients. Let stand at room temperature 1 hour.

*5 cups*

*Salsa may be prepared 1 day in advance, covered and refrigerated. Bring to room temperature before serving.*

155

# PORK

## Crockpot Barbecue

Crockpot Barbecue
is easy and delicious.
Published first in the
**Lamar School Cookbook,**
it has made the rounds.
R.P. is required to bring
this recipe for her
friends and family
at the cabin on
Lake Superior.

| | | | |
|---|---|---|---|
| 1 | (5-pound) Boston butt roast | ½-1 | cup firmly packed brown sugar |
| | Salt | 1 | (18-ounce) bottle barbecue sauce |
| | Ground black pepper | | |
| 1 | cup white vinegar | 1 | onion, halved |

Salt and pepper roast. Place in the crockpot and add vinegar. Cook on high 1 hour. Turn to low and cook 12 hours or overnight. Drain and shred roast into pieces. Place meat back into crockpot. Mix brown sugar and barbecue sauce. Pour over meat. Place onion halves on top of the meat. Cook on low until onion is done, about 2 to 3 hours.

*10 servings*

*Note: Must cook 15 hours.*

Everyone loves to
barbecue, especially
during the summer. To
ensure the safety of
your barbecued food, do
not ever put cooked
chicken, fish or meat
back onto the same
plate you used for raw
meats. Instead use a
clean platter and also
clean utensils. Raw food
can contaminate the
cooked meat.

## Fall Off The Bone Ribs

*Try these nontraditional ribs for your next 4th of July party*

| | | | |
|---|---|---|---|
| 5 | pounds baby back ribs | 2 | yellow bell peppers, sliced |
| | Lawry's Seasoned Salt | | |
| | Freshly cracked black pepper | 2 | red bell peppers, sliced |
| | | 2 | onions, sliced |
| 2 | green bell peppers, sliced | 6 | cloves garlic, chopped |
| | | 2 | jalapeño peppers, sliced |

Generously sprinkle ribs with Lawry's and black pepper. Lay all remaining ingredients on ribs and wrap in foil. Refrigerate 24 hours. Let ribs come to room temperature. Preheat oven to 400°F. Place ribs in oven and immediately lower temperature to 300°F. Cook 5½ to 6 hours.

*6 to 8 servings*

*Note: Must marinate ribs 24 hours before cooking.*

# Ham and Wild Rice Casserole

*Wonderful for leftover ham*

| | | | |
|---|---|---|---|
| 1 | (6-ounce) package long grain and wild rice mix | 1 | (10¾-ounce) can cream of mushroom soup |
| 2 | chicken bouillon cubes | ½ | cup water |
| 2 | tablespoons butter or margarine | 1 | (8-ounce) jar sliced mushrooms, drained |
| 2 | cups chopped cooked ham | 1 | (2-ounce) jar diced pimiento, drained |
| 1 | medium onion, chopped | 1 | cup sliced almonds, toasted |
| 1 | medium green bell pepper, chopped | | |

Preheat oven to 350°F. Cook rice according to package directions adding bouillon cubes. In a skillet over medium high heat, melt butter and sauté ham, onion and bell pepper until tender. Stir in rice. In a large bowl, combine soup, water, mushrooms and pimiento. Stir in ham mixture. Spoon into a lightly greased 2-quart baking dish. Bake 30 minutes. Sprinkle with almonds and bake 5 minutes.

*6 to 8 servings*

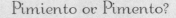

## Pimiento or Pimento?

Pimiento is used in stuffing green olives or in the making of paprika. Pimento is a tree used in producing allspice.

## Barbeque Sauce

**1 quart ketchup**

**1 (1-pound) box brown sugar**

**5 tablespoons Worcestershire sauce**

**6 tablespoons yellow mustard**

**6 tablespoons vinegar**

**1½ teaspoons salt**

**4 teaspoons liquid smoke**

In a saucepan, combine all ingredients. Simmer over low heat 20 minutes, stirring occasionally. Cool completely and store in refrigerator.

*5 cups*

# PORK

## Marmalade Glazed Ham with Sweet Orange Tea Sauce

### Pineapple Mint Relish

½ large pineapple, peeled, cored, and cut into ¼-inch pieces

½ cup finely chopped green bell pepper

½ cup finely chopped red onion

¼ cup chopped fresh mint

2 teaspoons lemon zest

⅛ teaspoon salt, or to taste

⅛ teaspoon pepper, or to taste

*In a bowl, stir all ingredients to blend.*

*4 cups*

*May be prepared 1 day ahead and refrigerated.*

### Ham

| | | | |
|---|---|---|---|
| 1 | (16 to 19-pound) smoked fully cooked bone-in ham | ¼ | cup Dijon mustard |
| 36 | whole cloves | 1½ | cups plus 2 tablespoons water, divided |
| 1 | cup orange marmalade | | |

### Sauce

| | | | |
|---|---|---|---|
| 2 | cups water | 1 | tablespoon Dijon mustard |
| 4 | orange spice herb tea bags or black tea bags | 1 | tablespoon cornstarch dissolved in 1 tablespoon water |
| 2 | cups canned low sodium chicken broth | | Salt |
| 1 | cup orange juice | | Ground black pepper |
| 3 | tablespoons orange marmalade | | Pineapple Mint Relish (see accompanying recipe) |

To prepare ham, preheat oven to 325°F. Trim any rind and excess fat from ham, leaving ¼-inch layer of fat. Score fat in 1-inch diamond pattern and place a clove in center of each diamond. Place ham in a large roasting pan. Bake 3 hours and 45 minutes or until thermometer inserted in center of ham registers 120°F. In a saucepan over medium heat, melt 1 cup marmalade. Whisk in ¼ cup mustard and 2 tablespoons water. Boil 6 minutes or until mixture thickens. Set aside. Remove ham from the roasting pan. Increase oven temperature to 425°F. Place the roasting pan on a burner over medium heat. Whisk in 1½ cups water, scraping up browned bits from bottom of the pan. Skim off fat and set pan juices aside. Line the roasting pan with foil and return ham to pan. Generously spoon marmalade mixture over ham. Bake 20 minutes or until glaze is set and begins to caramelize. Let ham stand 20 minutes.

For sauce, bring 2 cups water to a boil in a saucepan. Add tea bags, cover, and let steep for 10 minutes. Discard tea bags. Stir in chicken broth, orange juice and 3 tablespoons marmalade. Boil 12 minutes or until mixture is reduced to 3 cups. Whisk in 1

*Marmalade Glazed Ham continued*

tablespoon Dijon mustard and reserved pan juices. Return to boil. Whisk in cornstarch mixture. Boil 4 minutes. Season with salt and pepper to taste. Carve ham. Serve with sauce and Pineapple Mint Relish.

*12 to 16 servings*

# Red Beans and Rice

| | | | |
|---|---|---|---|
| 1 | pound dried red kidney beans | 2 | teaspoons salt |
| 1 | pound sausage, sliced | 1 | teaspoon ground black pepper |
| ¼ | cup butter, melted | 1 | teaspoon dried oregano |
| 2 | large white onions, chopped | 1 | teaspoon dried basil |
| 5 | green onions, chopped | 1 | teaspoon dried thyme |
| 5-6 | stalks celery, chopped | ¾ | teaspoon liquid crab boil |
| 5 | cloves garlic, minced | 4-5 | bay leaves |
| | | | Cooked rice |

In a covered saucepan, soak beans in water overnight. Drain and rinse soaked beans. Place beans in a stockpot. Generously cover with water. In a skillet, brown sausage in butter until sausage begins to stick to skillet. Add to beans. In the same skillet, sauté onions, green onions, celery and garlic until tender. Add to beans. Deglaze the skillet by adding a little water and scraping up browned bits. Add to beans. Stir in seasonings and adjust to taste. Simmer over low heat 4 to 5 hours or until beans are tender and thick. Discard bay leaves. Serve in individual bowls or plates over hot rice.

*8 servings*

*Note: Beans must be soaked overnight.*

## BBQ Sauce

**1 cup vinegar**

**1 clove garlic, minced**

**1 tablespoon olive oil**

**1 teaspoon salt**

**1 teaspoon paprika**

**1 tablespoon Tabasco sauce**

**1 tablespoon sugar**

**½ cup ketchup**

**1 teaspoon dry mustard**

**¼ teaspoon ground black pepper**

**2½ tablespoons Worcestershire sauce**

In a saucepan, combine all ingredients. In a well ventilated area, simmer over low heat 30 minutes, stirring often. Cool completely and store in refrigerator.

*1½ cups*

# Lamar School Fundraising Barbecue for 3000

| | | | |
|---|---|---|---|
| 1000 | pounds Boston butts, cut in chunks about the size of 2 large fists | 30 | pounds lemons, squeezed and reserve peelings |
| 2600 | pounds dressed halved chicken fryers, small size | 30 | pounds green bell pepper |
| 18 | gallons tomato ketchup | 20 | pounds bacon |
| | | 100 | pounds onion |
| 1 | case Durkee's dressing | 800 | pounds cabbage |
| 120 | gallons pork and beans | 32 | pounds carrots |
| 1 | case Louisiana Hot sauce | 8 | gallons slaw dressing |
| | | 50 | pounds salt |
| 4 | gallons Worcestershire sauce | 2 | pounds ground red pepper |
| | | 10 | pounds ground black pepper |
| | | 1 | gallon vegetable oil |
| | | 3000 | slices bread or rolls |

First, build a series of fires in a long, narrow row. Allow the fires to burn down to coals. Place meat in washtubs. Add water, red pepper, black pepper, salt, lemon peel, Worcestershire and Louisiana Hot sauce. Boil meat over the charcoal fire until it is fully cooked. The washtubs should rest on metal racks placed about 1 foot above the heat. Remove the washtubs with hooks attached to 6-foot poles. Add sauce and return the meat to the charcoal fires. Roast 30 minutes to 1 hour. Slice with an electric knife. Store in large metal cans until serving time.

To prepare peppers, bacon and onions, cut bacon into small pieces and dice bell peppers and onions. Heat cooking oil. Fry bacon, bell peppers and onions together.

To prepare beans, open several gallons of beans. Drain and discard liquid. Add in share of pepper, bacon and onion mix. Add some barbecue sauce. Mix and blend to flavor. Heat and serve.

For sauce, mix lemon juice, Durkee's dressing, and ketchup. Add 3 bottles hot sauce. Add salt, black pepper and a little red pepper to taste. Hide the extra red pepper!

To prepare slaw, combine shredded cabbage, carrots and slaw dressing. Keep refrigerated.

*3000 - Please let us know when you test this recipe!*

---

Lamar's first fundraising barbecue was held in the mid 1960's. D.C. created this ingredient list from memory. Some of his greatest satisfaction in life has been working with wonderful friends of Lamar.

## Basting Sauce for Smoked Meats

2 cups butter or margarine

2 cloves garlic, minced

⅔ cup sherry

2 tablespoons Worcestershire sauce

2 tablespoons soy sauce

½ cup chopped fresh parsley

2 teaspoons salt

1 cup water

In a saucepan, combine all ingredients. Simmer 30 minutes. May be kept in refrigerator up to 3 months.

*3½ cups*

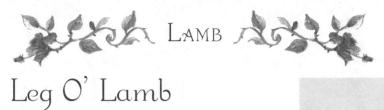

# Leg O' Lamb

1  (6 to 7-pound) leg of
   lamb
3  cloves garlic, halved
   Salt
   Ground black pepper
   All-purpose flour

1  large yellow onion,
   sliced and separated
   into rings, divided
   Boiling water

Preheat oven to 450°F. Wash and dry lamb. Cut six slits around lamb and insert garlic half in each slit. Sprinkle with salt and pepper on both sides. Dredge thoroughly in flour. Place half of onions on bottom of a metal or enamel pan. Lay lamb on top of onions. Top with remaining onion. Bake 25 to 30 minutes or until onion is browned. Lower oven temperature to 325°F. Fill pan 1-inch deep with boiling water. Do not pour water over lamb. Bake 2½ to 3 hours. Remove lamb. Reserve pan juices and make gravy.

*12 servings*

# Rack of Lamb

1    (1-pound) rack of lamb
1-2  tablespoons Dijon
     mustard
2    tablespoons regular
     cornmeal
1    teaspoon minced fresh
     rosemary

2    cloves garlic, minced
½    teaspoon kosher salt
⅛    teaspoon freshly
     ground black pepper,
     or to taste

Preheat oven to 450°F. Lightly brush fat side of lamb with mustard. In a small bowl, combine remaining ingredients. Dredge lamb with meal mixture. Bake 10 minutes. Reduce heat to 400°F and bake 15 minutes. Let rest before slicing.

*4 servings*

## Pan Gravy

2 tablespoons fat from
pan drippings

1-2 tablespoons
all-purpose flour

Degreased pan juices

Water

Salt

Ground black pepper

Dried rosemary

Strain drippings if desired. Separate fat from meat juices. Heat fat and whisk in enough flour until mixture is the consistency of heavy cream. Continue to cook slowly and stir constantly while adding degreased pan juices and enough water to make 1 cup. Season with salt, pepper and rosemary to taste.

*1 cup*

*This gravy may be used for any meat dish. May season with your favorite herbs.*

# Lost Island Duck Gumbo

Lost Island Duck Gumbo was an all time favorite at a duck camp in Arkansas, owned by the Meyers family who originated Brown and Serve Rolls. The cook entrusted B.R. with the recipe. The original recipe called for 3 flat soup bowls overflowing with fresh chopped onion. For convenience, we substituted frozen chopped onion. Lost Island Duck Gumbo will require some effort. Some good things just take time.

| | | | | |
|---|---|---|---|---|
| 6 | ducks | 1 | tablespoon dried thyme |
| 1½ | cups butter | 3 | tablespoons salt, or to taste |
| 3 | cups all-purpose flour | 3 | tablespoons ground black pepper, or to taste |
| 4 | (10-ounce) packages frozen chopped onion | | |
| 3 | bunches celery, finely chopped | 1½ | tablespoons crushed red pepper |
| 9 | cloves garlic, finely chopped | 1 | tablespoon cayenne pepper |
| 3 | bunches fresh parsley, finely chopped | 2 | tablespoons Accent |
| 6 | quarts reserved duck stock (add chicken broth to make 6 quarts) | 1 | tablespoon dried oregano |
| | | 6 | pounds shrimp, peeled and deveined |
| 3 | (6-ounce) cans tomato paste | 3 | tablespoons gumbo filé (optional) |
| 4 | (14½-ounce) cans tomatoes | | Cooked rice, wild rice or mixture of both |
| 9 | large green bell peppers, chopped | | Chopped fresh parsley, for garnish |
| 3 | bunches green onions, chopped | | |

Boil ducks until tender in salted water to cover. Drain, reserving stock. Debone ducks and cut meat into small pieces.

In a heavy cast iron skillet, melt butter and stir in flour. Stir constantly to make a medium dark roux. This must be done slowly to prevent burning. Add onion and celery. Reduce heat and cook until onion and celery are browned. Transfer roux mixture to a 21-quart stockpot. Add garlic and parsley. Gradually add duck stock, stirring to keep mixture smooth. Add remaining ingredients except shrimp and gumbo filé. Boil rapidly 30 minutes. Add shrimp. Simmer until shrimp turn pink. Remove from heat. Add gumbo filé and stir well. Serve in bowls over rice. Top with chopped parsley.

*5 gallons*

*Gumbo filé may be omitted or sprinkled on rice before pouring gumbo over it.*

# GAME

## Plantation Wild Duck

| | | | |
|---|---|---|---|
| 2 | ducks | 2 | bay leaves |
| | Salt | 2 | cups sliced fresh |
| | Ground black pepper | | mushrooms |
| 2 | onions, sliced | ¼ | teaspoon dried thyme |
| 1 | cup butter or | 4 | tablespoons all- |
| | margarine | | purpose flour |
| 4 | cups water | | Cooked wild rice |

Preheat oven to 250°F. Prepare ducks for roasting. Sprinkle with salt and pepper. Cut up ducks at joints and brown with onions in butter. Add water and bay leaves. Bake 1½ hours. Sauté mushrooms. Stir in thyme and flour. Spoon mushroom mixture over ducks. Bake 30 minutes. Discard bay leaves. Serve with wild rice.

*4 servings*

## Deer Wraps

| | | | |
|---|---|---|---|
| 1 | (2-pound) venison roast or loin, rectangular cut | ¾ | cup Italian dressing |
| 1 | (12-ounce) package sliced bacon | 1 | tablespoon mesquite powdered seasoning |
| ¾ | cup Moore's Marinade | ½ | teaspoon ground black pepper |

Slice venison in lengthwise strips, approximately ¼ inch thick by 8 to 10 inches long. Pound venison to tenderize. Cut bacon strips in half lengthwise. Place bacon on flat surface, lay venison strip on top. Roll up with bacon on the outside. Skewer with a toothpick. Continue until all strips are wrapped. In a large bowl, mix Moore's and dressing. Add wraps to marinade mixture. Sprinkle with mesquite seasoning and pepper. Marinate at least 6 hours. Prepare grill. Grill, medium to well done, 10 to 15 minutes.

*4 servings*

*For shish-ka-bobs, marinate venison tenderloin cubes, green bell pepper pieces, onion pieces, whole mushrooms and bacon in marinade. Skewer, placing bacon next to venison. Broil or grill until medium to well done.*

## Easy Venison Roast and Gravy

*Makes its own delicious gravy*

1 venison roast

1 stalk celery, cut into small slivers

2-3 cloves garlic, cut into slivers

1 onion, sliced

4-6 slices bacon

Seasoning salt

Ground black pepper

1-2 (10¾-ounce) cans cream of mushroom soup

Cooked rice or mashed potatoes

Preheat oven to 350°F. Punch several holes in both sides of roast. Into each hole, slide slivers of celery and garlic. Place in a roasting pan. Top roast with sliced onion. Cover onion with crisscrossed bacon slices. Sprinkle with salt and pepper. Bake covered 20 to 25 minutes per pound. Remove from oven 30 minutes before roast is done. Add 1 to 2 cans cream of mushroom soup around sides of roast. Bake uncovered 30 minutes. Serve with rice or mashed potatoes.

*4 to 6 servings*

# Tender Venison Shoulder
*Very tender and tasty*

| | | | |
|---|---|---|---|
| 1 | whole deer shoulder | | Tony Chachere's |
| 6 | potatoes, peeled and | | Seasoning |
| | sliced | ½ | cup Worcestershire |
| 4 | onions, sliced | | sauce, or to taste |
| 1 | pound carrots, peeled | | |
| | and sliced | | |

Prepare grill or preheat oven to 250°F. Place shoulder in a shallow disposable aluminum pan. Cover with potatoes, onions, carrots or any other vegetables desired. Sprinkle liberally with Chachere's. Add Worcestershire. Cover with extra heavy duty aluminum foil. Seal tightly around the edges so that no steam can escape. Place on a grill or in the oven. Cook a small shoulder for 4 hours, a medium shoulder for 6 hours and a large shoulder for 8 hours. The longer the shoulder cooks, the more tender it gets.

*Smoked sausage or mushrooms may be added to the pan with vegetables.*

*For a different flavor, coat shoulder with barbecue sauce or Italian dressing.*

*1 deer shoulder*

## Preparing Venison

Before turning down a hunter's gift of venison, try these methods for taming wild game!

Soak meat in ⅓ cup vinegar, 1 tablespoon salt and water. Let soak overnight in the refrigerator.

Soak venison in Italian salad dressing following vinegar solution process. Some wild game chefs prefer to leave venison in the dressing overnight.

Always remove the white membrane or sinew before cooking venison.

# Baked Dove Breasts

| | | | |
|---|---|---|---|
| 18 | dove breasts | | Zest of ½ lemon |
| 2 | tablespoons butter or margarine | | Juice of ½ lemon |
| 2 | tablespoons canola oil | 2 | teaspoons liquid smoke |
| ⅛ | teaspoon salt, or to taste | 1 | tablespoon Worcestershire sauce |
| ⅛ | teaspoon ground black pepper, or to taste | 4 | slices bacon |
| ⅛ | teaspoon garlic salt | ¼ | cup sherry |
| | | ¼ | cup water |

Preheat oven to 325°F. In a skillet, brown dove breasts in butter and oil. Sprinkle with salt and pepper liberally while browning. Remove dove breasts from the skillet and place in a 13x9-inch baking dish. Sprinkle with garlic salt, lemon zest and juice, liquid smoke and Worcestershire. Cover doves with bacon slices. Deglaze the skillet with sherry and water. Pour over dove breasts. Bake covered 1½ hours.

*Serves 6 if 3 dove breasts per person are enough…*
*but no one will be satisfied with 3!*

## Grilled Doves

2 cups orange juice

1 cup Italian dressing

¼ cup dry sherry

4 tablespoons Worcestershire sauce

24 dove breasts

Olive oil

1 teaspoon seasoning salt

1 tablespoon coarse ground black pepper

1 pound thinly sliced bacon

Combine orange juice, Italian dressing, sherry and Worcestershire to form marinade. Place dove breasts in a sealable plastic container. Completely cover with marinade. Refrigerate overnight. Prepare grill. Drain dove breasts and pat dry with paper towels. Coat each dove breast with olive oil. Lightly sprinkle with seasoning salt and pepper. Wrap each dove breast with ½ slice bacon and secure with a toothpick. Place in a grilling basket and cook slowly over a medium charcoal fire. Grill 15 to 20 minutes or until bacon is fairly crisp.

*6 to 8 servings*

*Note: Must marinate overnight.*

# GAME

It is recommended that hunters in the elementary division of Lamar School refrain from bringing deer hearts to class for anatomy lessons. This method of instruction was once attempted when B.B. brought his recent trophy to Mrs. Lee's fifth grade classroom for "Show and Tell." Several of his former classmates recall that they "fainted dead away."

## Wonderful Wild Goose with Sour Cream and Mushrooms

| | | | |
|---|---|---|---|
| 1 | (5 to 8-pound) goose | 4 | tablespoons all-purpose flour, divided |
| 1½ | teaspoons salt, divided | ½ | teaspoon dried rosemary |
| | Garlic salt | | |
| | Paprika | | |
| 1½ | stalks celery, chopped | ¼ | teaspoon dried thyme |
| 1 | carrot, peeled and chopped | 1 | (8-ounce) carton sour cream |
| 1 | onion, chopped | 1 | (4-ounce) can button mushrooms, drained |
| 2 | tablespoons canola oil | | |

Preheat oven to 325°F. Remove neck and wing tips from goose. In a saucepan, cover neck and tips with water seasoned with ¾ teaspoon salt, simmer 45 minutes to 1 hour. Reserve stock.

Season goose inside and out with garlic salt and paprika. Place on a rack in a shallow pan. Roast uncovered 1 hour or until brown and fat has cooked off. In a saucepan, sauté celery, carrot and onion in canola oil until soft and golden. Stir in 2 tablespoons flour. Blend in 1 cup reserved stock. Season with rosemary, thyme and remaining salt. Stir remaining flour into sour cream to prevent curdling during roasting. Blend sour cream mixture into gravy. Transfer goose to a roasting pan. Pour gravy and mushrooms over goose. Cover and roast 2 hours.

*6 servings*

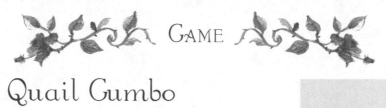

# Quail Gumbo

| | | | |
|---|---|---|---|
| 4 | tablespoons all-purpose flour | 1 | cup chopped green onion |
| 2 | tablespoons bacon grease or vegetable oil | 1 | teaspoon ground white pepper |
| ¼ | cup cooked crumbled bacon | 6 | quail |
| 1 | cup diced onion | 1 | pound link sausage, cut into bite-size pieces |
| 4 | cups hot water | 1 | pound shrimp, peeled and deveined (optional) |
| 1 | cup chopped fresh parsley | 3 | tablespoons gumbo filé |
| 1 | teaspoon dry mustard | | Cooked rice |
| 1 | teaspoon seasoning salt | | |

In a skillet, combine flour and grease. Cook, stirring constantly, until roux is the color of a new penny. Transfer roux into a stockpot. Add bacon and onion. Cook until onion is soft. Stir in water, parsley, dry mustard, seasoning salt, green onion and white pepper. Add quail. Simmer 1 hour. In a skillet, brown sausage and drain well. Remove quail, debone and cut into bite-size pieces. Return quail pieces to liquid. Add sausage and shrimp. Prior to serving, stir in gumbo filé. Serve in individual bowls over rice.

*6 to 8 servings*

## Quail in Wine

6-8 quail, split in half

Salt, to taste

Ground black pepper, to taste

½ cup butter, divided

1 carrot, peeled and diced

1 small onion, chopped

½ cup chopped fresh mushrooms

2 tablespoons green bell pepper, chopped

1 tablespoon all-purpose flour

1 cup chicken stock or broth

½ cup white wine or sherry

Preheat oven to 350°F. Season quail with salt and pepper. In a skillet, lightly brown quail in ¼ cup butter. Remove to a buttered baking dish. In the same skillet, sauté vegetables in remaining butter 5 minutes. Stir in flour. Gradually add stock. Simmer 10 minutes. While sauce is simmering, pour wine over quail. Cover with sauce. Tightly cover with foil. Bake 1½ hours.

*3 to 4 servings*

# Wild Turkey Tetrazzini

A Brunswick stew recipe was once part of an antique club's program on historic recipes. Several ladies, entranced by its unusual flavor, insisted on full disclosure of the secret ingredient. One lady's false teeth landed straight in the punch bowl when she learned that she had just eaten a large bowlful of squirrel!

| | | | |
|---|---|---|---|
| 4 | chicken bouillon cubes | 2 | tablespoons dried parsley flakes |
| ½ | wild turkey breast | 1 | teaspoon salt |
| 1 | (12-ounce) package thin spaghetti | 1 | teaspoon ground black pepper |
| ½ | green bell pepper, diced | 1 | (2-ounce) jar diced pimientos |
| 6 | shallots, finely chopped | | |
| ½ | cup butter or margarine | 1 | (10¾-ounce) can cream of mushroom soup |
| ½ | cup slivered almonds | | |
| ¼ | cup dry sherry | ½ | cup grated Parmesan cheese |
| 1 | (4-ounce) can sliced mushrooms | | |
| ½ | cup chicken broth | | |
| 1 | teaspoon sugar | | |

Preheat oven to 350°F. In a stockpot, place bouillon cubes and turkey breast and cover with water. Boil until tender. Remove breast from broth and cube. Reserve broth. Cook spaghetti according to package directions in reserved broth instead of water. In a skillet, sauté bell pepper and shallots in butter until soft. To prepare sauce, combine sautéed mixture with remaining ingredients except Parmesan cheese. Add turkey and spaghetti. Pour into a greased 13x9-inch casserole. Sprinkle with Parmesan cheese. Bake 30 minutes.

*10 to 12 servings*

## Critter Chili

| | | | | |
|---|---|---|---|---|
| ½ | cup all-purpose flour | | 2 | pounds smoked rabbit meat (see accompanying recipe) |
| ½ | cup bacon grease | | | |
| 3 | large onions, chopped | | | |
| 4 | cloves garlic, minced | | 2 | pounds uncooked wild turkey meat, cut into chunks |
| | Chili powder, 3 different brands, divided | | | |
| 1 | (10-ounce) can tomatoes with green chilies | | 2 | pounds venison sausage |
| | | | ⅛ | teaspoon salt, or to taste |
| 4 | (16-ounce) cans dark red chili beans, drained | | | Shredded Cheddar cheese, for garnish |
| | | | | Chopped green onions, for garnish |
| 2 | quarts water | | | Sliced stuffed green olives, for garnish |

In a skillet, combine flour and bacon grease. Heat slowly and stir constantly until roux becomes dark brown. Stir in onions and garlic. Simmer 4 to 5 minutes. Transfer roux mixture to a stockpot. Add ¼ cup chili powder, tomatoes, beans and water. Sprinkle each meat with a different brand of chili powder. Separately brown meats. Add browned meats to tomato mixture. Simmer 3 hours. Add salt. Garnish each serving with cheese, onions and olives.

*25 to 30 servings*

### Smoked Rabbit

**8 (3 to 5-pound) rabbits**

**8 tablespoons liquid crab boil**

In a large stockpot, add sufficient water to cover 8 rabbits. Bring to a rolling boil. Add crab boil. Boil 5 minutes, reduce heat and simmer 30 minutes. Leave rabbits in stock and cool in refrigerator or in a sink filled with ice. Cool overnight. Remove, drain and save stock. Prepare Cajun water bath smoker using rabbit stock for the water bath. Place 4 rabbits on each rack. Smoke 1 hour with mesquite or wild cherry as smoking wood. Quarter rabbits and serve or debone for use in other recipes. Freezes well.

*8 rabbits*

*Note: Must be cooled overnight.*

# Crawfish Fettuccine with Andouille

## Romano Shrimp Pasta

¾ cup butter

12 jumbo shrimp, peeled and diced

6 large fresh mushrooms, diced

2 cloves garlic, minced

8 ounces vermicelli, cooked al dente, drained

½ cup freshly grated Romano cheese, divided

¼ teaspoon salt

⅛ teaspoon freshly ground black pepper

Freshly chopped parsley

In a large, heavy skillet over medium heat, melt butter and sauté shrimp and mushrooms 1 minute. Add garlic and sauté 1 to 2 minutes. Stir in hot vermicelli, 6 tablespoons cheese, salt and pepper. Toss carefully until very hot, but do not allow butter to brown. Place in a serving dish. Sprinkle with remaining cheese and parsley. Serve immediately.

*4 servings*

| | |
|---|---|
| 3 | cups seafood stock or 3 (8-ounce) bottles clam juice |
| 4 | cups whipping cream |
| ½ | cup butter |
| 1 | medium onion, minced |
| 1 | medium green or red bell pepper, minced |
| 3 | cloves garlic, minced |
| 1 | teaspoon dried basil |
| 1 | pound peeled crawfish tails |
| 4-8 | ounces diced andouille sausage |
| ⅛ | teaspoon salt, or to taste |
| ½ | teaspoon cayenne pepper |
| ½ | teaspoon freshly ground black pepper |
| 3 | tablespoons melted butter blended with 3 tablespoons flour |
| 6 | green onions, chopped |
| 1 | pound fettuccine, cooked according to package directions |
| | Freshly grated Parmesan cheese |

In a saucepan, boil stock or clam juice until reduced by half. Add cream and reduce again by half. Set aside. In a deep skillet, melt ½ cup butter. Stir in onion, bell pepper, garlic and basil. Sauté until onion is transparent. Add crawfish, andouille, salt and peppers. Cook several minutes to combine. Remove from heat. Bring cream mixture to a boil. Whisk in butter and flour mixture, a little at a time until all is incorporated and the sauce has thickened. Stir cream mixture into crawfish mixture and heat through. Add green onions. Serve over fettuccine. Sprinkle with cheese.

*6 to 8 servings*

# Cajun Style Linguine

| | | | |
|---|---|---|---|
| 1 | pound smoked sausage, sliced | ½ | cup Italian dressing |
| 3 | boneless, skinless chicken breast halves, cut into bite-size strips | 1 | small onion, diced |
| | | 3 | (1.6-ounce) packages Alfredo sauce, prepared according to package directions |
| 2 | tablespoons butter | 2 | (6-ounce) packages frozen precooked salad shrimp |
| 2 | tablespoons dried rosemary | | |
| 1 | teaspoon ground black pepper | 1 | pound linguine, prepared according to package directions |
| 1 | teaspoon cayenne pepper | | Grated Parmesan cheese |
| 1 | teaspoon chili powder | | |
| 1 | teaspoon Cajun seasoning (optional) | | |

In a skillet, cook sausage over medium heat and remove. To the skillet, add chicken and cook until almost done. Remove chicken from skillet and drain fat. In the skillet, melt butter and stir in all seasonings, dressing and onion. Sauté 1 minute. Add chicken and sausage. Stir in Alfredo sauce. Add shrimp and heat thoroughly. Serve hot over linguine. Sprinkle with Parmesan cheese.

*6 to 8 servings*

Over the years, S.P. has literally worn out two copies of Lamar School's first cookbook, **Kitchen Gems**. They are held together with red yarn and the pages are worn and stained with various recipe ingredients. Hopefully she and her granddaughter, A.J., will wear out several copies of **Prime Meridian** as they continue the family's cooking tradition.

# Lemon Linguine with Fresh Tomato Sauce and Grilled Chicken

*A beautiful presentation*

### Tomato Sauce

| | | | | |
|---|---|---|---|---|
| 4 | cups fresh plum tomatoes, washed, cored and cut into wedges | 2 | tablespoons snipped Italian or flat-leafed parsley |
| ⅛ | teaspoon salt, or to taste | 2-4 | cloves garlic, crushed |
| 6 | fresh basil leaves, torn | 4 | tablespoons olive oil |
| | | | Juice of 1 lemon |
| | | | Freshly ground black pepper |

### Chicken

| | | | |
|---|---|---|---|
| 6 | boneless, skinless chicken breast halves | 2 | tablespoons olive oil |
| | Juice of 1 lemon | 1 | tablespoon dried oregano |

### Lemon Sauce

| | | |
|---|---|---|
| 4 | tablespoons butter | Zest of 2 lemons |
| 1 | cup whipping cream | Juice of 2 lemons |

### Pasta

| | | | |
|---|---|---|---|
| 8 | ounces linguine, cooked al dente, drained | 18 | very thin lengthwise slices red and/or yellow bell pepper, for garnish |
| 1 | cup freshly grated Parmesan cheese, divided | | |

For tomato sauce, place tomatoes in a large bowl. Sprinkle with salt, basil, parsley, garlic and olive oil. Stir gently just to mix. Sprinkle with lemon juice and pepper. Set aside to marinate 1 hour.

To prepare chicken, place chicken breasts in a zip-top plastic bag. Add lemon juice, olive oil, and oregano. Marinate 1 hour. Grill chicken breasts over hot coals 7 to 10 minutes, turning once, taking care not to overcook. Diagonally slice chicken breasts thinly, keeping them intact. Keep warm.

Lemon Linguine continued

For lemon sauce, heat butter and cream in a large skillet. When cream begins to boil, add lemon zest and juice. Stir thoroughly. Cook over high heat, stirring constantly, until cream is reduced by half. At this point, sauce may be put on hold by simply removing it from the heat. Reheat before assembling dish.

To assemble dish, toss hot pasta with ½ cup cheese and lemon sauce. Divide pasta into 6 servings. Top each serving with tomato sauce and a layer of sliced chicken breast. Garnish with pepper slices. Sprinkle with remaining cheese.

*6 servings*

# Spicy Shrimp and Pasta

| | | | |
|---|---|---|---|
| 2 | tablespoons butter | 8 | ounces angel hair pasta, cooked according to package directions |
| ½ | cup chopped green onion | | |
| 2 | cloves garlic, minced | ⅓ | cup grated Parmesan cheese |
| 2 | teaspoons Cajun seasoning | ½ | teaspoon crushed red pepper |
| 1 | pound medium fresh shrimp, peeled and deveined | ¼ | cup freshly chopped parsley |
| ½ | cup whipping cream | | |
| ¼ | cup dry white wine | | |

In a large skillet, melt butter and sauté onion and garlic until tender. Stirring constantly, add Cajun seasoning and cook 1 minute. Reduce heat. Add shrimp and cream. Simmer 3 minutes, stirring often. Add wine and simmer 3 minutes, stirring often. Gently stir in pasta, cheese and pepper. Heat thoroughly. Stir in parsley and serve.

*4 to 6 servings*

# Cannelloni

Cannelloni are large round pasta tubes typically stuffed and baked with sauce.

### Tomato Sauce

| | | | |
|---|---|---|---|
| 4 | tablespoons olive oil | 6 | tablespoons tomato paste |
| 1 | cup finely chopped onion | 2 | teaspoons dried basil |
| 4 | cups canned tomatoes, coarsely chopped, reserve liquid | 2 | teaspoons sugar |
| | | 1 | teaspoon salt |
| | | ⅛ | teaspoon ground black pepper, or to taste |

### Meat Filling

| | | | |
|---|---|---|---|
| 2 | tablespoons olive oil | 5 | tablespoons grated Parmesan cheese |
| ¼ | cup finely chopped onion | 2 | tablespoons whipping cream |
| 1 | teaspoon garlic, minced | 2 | eggs, lightly beaten |
| 1 | (10-ounce) package frozen chopped spinach, thawed and squeezed dry | ½ | teaspoon oregano |
| | | ⅛ | teaspoon salt, or to taste |
| 1 | tablespoon butter | ⅛ | teaspoon ground black pepper, or to taste |
| 1 | pound ground round | | |

### Besciamella

| | | | |
|---|---|---|---|
| 4 | tablespoons butter | 1 | cup whipping cream |
| 4 | tablespoons all-purpose flour | 1 | teaspoon salt |
| 1 | cup milk | ⅛ | teaspoon ground white pepper |

### Cannelloni

| | | | |
|---|---|---|---|
| 2 | (12-ounce) boxes jumbo pasta shells, prepared according to package directions | 4 | tablespoons grated Parmesan cheese |
| | | 2 | tablespoons butter, cut into pieces |

For tomato sauce, heat oil in a 2 or 3-quart saucepan. Add onion and cook until soft. Stir in tomatoes, tomato liquid and remaining sauce ingredients. Reduce heat to low and simmer 40 minutes with pan partially covered. Stir occasionally. Blend tomato mixture in blender.

To prepare meat filling, heat oil in a skillet over medium heat. Sauté onion and garlic 7 to 8 minutes until soft, stirring frequently. Stir in spinach and cook 3 to 4 minutes, stirring constantly. When

Cannelloni continued

all moisture has cooked away, transfer to a large mixing bowl. In the same skillet, melt butter and lightly brown meat. Drain and add to spinach mixture. Stir in cheese, cream, eggs and oregano. Season with salt and pepper.

For besciamella, melt butter in a heavy 2 or 3-quart saucepan over medium heat. Remove from heat and stir in flour. Add milk and cream all at once, stirring constantly with a whisk. Return to heat. When sauce comes to a boil and is smooth, reduce heat. Simmer, still stirring, 2 to 3 minutes or until sauce heavily coats the whisk wires. Remove from heat. Season with salt and white pepper.

Preheat oven to 375°F. To assemble cannelloni, pour a light film of tomato sauce into two 14x10-inch baking dishes. Stuff each shell with meat filling. Place in the dishes, side by side, on top of tomato sauce. Pour besciamella over pasta shells. Spoon remaining tomato sauce on top. Sprinkle with cheese and dot with butter. Bake uncovered 20 minutes or until cheese is melted and sauce bubbles.

*12 to 15 servings*

*Tomato sauce may be prepared ahead and refrigerated for one week.*

*Once assembled, cannelloni may be refrigerated for one day or may be frozen.*

# Linguine with Clam Sauce

Don't throw out all that leftover wine. Freeze into ice cubes for future use in sauces and casseroles.

| | | | |
|---|---|---|---|
| 3 | (6½-ounce) cans minced clams | ⅛ | teaspoon thyme |
| | Bottled clam juice | ¼ | cup chopped parsley |
| ¼ | cup butter or margarine | 1 | tablespoon fresh lemon juice |
| 1 | teaspoon minced garlic | ⅛ | teaspoon salt, or to taste |
| 2 | tablespoons all-purpose flour | ⅛ | teaspoon ground black pepper, or to taste |
| ½ | cup white wine or chicken broth | 1 | pound linguine, cooked according to package directions |
| ⅛ | teaspoon crushed red pepper | | |

Drain juice from clams into a 2-cup measuring cup. Add bottled clam juice to make 2 cups liquid. In a skillet over low heat, melt butter and sauté garlic for 1 minute. Remove from heat and stir in flour. Return to low heat and cook 1 minute, stirring constantly. Gradually add clam liquid, wine, red pepper and thyme. Bring to a boil and simmer 1 to 2 minutes. Stir in clams, parsley, and lemon juice. Heat thoroughly. Add salt and pepper to taste. Serve over linguine.

*4 to 6 servings*

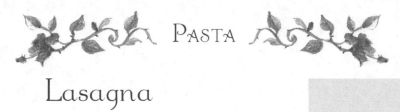

# Lasagna

### Sauce

| | | | |
|---|---|---|---|
| 2 | tablespoons olive oil | ¼ | cup chopped celery |
| 1 | medium onion, chopped | 2 | tablespoons freshly chopped parsley |
| 1 | clove garlic, minced | 2 | teaspoons salt |
| 1 | pound ground beef | 1 | teaspoon sugar |
| 3½ | cups whole tomatoes | ⅛ | teaspoon ground black pepper |
| 1 | (6-ounce) can tomato paste | 1 | bay leaf |
| ¼ | cup water | ½ | teaspoon dried basil |

### Lasagna

| | | | |
|---|---|---|---|
| 1 | pound lasagna noodles | ½ | cup grated Romano cheese |
| 1 | cup cottage cheese | | |
| 1 | cup ricotta cheese | ½ | cup grated Parmesan cheese |
| 4 | cups shredded mozzarella cheese | | |

To prepare sauce, heat oil in a saucepan. Sauté onion and garlic 5 minutes. Add ground beef and brown. Stir in remaining sauce ingredients. Bring to a boil and reduce heat. Simmer 3 hours, stirring occasionally. Remove bay leaf and skim off fat.

Boil noodles about 15 minutes until al dente, stirring frequently to avoid sticking. Drain and cover with cold water. Lightly oil a 13x9-inch baking dish. In a separate bowl, combine cottage and ricotta cheeses. In another bowl, combine mozzarella, Romano and Parmesan cheeses.

Preheat oven to 350°F. Line bottom of the baking dish with a single layer of noodles. Top with ¼ of sauce and ¼ of each cheese mixture. Repeat layers of noodles, sauce, and cheeses 3 times to make 4 layers. Bake 30 minutes. Let stand 15 minutes before serving.

*10 to 12 servings*

## Low-Fat Spinach Stuffed Pasta Shells

1 tablespoon margarine

1 small onion, chopped

1 (24-ounce) carton low-fat cottage cheese

1 (12-ounce) package grated mozzarella cheese

1 (10-ounce) package frozen chopped spinach, thawed and well drained

1 teaspoon salt

½ teaspoon ground black pepper

1 (12-ounce) box jumbo pasta shells, prepared according to package directions

1 (26-ounce) jar spaghetti sauce

Preheat oven to 350°F. In a large skillet, melt margarine. Sauté onion until tender. Add cheeses, spinach, salt and pepper. Stuff shells with spinach mixture. Place shells in a greased 13x9-inch baking dish. Pour sauce over shells. Cover with foil. Bake 30 to 40 minutes or until hot.

*6 to 8 servings*

# Baked Spaghetti

1 cup chopped onion
1 cup chopped green bell pepper
1 tablespoon oil
1 pound ground beef
2 (14½-ounce) cans diced tomatoes, undrained
1 (2¼-ounce) can sliced ripe olives, drained
1 (4-ounce) can sliced mushrooms, drained
1 (10¾-ounce) can cream of mushroom soup
1 teaspoon salt
1 teaspoon ground black pepper
1 (12-ounce) package spaghetti, cooked according to package directions
8 ounces shredded sharp Cheddar cheese

Preheat oven to 350°F. In a skillet, sauté onion and bell pepper in oil until tender. Remove from skillet. Brown ground beef and drain. Combine all ingredients except spaghetti and cheese. In a greased 13x9-inch baking dish, layer ⅓ of spaghetti, ⅓ of sauce, and ⅓ of cheese. Repeat layers twice. Bake 40 minutes.

*8 servings*

# Black Bean Lasagna

*A delicious vegetarian entrée*

| | | | |
|---|---|---|---|
| 2 | (15-ounce) cans black beans, rinsed and drained | 1 | (12-ounce) carton low-fat cottage cheese |
| ½ | cup chopped onion | 1 | (8-ounce) package reduced fat cream cheese |
| ½ | cup chopped green bell pepper | ¼ | cup light sour cream |
| 2 | cloves garlic, minced | 1 | (8-ounce) package lasagna noodles, prepared according to package directions |
| 2 | (15-ounce) cans low sodium tomato sauce | | |
| ¼ | cup snipped fresh cilantro | | Tomato slices |

Preheat oven to 350°F. Mash 1 can of beans and set aside. Spray a large skillet with nonstick cooking spray. Sauté onion, bell pepper and garlic over medium heat until tender but not brown. Add mashed beans, whole beans, tomato sauce and cilantro. Heat thoroughly. In a large bowl, combine cheeses and sour cream. Set aside. Spray a 13x9-inch baking dish with nonstick cooking spray. Arrange three noodles in the dish. Top with ⅓ of bean mixture. Spread with ⅓ of cheese mixture. Repeat layers twice, ending with bean mixture. Reserve final cheese mixture layer. At this point, recipe may be frozen. Thaw before baking. Bake, covered 40 to 50 minutes. Dollop with reserved cheese mixture. Garnish with tomato slices. Let stand 10 minutes before serving.

*10 to 12 servings*

# Tomato and Artichoke Pasta Sauce

*Super meatless meal*

| | | | |
|---|---|---|---|
| 2 | (6-ounce) jars marinated artichoke hearts in oil, reserve marinade | ⅛ | teaspoon crushed red pepper |
| ¼ | cup olive oil | 1 | (28-ounce) can plum tomatoes, quartered, with juice |
| 1 | cup chopped onion | 4 | ounces fresh mushrooms, sliced |
| 2 | tablespoons minced garlic | ¼ | cup freshly grated Parmesan cheese |
| 1½ | teaspoons fresh oregano | ¼ | cup chopped fresh parsley |
| 1½ | teaspoons fresh basil | | Pasta, prepared according to package directions |
| 1 | teaspoon coarsely ground black pepper | | |
| ½ | teaspoon salt | | |

Quarter artichoke hearts. In a large saucepan, heat olive oil. Add onion, garlic, oregano, basil, black pepper, salt, red pepper and reserved marinade. Over medium-low heat, sauté 10 minutes or until onion and garlic are soft and translucent. Stir in tomatoes and simmer 30 minutes. Add artichoke hearts, mushrooms, Parmesan and parsley. Stirring gently, simmer 5 minutes. Serve over hot pasta.

*4 servings*

# Side Dishes

# Transporting Past
## Success into
### Future Prosperity

*Located near the entrance of the Hotel Meridian, highway signs indicate Meridian's position as one of Mississippi's travel and transportation cross-roads. With its location at the intersection of major roads and only two blocks from Union Station, the five-story Hotel Meridian served weary travelers of roads and rails. Opened in 1907, the hotel featured many electrical services, including lights, ceiling fans, and elevator. These conveniences secured its much-advertised reputation as the first fireproof hotel in Meridian.*

*Two blocks away, Meridian's Union Station Multi-Modal Transportation Center salutes its past as a depot and anticipates its future as a national model for small city inter-modal transportation operations. Constructed in the late 1990's, Union Station is similar in appearance to the original turn-of-the-century Meridian depot, noted for its Mission Revival architecture. Today, Union Station functions as a transfer point for several modes of passenger transportation, from trains to buses. Because of its diverse operations, Union Station has received much national acclaim and has ensured Meridian's place as a transportation center vital to the success of the Southeast.*

# Carrot Soufflé

*You won't believe it's carrots!*

| | | | |
|---|---|---|---|
| 3 | pounds carrots, peeled and sliced | 3 | cups sugar |
| 1½ | cups margarine | ¼ | teaspoon ground cinnamon |
| 6 | large eggs | | Powdered sugar (optional) |
| ½ | cup all-purpose flour | | |
| 1 | tablespoon baking powder | | |

Preheat oven to 350°F. Cook carrots in boiling water 15 minutes or until tender. Drain well. Process carrots, margarine, eggs, flour, baking powder, sugar and cinnamon until smooth. Spoon into 2 lightly greased 1½-quart soufflé or baking dishes. Bake 1 hour or until set and lightly browned. Lightly sift powdered sugar over top before serving.

*12 servings*

# Green Beans and Mushrooms Amandine

| | | | |
|---|---|---|---|
| 1 | pound whole fresh green beans | ⅛ | teaspoon ground black pepper |
| 1 | tablespoon butter | 2 | tablespoons sliced almonds, toasted |
| ¼ | cup chopped onion | 1 | teaspoon whipping cream |
| ½ | pound sliced fresh mushrooms | 4 | tablespoons evaporated milk |
| ¾ | teaspoon salt | | |

In a saucepan, cook green beans until tender and drain. Return beans to the saucepan. In a skillet, melt butter. Sauté onion 5 minutes. Add mushrooms and sauté 5 minutes. Stir in salt, pepper and almonds. Cook 1 minute, stirring constantly. To beans add cream and milk. Heat until milk almost boils. Transfer bean mixture to a serving dish. Top with sautéed mixture.

*6 servings*

## Horseradish Sauce

*Great with roast, broccoli or green beans*

4 tablespoons butter, melted

¾ cup mayonnaise

1 tablespoon horseradish

½ teaspoon onion powder

¼ teaspoon salt

¼ teaspoon dry mustard

¼ teaspoon cayenne pepper

In a bowl, combine all ingredients. Refrigerate until ready to use. Keeps in refrigerator for 2 weeks.

*1 cup*

# Scalloped Tomatoes

| | | | |
|---|---|---|---|
| 1 | (28-ounce) can whole tomatoes | 1 | teaspoon salt |
| 2 | medium onions, finely chopped | ¼ | teaspoon ground black pepper |
| 1 | cup prepared herb flavored stuffing mix, divided | 2 | tablespoons butter, cut into pieces |

Preheat oven to 300°F. In a bowl, combine all ingredients, reserving ⅓ cup stuffing mix. Place in a buttered 1½-quart baking dish. Sprinkle reserved stuffing mix on top. Bake, uncovered, 3 hours. Must be baked for the entire 3 hours!

*6 servings*

*May be partially baked ahead, completing cooking time later.*

# Asparagus with Garlic Mustard

| | | | |
|---|---|---|---|
| 1 | pound asparagus spears, trimmed | 2 | tablespoons Dijon mustard |
| ¼ | cup butter or margarine | ¼ | teaspoon freshly ground black pepper |
| 2 | cups sliced fresh mushrooms | ⅛ | teaspoon salt |
| | | 1 | teaspoon minced garlic |

In a 10-inch skillet, place asparagus spears. Add enough water to cover. Bring to a full boil. Cook over medium heat 5 to 7 minutes or until asparagus is tender crisp. Drain. Return to skillet. Add butter, mushrooms, mustard, pepper, salt and garlic, pushing asparagus to the side just until butter is melted. Cook over medium heat, stirring occasionally, until thoroughly heated.

*4 to 6 servings*

## Hollandaise and Béarnaise Sauces

**2 egg yolks**

**3 tablespoons lemon juice**

**½ cup very cold butter, divided**

**1 tablespoon chopped fresh parsley (for Béarnaise)**

**½ teaspoon dried tarragon (for Béarnaise)**

For Hollandaise sauce, stir together egg yolks and lemon juice in a small saucepan. Add ¼ cup butter, stirring constantly over low heat until butter is almost completely melted. Butter must melt slowly to thicken sauce without curdling. Add remaining butter. Continue stirring until all butter is melted and sauce is thick.

For Béarnaise sauce, add parsley and tarragon to Hollandaise sauce.

*1 cup*

*Use Hollandaise Sauce or Béarnaise Sauce to embellish vegetable, fish and egg dishes. Béarnaise Sauce is also a wonderful enhancement for meat.*

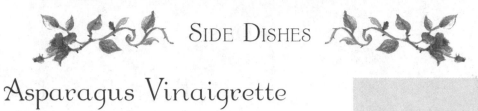

# Asparagus Vinaigrette

| | | | | |
|---|---|---|---|---|
| ¼ | cup white vinegar | | ¼ | cup finely chopped fresh parsley |
| 1 | teaspoon sugar | | 2 | tablespoons chopped pimiento |
| 3 | tablespoons finely chopped green onion | | 3 | tablespoons sweet pickle relish |
| 3 | tablespoons finely chopped green bell pepper | | ½ | cup vegetable oil |
| 3 | tablespoons finely chopped chives | | 1 | (15-ounce) can green asparagus spears, drained |

In a saucepan, heat vinegar and sugar until sugar dissolves. Remove from heat. Stir in onion, bell pepper, chives, parsley, pimiento, relish and oil. Pour vinaigrette over asparagus, which are either warm or room temperature.

*4 servings*

# Asparagus Casserole

| | | | | |
|---|---|---|---|---|
| ¼ | cup margarine | | 1 | (10¾-ounce) can cream of mushroom soup |
| ¼ | cup slivered toasted almonds | | ¼ | cup milk |
| 1 | cup cooked rice | | | Shredded sharp Cheddar cheese |
| 2 | (15-ounce) cans asparagus spears, drained, liquid reserved | | | Crispy rice cereal |

Preheat oven to 350°F. Melt margarine in a 9x9-inch baking dish in microwave. Add almonds and rice. Place drained asparagus on top. Mix soup, milk and enough asparagus liquid to reach desired consistency. Pour over asparagus. Top with cheese and cereal. Bake 30 minutes or until cheese melts and cereal is brown.

*6 to 8 servings*

## Asparagus Tomato Parmesan

**1 pound fresh asparagus, cleaned and trimmed**

**1 medium tomato, thinly sliced**

**Butter**

**Grated Parmesan cheese**

Preheat oven to 350°F. Layer asparagus in bottom of an 8x8-inch baking dish. Place tomato slices on top. Dot with butter. Sprinkle with cheese. Bake 15 to 20 minutes.

*4 servings*

## Green Bean Bundles

*Men will love these as well as children*

| | | | |
|---|---|---|---|
| ½ | pound sliced bacon | | Garlic salt |
| 2 | (14¼-ounce) cans whole green beans, drained | 6 | tablespoons margarine |
| | | ½ | cup firmly packed light brown sugar |

Preheat oven to 325°F. Cut each strip of bacon into thirds. Wrap 6 to 8 green beans in a piece of bacon. Secure with toothpick or place bundles with area where bacon overlaps down in a 1½-quart baking dish. Sprinkle with garlic salt. In a small saucepan, melt margarine. Add brown sugar. Cook 1 minute or until sugar melts. Pour over beans. Bake, uncovered, 30 to 40 minutes or until bacon is browned.

*6 to 8 servings*

*A family favorite for years! Someone is always asking for the recipe!*

## Swiss Cheese Broccoli

| | | | |
|---|---|---|---|
| 1 | pound broccoli, coarsely chopped | 3 | tablespoons chopped onion |
| 2 | teaspoons salt, divided | 1¼ | cups milk |
| 3 | tablespoons butter or margarine | 2 | cups shredded Swiss cheese |
| 2 | tablespoons all-purpose flour | 2 | eggs, beaten |

Preheat oven to 325°F. Place broccoli and ½ teaspoon salt in a medium saucepan. Add 1 inch of water and bring to a boil. Cover and cook 10 minutes. Drain and set aside. In a medium saucepan over medium heat, melt butter. Stir in flour and 1½ teaspoons salt until smooth. Add onion and cook 1 minute. Slowly stir in milk. Cook, stirring constantly, until mixture thickens and begins to boil. Remove from heat. Stir cheese and broccoli into mixture until cheese melts slightly. Stir in beaten eggs. Pour into a greased 8x8-inch baking dish. Bake 30 minutes or until center is firm to the touch.

*6 to 8 servings*

---

### Pasta with Broccoli

2 heads fresh broccoli, cut into florets

½ cup olive oil

10 cloves garlic, minced

½ cup margarine

1 (16-ounce) box penne or cut ziti pasta, cooked according to package directions

½ cup grated Parmesan or Romano cheese

Steam broccoli 4 to 5 minutes. In a large saucepan, heat olive oil. Add garlic and margarine. When margarine has melted, add broccoli and stir. Cover and cook over low heat 4 to 5 minutes. Add pasta and toss. To serve, sprinkle with cheese.

*8 servings*

*For a main dish, add grilled chicken.*

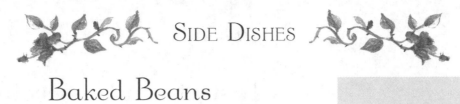

# Baked Beans

| | | | |
|---|---|---|---|
| ¼ | pound smoked sausage, cut into ½-inch slices and quartered | 1 | cup firmly packed brown sugar |
| ¼ | pound ground beef | ¾ | cup plus 2 tablespoons hickory smoked barbecue sauce |
| 1 | small onion, chopped | 2 | tablespoons ketchup |
| ¼ | green bell pepper, chopped | 1 | (10-ounce) can pineapple chunks, drained |
| 1 | (32-ounce) can baked beans | ¼ | pound bacon, cooked and crumbled |

Preheat oven to 350°F. In a skillet, brown sausage and ground beef. Remove meat with a slotted spoon and set aside. In the same skillet, sauté onion and bell pepper in reserved drippings. Drain well. Combine all ingredients except bacon and pour into a 3-quart baking dish. Bake 1 hour. Top with crumbled bacon.

*6 to 8 servings*

# Broccoli in Olive Butter

| | | | |
|---|---|---|---|
| ⅓ | cup sliced ripe olives | 1 | red bell pepper, sliced into strips |
| ⅓ | cup butter, melted | ½ | pound sliced fresh mushrooms |
| 1 | teaspoon lemon zest | | |
| 3 | tablespoons fresh lemon juice | 1 | (7-ounce) can baby corn |
| 1 | bunch broccoli, trimmed | | |

In a bowl, combine olives, butter, lemon zest and juice. Set aside. Steam broccoli and red bell pepper 5 minutes. Add mushrooms and corn. Steam an additional 2 minutes. Pour olive butter sauce over broccoli.

*6 servings*

## Broccoli Casserole

1 onion, chopped

¾ cup chopped celery

¼ cup margarine

1 (10-ounce) package frozen chopped broccoli, thawed

1 cup instant rice, uncooked

1 (10¾-ounce) can cream of chicken soup

1 (8-ounce) jar processed cheese spread

Preheat oven to 350°F. In a skillet, sauté onion and celery in margarine. In another bowl, mix broccoli, rice, soup and cheese. Stir in sautéed vegetables. Transfer to a greased 1½-quart baking dish. Bake 35 minutes.

*4 to 6 servings*

## Skillet Black-Eyed Peas

¼ pound sliced bacon

2 cups chopped celery

2 cups chopped green bell pepper

2 cups chopped onion

2 (14½-ounce) cans chopped tomatoes

2 (15-ounce) cans black-eyed peas

Cook bacon in a large skillet until brown and crispy. Remove from skillet and set aside. Sauté celery, bell pepper and onion in bacon drippings until tender. Add tomatoes and peas. Crumble bacon in skillet and simmer 10 minutes.

*6 to 8 servings*

## Tasty Corn Casserole

| | | | |
|---|---|---|---|
| 1 | (14¾-ounce) can cream style corn | 2 | eggs, beaten |
| ½ | cup chopped green bell pepper | 1 | tablespoon all-purpose flour |
| 2 | tablespoons brown sugar | 2 | tablespoons milk |
| 1 | tablespoon bacon drippings | 4 | slices bacon, slightly cooked |

Preheat oven to 350°F. Mix all ingredients except bacon. Pour in a 1-quart baking dish. Top with bacon slices. Bake 45 minutes.

*4 servings*

## Eggplant Parmigiana
*May be a side dish or a vegetarian entrée*

| | | | |
|---|---|---|---|
| 6 | tablespoons butter or margarine, melted | 2 | eggs, lightly beaten |
| 1 | cup bread crumbs | 2 | (8-ounce) cans tomato sauce |
| ½ | cup grated Parmesan cheese | 1 | teaspoon dried oregano |
| 1 | teaspoon salt | 1 | teaspoon sugar |
| ⅛ | teaspoon ground black pepper | ⅛ | teaspoon onion salt |
| 1 | medium eggplant | 4 | (1-ounce) slices mozzarella cheese, halved |

Preheat oven to 400°F. Pour melted butter into a 13x9-inch baking dish and set aside. Combine bread crumbs, Parmesan cheese, salt and pepper. Stir well. Set aside. Peel eggplant and slice into ¾-inch slices. Dip each slice in egg and coat with crumb mixture. Arrange in baking dish. Bake 20 minutes. Turn over eggplant. Bake 15 minutes.

In a small saucepan, combine tomato sauce, oregano, sugar and onion salt. Bring to a boil, stirring occasionally. Pour sauce over eggplant. Top with mozzarella slices. Bake an additional 3 minutes or until cheese is slightly melted.

*4 to 6 servings*

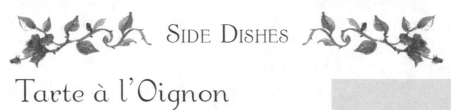

# Tarte à l'Oignon

| | | | | |
|---|---|---|---|---|
| 1 | (9-inch) prepared pie crust | 1 | cup shredded Gruyère or Emmenthaler cheese |
| 3 | tablespoons butter | 5 | egg yolks |
| 3 | Vidalia or sweet onions, thinly sliced | 1 | cup whipping cream |
| ½ | teaspoon salt, or to taste | | Freshly grated nutmeg |
| ¼ | teaspoon ground black pepper, or to taste | | Whole fresh chives, for garnish |

Preheat oven to 450°F. Press pie crust into a 9-inch tart pan. Bake 10 minutes or until lightly golden. Remove from oven and set aside. Reduce heat to 375°F. In a heavy saucepan over medium heat, melt butter. Add onions, salt and pepper. Stir. Cover and steam until onions are just tender. Remove from heat and mix gently with cheese. Place in pie crust. Whisk egg yolks and cream together. Pour over onion mixture. Sprinkle with nutmeg. Bake 25 to 35 minutes or until custard is just set. Remove sides of the tart pan and place on a serving plate. Garnish with chives.

*6 to 8 servings*

Mary Peavey, wife of Hartley Peavey,
Peavey Electronics Corporation, Meridian, MS

Peavey Electronics Corporation

Hartley Peavey is the founder and CEO of Peavey Electronics Corporation, one of the largest manufacturers of musical and pro-audio equipment in the world. Peavey Electronics produces over 3000 products, shipping them to 130 countries, with facilities in the United States, Canada and England. In 1990, Peavey was inducted into the RockWalk of Fame, and in 2001, he was inducted into the Mississippi Musicians Hall of Fame in recognition for his outstanding contribution to the music industry.

## Sweet Potato Casserole

### Casserole

3 cups cooked,
mashed sweet potatoes

½ cup sugar

½ cup butter, melted

2 eggs, beaten

1 teaspoon vanilla

⅓ cup milk

### Topping

⅓ cup butter, melted

1 cup firmly packed
light brown sugar

½ cup all-purpose flour

1 cup chopped pecans

Preheat oven to 350°F.
Combine all casserole
ingredients and pour into a
greased 13x9-inch baking
dish. Combine all topping
ingredients. Sprinkle over
casserole. Bake 25 minutes.

*10 to 12 servings*

# Spinach Madeline

| | | | |
|---|---|---|---|
| 2 | (10-ounce) packages frozen chopped spinach | ¼ | teaspoon cayenne pepper |
| 4 | tablespoons butter | ¾ | teaspoon celery salt |
| 2 | tablespoons all-purpose flour | ¾ | teaspoon garlic salt |
| 2 | tablespoons chopped onion | 1 | (6-ounce) roll jalapeño cheese or 6-ounces Mexican Hot Velveeta |
| ½ | cup evaporated milk | 1 | teaspoon Worcestershire sauce |
| ½ | cup liquid reserved from spinach | ½ | cup herb flavored stuffing mix or buttered bread crumbs |
| ½ | teaspoon ground black pepper | | |

Preheat oven to 350°F. Cook spinach according to package directions. Drain and reserve ½ cup liquid. In a saucepan over low heat, melt butter. Stir in flour and blend until smooth but not brown. Add onion and cook until soft. Stir in milk and spinach liquid slowly to avoid lumps. Cook until smooth and thick. Add peppers, salts, cheese, and Worcestershire. Stir until cheese is melted. Stir in spinach. Pour into a greased 1½-quart baking dish. Bake 30 minutes. Sprinkle stuffing or bread crumbs on top. Return to oven and bake 5 minutes.

*6 to 8 servings*

*Flavor improves if refrigerated overnight prior to baking.*

*May be served warm as an appetizer with wheat crackers.*

# Spinach and Artichoke Casserole

| | | | |
|---|---|---|---|
| 2 | (10-ounce) packages frozen chopped spinach | ½ | cup grated Parmesan cheese |
| ½ | cup margarine | 1 | (14-ounce) can artichoke hearts, drained |
| 1 | (8-ounce) carton sour cream | ½ | teaspoon salt |
| ½ | cup chopped green onion | ¼ | teaspoon ground black pepper |

Preheat oven to 350°F. Cook spinach according to package directions. Drain well. In a 9x9-inch baking dish, melt margarine. In a bowl, combine spinach and remaining ingredients. Pour into baking dish. Bake, uncovered, 25 minutes or until bubbly and thoroughly heated.

*8 servings*

# Spinach Stuffed Squash

| | | | |
|---|---|---|---|
| ½ | cup chopped onion | 2 | tablespoons red wine vinegar |
| 2 | tablespoons butter | 4 | yellow squash |
| 2 | (10-ounce) packages frozen chopped spinach, cooked and drained | | Squeeze butter |
| | | | Salt |
| | | | Ground black pepper |
| 1 | teaspoon salt | 1 | cup grated Parmesan cheese, divided |
| 1 | cup sour cream | ½ | cup bread crumbs |

Preheat oven to 350°F. In a skillet, sauté onion in butter. Add spinach, salt, sour cream and vinegar. Blend well and set aside. In boiling salted water, cook squash 10 minutes or until tender but still firm. Let cool. Cut into halves lengthwise and scoop out seeds. Sprinkle each shell with squeeze butter, salt, pepper and ½ cup cheese. Stuff each shell with spinach mixture. Top with remaining cheese and bread crumbs. Bake 15 minutes.

*8 servings*

## English Pea Casserole

1 (15-ounce) can English peas, drained

⅛ teaspoon salt, or to taste

⅛ teaspoon ground black pepper, or to taste

1 (10¾-ounce) can cream of chicken soup

½ cup blanched almonds or coarsely chopped pecans

1 (2-ounce) jar chopped pimiento, drained

½ cup shredded Cheddar cheese

1 tablespoon Worcestershire sauce

Round buttery crackers, crushed

Butter

Preheat oven to 350°F. Combine all ingredients except crackers and butter. Pour into a buttered 9x5-inch baking dish. Sprinkle cracker crumbs on top and dot with butter. Bake 30 minutes.

*4 servings*

# Squash Dressing

| | | | | |
|---|---|---|---|---|
| 1 | (8½-ounce) box cornbread mix, prepared according to package directions | 2 | (15-ounce) cans yellow squash, drained and mashed |
| 1 | medium onion, chopped | 1 | (10¾-ounce) can cream of chicken soup |
| ½ | green bell pepper, chopped | 2 | eggs, lightly beaten |
| ½ | cup margarine | | |

Preheat oven to 350°F. Crumble cornbread into a large mixing bowl. In a skillet, sauté onion and bell pepper in margarine. Add to cornbread. Stir in squash, soup and eggs. Mix well. Pour into a greased 10-inch square baking dish. Bake 30 to 40 minutes or until top is golden brown. Freezes well.

*6 to 8 servings*

*Two (16-ounce) packages frozen yellow squash, cooked, drained and mashed, may be substituted for canned squash.*

*For a one dish meal, add sautéed chicken. In 2 tablespoons margarine, lightly sauté 2 chopped, boneless, skinless chicken breasts. Add to dressing mixture before baking.*

---

## Better Beets

*Healthy and low calorie*

1 tablespoon butter

¼ teaspoon dried basil

1 tablespoon chopped fresh parsley

¼ teaspoon salt, or to taste

¼ teaspoon ground black pepper, or to taste

1 (15-ounce) can sliced beets, drained well

In a saucepan, melt butter. Stir in all spices and blend well. Add beets. Heat until thoroughly warm.

*4 servings*

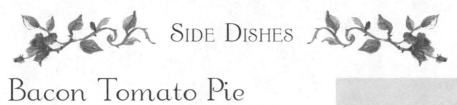

# Bacon Tomato Pie

| | | | |
|---|---|---|---|
| 4 | large tomatoes, peeled and thinly sliced | ½ | teaspoon dried basil |
| 1 | (9-inch) pie crust, baked | ⅛ | teaspoon salt, or to taste |
| 2 | tablespoons finely chopped green onion | ⅛ | teaspoon ground black pepper, or to taste |
| 6 | slices bacon, cooked crisp and crumbled | ½ | cup mayonnaise |
| 1 | teaspoon sugar | 2 | cups shredded Cheddar cheese or mozzarella cheese |

Preheat oven to 350°F. Layer tomatoes in pie crust. Sprinkle onion and bacon over tomatoes. Mix sugar, basil, salt and pepper. Sprinkle over pie. Combine mayonnaise and cheese. Spread over top of pie. Bake 30 minutes.

*6 servings*

*The fewer the seeds in tomatoes, the better. The tomatoes should be firm to prevent pie from being soupy.*

Four ounces of cheese shredded equals one cup shredded cheese.

Ever run across an old recipe that calls for a #10 can? You have to search the grocery store for the oldest female to ask her what size that is! Well search no more! Below is a conversion chart for the sizes of some common numbered cans.

| Can Size | Average Weight |
|---|---|
| 300 | 14-16 ounces |
| 303 | 15-17 ounces |
| 2 | 20 ounces |
| 10 | 6 pounds 9 ounces to 6 pounds 14 ounces |

## French Onion Rice

½ cup margarine

1 cup white rice, uncooked

1 (10¾-ounce) can
French onion soup

1 soup can of water

Preheat oven to 350°F.
Melt margarine in a 1½-quart
baking dish. Add rice. Pour in
soup and water. Stir to mix.
Bake, uncovered, 30 to
45 minutes or until
rice is tender.

*6 to 8 servings*

*For a Mexican side dish, add
1 (10-ounce) can diced
tomatoes with chiles and
reduce water to ½ soup can.*

# Pesto Vegetable Ribbons

*A beautiful and different way to serve vegetables!*

| | | | |
|---|---|---|---|
| 3 | large carrots, peeled | ⅛ | teaspoon salt, or to taste |
| 2 | medium zucchini | | |
| 2 | medium yellow squash | ⅛ | teaspoon ground black pepper, or to taste |
| ¼ | cup prepared basil pesto (or see index) | | Fresh basil leaves, for garnish |

Using a vegetable peeler, cut ribbon-like slices from carrots, zucchini and yellow squash, using as much of vegetable as possible. Draw the peeler in lengthwise motions to make ribbons. In a medium saucepan, add ½ inch of water and heat to boiling. Add carrots, cover and cook over medium heat 2 to 3 minutes. Add zucchini and yellow squash. Cook 1 to 2 minutes. Drain well. Place in a serving bowl. Add pesto. Season with salt and pepper. Toss to coat. Garnish with fresh basil leaves. Serve immediately.

*4 to 6 servings*

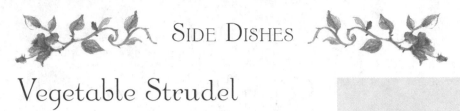
# Vegetable Strudel

| | | | | |
|---|---|---|---|---|
| 3 | tablespoons margarine, melted | 6 | ounces feta or Cheddar cheese, crumbled or sliced |
| 3 | tablespoons olive oil | ½ | teaspoon salt |
| 10 | (12x6-inch) phyllo pastry sheets | ½ | teaspoon ground black pepper |
| ½ | pound squash or zucchini, sliced thinly and steamed | 1½ | tablespoons chopped fresh thyme |
| ½ | pound broccoli, finely chopped and steamed | 1 | tablespoon chopped fresh tarragon |
| ¼ | pound thin green beans, julienned and steamed | 1 | egg, beaten |

Preheat oven to 375°F. Combine melted margarine with olive oil. Brush 5 of the phyllo pastry sheets with mixture. Layer them on top of each other. In a bowl, mix vegetables with cheese. Season with salt and pepper. Add thyme and tarragon. Spread ½ of vegetable mixture over layered pastry, leaving a 2-inch margin all around. Fold short edges in and roll up from the long side in a jelly roll fashion. Brush surface with beaten egg. Place on a well greased baking sheet. Repeat process with remaining phyllo sheets and remaining vegetable mixture to make a second strudel. Bake 30 to 40 minutes or until golden brown and crisp. Let stand for a few minutes before slicing. Serve on a warm dish.

*6 to 8 servings*

## Potato Wedges

4 medium russet potatoes

½ cup oil

2 tablespoons grated Parmesan cheese

1 teaspoon salt

½ teaspoon garlic salt

½ teaspoon paprika

½ teaspoon ground black pepper

Preheat oven to 350°F. Cut each potato into 4 wedges. Place in a 13x9-inch baking dish. Mix remaining ingredients. Pour over wedges and toss. Stirring several times, bake 45 minutes or until potatoes are tender.

*4 servings*

# Cajun Roasted Sweet Potatoes with Balsamic Vinaigrette

*A tangy, sweet dish that's decidedly different*

## Caramelized Onions

2 tablespoons butter

1 tablespoon olive oil

2 large sweet onions, diced or thinly sliced

1 teaspoon sugar

In a large skillet, melt butter. Add oil and heat. Add onions, stir to coat and reduce heat to low. Cook onions stirring occasionally, 45 minutes to 1 hour or until deep brown in color. Sprinkle with sugar and continue cooking a few minutes.

| | | | |
|---|---|---|---|
| 1 | teaspoon garlic powder | 6 | tablespoons olive oil |
| 1 | teaspoon onion powder | 2 | tablespoons balsamic vinegar |
| 1 | teaspoon paprika | | |
| ½ | teaspoon ground thyme | ⅓ | cup sugar or 8 packages artificial sweetener |
| ½ | teaspoon ground oregano | 1 | tablespoon chopped parsley |
| ½ | teaspoon cayenne pepper (optional) | ¼ | cup chopped green onion |
| 2 | large sweet potatoes, peeled, cut into ¾-inch cubes | 1 | tablespoon bacon, cooked and crumbled |
| ⅛ | teaspoon salt, or to taste | | Caramelized Onions (See accompanying recipe) |
| ⅛ | teaspoon pepper, or to taste | | |

Preheat oven to 400° F. Combine garlic powder, onion powder, paprika, thyme, oregano and cayenne pepper for seasoning mix. Place sweet potatoes in a 13x9-inch baking dish. Sprinkle with salt, pepper and seasoning mix. In a separate bowl, combine olive oil and balsamic vinegar. Pour over sweet potatoes and toss. Bake 50 minutes or until potatoes are tender, stirring every 15 minutes. Remove from oven. Sprinkle with sugar, parsley and green onion. Top with bacon and Caramelized Onions, if desired.

*4 to 6 servings*

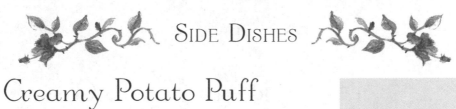

# SIDE DISHES

## Creamy Potato Puff

| | | | | |
|---|---|---|---|---|
| 1 | (8-ounce) package cream cheese, softened | 1 | egg, beaten | |
| | | 1/3 | cup chopped onion | |
| 4 | cups hot Perfect Mashed Potatoes (see accompanying recipe) | 1/2 | cup diced pimiento | |
| | | 1 | teaspoon salt | |
| | | 1/8 | teaspoon ground black pepper, or to taste | |

Preheat oven to 350°F. Combine cream cheese and potatoes. Mix well. Stir in remaining ingredients. Pour into a 1-quart greased baking dish. Bake 45 minutes.

*6 to 8 servings*

## Swiss Scalloped Potatoes

| | | | | |
|---|---|---|---|---|
| 1½ | cups shredded Swiss cheese, divided | 1 | teaspoon salt | |
| 1/2 | cup chopped green onion | 1 | cup milk | |
| | | 1 | cup sour cream | |
| 1 | teaspoon dried dill weed | 4 | large russet potatoes, peeled, cooked and sliced | |
| 6 | tablespoons butter, divided | | | |
| 2 | tablespoons all-purpose flour | 1/4 | cup bread crumbs | |

Preheat oven to 350°F. In a small bowl combine 1 cup cheese, onion and dill. Set aside. In a 1-quart saucepan over medium heat, melt 2 tablespoons butter. Stir in flour and salt. Add milk stirring constantly until thickened. Cook 2 more minutes. Remove from heat and stir in sour cream. In a greased 13x9-inch baking dish, layer 1/3 potatoes, 1/2 cheese mixture and 1/2 sour cream mixture. Repeat layers. Top with remaining potatoes. Melt remaining butter. Combine with remaining cheese and breadcrumbs. Sprinkle over casserole. Bake 30 minutes or until bubbly.

*8 to 10 servings*

### Perfect Mashed Potatoes

1½ pounds baking potatoes, peeled and cut into large pieces

½ cup milk

½ cup whipping cream

6 tablespoons unsalted butter or margarine

1/8 teaspoon salt, or to taste

1/8 teaspoon ground black pepper, or to taste

In a saucepan cover potatoes with cold water. Bring to a boil and reduce heat. Gently boil until potatoes are tender. Drain potatoes and let dry. Beat with an electric mixer. In a separate pan, warm milk and cream. Gradually add to potatoes. Stir in butter, salt and pepper.

*4 cups*

Drying boiled potato pieces, makes fluffier mashed potatoes. Always warm milk or cream. If cold, mashed potatoes will be gummy. Add butter after warmed milk or cream. If added all at once, mashed potatoes will be watery and loose.

195

# Hearty Potato Casserole

### Apricot Rice

*Delicious with game, pork or turkey!*

**3 tablespoons unsalted butter**

**1 small onion, finely chopped**

**½ cup finely chopped celery**

**1¼ cups long grain white rice**

**¼ teaspoon ground ginger**

**2 cups chicken broth, divided**

**1 cup water**

**⅓ cup raisins**

**1 cup dried apricots, diced**

**½ cup sliced almonds, toasted**

In a deep saucepan, melt butter. Sauté onion and celery until soft. Add rice. Continue to sauté until grains of rice are coated with butter. Add ginger to 1 cup broth. Add gingered broth and water to rice. Bring to a boil. Lower heat and slowly simmer 15 minutes. Add remaining broth, raisins and apricots. Simmer 10 minutes or until rice is cooked. Remove from heat. Stir in almonds.

*6 to 8 servings*

| | | | |
|---|---|---|---|
| 8 | medium-size baking potatoes, peeled and cut into ¼-inch slices | 1 | (8-ounce) carton sour cream |
| ½ | cup butter, divided | 1 | cup shredded Gouda cheese |
| ¼ | teaspoon paprika | ¾ | cup diced cooked ham |
| ½ | teaspoon ground black pepper, divided | ½ | cup chopped green onion |
| 2 | tablespoons all-purpose flour | 6 | slices bacon, cooked and crumbled |
| 1½ | cups milk | | |

Preheat oven to 425°F. Arrange potato slices in a lightly greased 3-quart shallow baking dish. Melt 6 tablespoons butter. Add paprika and ¼ teaspoon pepper. Drizzle butter mixture over potato slices. Cover and bake 30 minutes. Remove cover and bake 15 minutes. In a heavy skillet over low heat, melt remaining butter. Add flour and cook 1 minute. Increase heat to medium, gradually add milk stirring constantly until thick and bubbly. Add sour cream, cheese and remaining pepper. Set aside and keep warm. Sprinkle ham and green onion over potatoes. Top with cheese sauce. Cover and bake 5 minutes or until hot and bubbly. Prior to serving, sprinkle with bacon.

*8 to 10 servings*

# SIDE DISHES

## French Risotto

*A traditionally Italian dish with a French Cajun twist*

| | | | | |
|---|---|---|---|---|
| ¼ | cup butter | 1 | tablespoon Cavender's Greek seasoning |
| 1 | small white onion, minced | ½ | teaspoon cracked black pepper |
| 2 | cups long grain white rice | 1 | (8-ounce) carton whipping cream, warmed |
| ½ | cup vermouth | ¾ | cup grated Parmesan cheese |
| 4 | cups chicken broth | | |
| 1 | bay leaf | | |

In a large skillet over medium heat, melt butter. Slowly sauté onion 5 to 10 minutes, or until soft. Be careful not to let onion brown. Lower heat and add rice. Slowly stir and sauté until rice becomes milky white. Add vermouth and boil down for one minute. Blend in chicken broth. Add bay leaf, Cavender's seasoning and pepper. Adjust heat and bring to a simmer. Stir thoroughly and place lid on skillet tightly. Simmer 15 minutes or until rice is tender. Remove from heat. Set aside, covered, 10 minutes. Discard bay leaf. Fold in cream and cheese.

*8 servings*

## Rice and Artichokes

| | | | | |
|---|---|---|---|---|
| 1 | (10.3-ounce) package chicken flavored Rice-A-Roni | 4 | green onions, finely chopped |
| 2 | (6-ounce) jars marinated artichoke hearts, reserve liquid | ½ | green bell pepper, finely chopped |
| | | ½ | cup mayonnaise |
| | | 12 | small green olives, sliced |

Preheat oven to 350°F. Prepare Rice-A-Roni according to package directions. Set aside. Slice artichoke hearts. Add to mix. Stir in all remaining ingredients including reserved artichoke liquid. Pour into a lightly greased 8x8-inch baking dish. Bake 30 minutes or until thoroughly heated.

*6 to 8 servings*

## Wonderful Wild Rice Casserole

2 cups pecan pieces

1 cup wild rice

4 cups water

1 teaspoon salt

2 (6.2-ounce) packages long grain and wild rice mix

3¾ cups chicken broth

2 cups finely chopped celery

1 cup finely chopped onion

½ cup butter

2 cups golden raisins

Preheat oven to 300°F. Spread pecan pieces on a cookie sheet. Bake 5 minutes. Set aside. Cook wild rice in salted water 1 hour. Preheat oven to 350°F. Prepare long grain and wild rice mix according to package directions, using chicken broth instead of water. Sauté celery and onion in butter. Combine all ingredients. Pour into 2 greased 13x9-inch baking dishes. Bake 20 to 30 minutes or until thoroughly heated.

*16 servings*

*For a main dish, add peeled and deveined shrimp.*

# Walnut Couscous Pilaf

| | | | |
|---|---|---|---|
| ½ | cup chopped walnuts | 1 | (10-ounce) package couscous |
| 2 | tablespoons margarine | 1 | tablespoon orange zest |
| 1 | clove garlic, minced | ¼ | cup chopped fresh parsley |
| ½ | cup finely chopped green onion | ½ | teaspoon ground black pepper |
| ¼ | cup finely chopped red bell pepper | ½ | teaspoon salt |
| 2¼ | cups chicken broth | | |

Preheat oven to 350°F. Place walnuts in a shallow pan. Bake, stirring often, 5 to 10 minutes or until toasted. In a large saucepan, melt margarine. Sauté garlic, onion and bell pepper until tender crisp. Stir in chicken broth and bring to a boil. Add couscous. Cover and remove from heat. Let stand 5 minutes. Stir in walnuts, orange zest, parsley, pepper and salt.

*8 to 10 servings*

## Bread and Butter Pickles

*A delightful compliment to southern vegetables*

10 medium cucumbers, thinly sliced

3 medium onions, thinly sliced

½ cup salt

3 cups white vinegar

3 cups sugar

½ tablespoon turmeric

2 tablespoons mustard seed

2 teaspoons celery seed

¼ teaspoon cayenne pepper

6 pint-size jars, sterilized

Cover cucumbers and onions in water. Add salt and soak 2 hours. Rinse. In a large stockpot, combine vinegar, sugar, turmeric, mustard seed, celery seed and cayenne pepper. Bring to a boil. Add cucumbers and reduce heat to low. Simmer 2 minutes, stirring. Fill jars to within ½-inch of top. Cap and process in boiling water bath 10 minutes.

*6 pints*

# Baked Orzo with Peppers and Cheese

| | | | | |
|---|---|---|---|---|
| 2 | quarts water | 1 | cup shredded Monterey Jack cheese | |
| 2 | teaspoons salt | 1 | cup sour cream | |
| 1 | cup orzo | 1 | cup freshly grated Parmesan cheese | |
| ⅓ | cup diced red bell pepper, sautéed in butter | 2 | tablespoons butter, cut into small pieces | |
| ⅓ | cup mild green chiles, chopped | | | |

Preheat oven to 450°F. In a stockpot, bring water to a boil. Add salt and sprinkle in orzo. When boiling resumes, cook 11 minutes or until tender. Drain. Combine orzo with bell pepper, chiles and Monterey Jack cheese. Place in an 11x8-inch baking dish. Spread sour cream evenly over the top. Sprinkle with Parmesan cheese, then dot with butter. On upper shelf of oven, bake 15 minutes or until top is golden and puffy and edges are bubbly. Serve hot.

*8 servings*

Orzo is a very tiny variety of pasta. Since it is smaller than a pine nut, it is a delightful substitute for rice and is often used in soups.

# Hot Pineapple and Cheese

*Great side dish with pork or ham*

| | | | |
|---|---|---|---|
| 1 | (20-ounce) can pineapple chunks, drained, reserve juice | 1 | cup shredded Cheddar cheese |
| ½ | cup sugar | ¼ | cup butter, melted |
| 3 | tablespoons all-purpose flour | ½ | cup crushed round buttery crackers |

Preheat oven to 350°F. In a medium bowl, combine 3 tablespoons pineapple juice, sugar and flour. Add cheese and pineapple chunks. Mix well. Pour into a lightly buttered 1½-quart glass baking dish. In a small bowl, combine butter and crackers. Place on top of pineapple mixture. Bake 20 to 30 minutes.

*6 to 8 servings*

Hot Pineapple and Cheese became very popular in Washington after a Meridian couple introduced it. If federal aid were dispensed according to culinary contributions, Mississippi would be in "High Cotton."

# Holiday Hot Fruit

| | | | |
|---|---|---|---|
| 1 | (20-ounce) can pineapple chunks, drained | 1 | (20-ounce) jar applesauce |
| 1 | (17-ounce) can blackberries, drained | 1 | cup firmly packed brown sugar |
| 2 | (14½-ounce) cans peeled apricots, drained | ¾ | cup sherry |
| | | 3 | tablespoons butter or margarine |
| | | | Sour cream (optional) |

Preheat oven to 350°F. In a large bowl, gently mix fruits, applesauce and brown sugar. Transfer to a buttered 13x9-inch baking dish. Pour sherry over fruit. Dot with pats of butter. Bake 30 minutes or until bubbly. Remove from oven. Top each serving with a dollop of sour cream.

*8 to 10 servings*

# Desserts

# A Lasting Home for a King and Queen

*Meridian's Rose Hill Cemetery contains the gravesites of at least eleven Romany gypsies. The first gypsy buried in the cemetery was Kelly Mitchell, former queen of the gypsy tribe. While in an Alabama gypsy camp, she suffered complications from giving birth to her fifteenth child. In an effort to save her life, King Emil Mitchell transported the queen to Meridian, the nearest city to their camp. Though his efforts were unsuccessful, King Mitchell appreciated the Meridian citizens' hospitality and chose the city as his wife's final resting place. Dressed in fine clothing and wearing elaborate jewelry, Mitchell's body was buried in a magnificent mahogany casket in February 1915. Her funeral procession was the grandest ever witnessed in Meridian and ended with a midnight tribal rite. In contrast, like those of the other gypsies buried in the cemetery, King Emil Mitchell's 1942 funeral was more sedate. Today, gypsies and tourists often leave trinkets and food at the gypsies' gravesites.*

# Torta D'Espresso E Cioccolata

*Chocolate Espresso Torte*
*The best chocolate dessert you'll ever put in your mouth!*

| | | | |
|---|---|---|---|
| 2 | cups butter | 6 | egg yolks, room |
| 1 | cup plus 2 tablespoons | | temperature |
| | sugar | | Powdered sugar |
| 1 | cup plus 2 tablespoons | | (optional) |
| | hot espresso coffee | | Chocolate Ganache |
| 16 | ounces semisweet | | Icing |
| | chocolate, chopped | | (see accompanying |
| | into small pieces | | recipe) |
| 6 | eggs, room temperature | | |

Preheat oven to 325°F. Generously butter an 8 or 9-inch springform pan. Line the bottom of the pan with parchment paper. Butter and flour the paper. In a heavy saucepan, combine butter, sugar and espresso. Cook over medium heat until sugar dissolves. Add chocolate pieces and stir until smooth. Remove from heat and let cool slightly. In a large bowl, whisk eggs and yolks until frothy. Whisk into chocolate mixture. Pour batter into the prepared pan. Place the pan on a baking sheet. Bake 1 hour or until edges puff and crack slightly but center is not completely set. Do not overbake. Cake will continue to set as it cools. Place pan on a rack to cool. Cover and refrigerate overnight. To remove from pan, run a knife around edge to loosen. Carefully release pan sides. Sift powdered sugar over cake or ice with Chocolate Ganache Icing.

*12 servings*

*Note: Must be refrigerated overnight.*

## Chocolate Ganache Icing

**8 ounces semisweet chocolate, cut into pieces**

**1 cup whipping cream**

In a heavy saucepan over very low heat, melt chocolate with cream until mixture is smooth and glossy. Place ½ mixture in a mixing bowl. Beat until thickened. Spread over torte as an undercoat. Pour remaining ganache over torte and smooth.

*1½ cups*

# Pumpkin Bread Pudding with Caramel Rum Raisin Sauce

## Pudding

| | | | | |
|---|---|---|---|---|
| 2 | cups milk | 4 | large eggs |
| 1½ | cups whipping cream | 3 | large egg yolks |
| 3 | cinnamon sticks, crushed | ½ | cup canned unsweetened pumpkin purée |
| 1½ | inches fresh peeled ginger, chopped | ½ | teaspoon salt |
| 1 | teaspoon vanilla | ½ | cup plus 3 tablespoons sugar, divided |
| 6 | whole cloves | 2 | teaspoons ground cinnamon |
| 1 | loaf brioche or French bread, cut into 1-inch cubes | | |

## Sauce

| | | | | |
|---|---|---|---|---|
| ¾ | cup dark rum | ½ | cup water |
| 1 | cup raisins | 1 | cup whipping cream |
| 3 | cups sugar | | |

Preheat oven to 375°F. For pudding, combine milk, cream, crushed cinnamon sticks, ginger, vanilla and cloves in a saucepan. Cook over medium heat until just steaming. Do not boil. Remove from heat, cover and let stand until milk is fragrant, about 30 minutes.

Lightly butter a 13x9-inch glass baking dish. On a rimmed baking sheet, toast cubed bread 8 minutes or until crisp and golden. Place an even layer of bread in the baking dish. Rewarm spiced milk until steaming. Strain into a heatproof medium bowl. In another medium bowl, combine eggs, egg yolks, pumpkin purée and salt. Whisk until blended and smooth. Whisk in ½ cup sugar. Gradually whisk in 1 cup hot milk mixture. Whisk pumpkin mixture into remaining milk. Blend well. Pour pudding evenly over bread and cover with plastic wrap. Let stand 30 minutes or until bread has absorbed pudding. In a small bowl, combine remaining sugar with ground cinnamon. Sprinkle over bread pudding. Place baking dish in a large roasting pan. Add enough hot water to reach halfway up the sides of the baking dish. Bake,

Pumpkin Bread Pudding continued

uncovered, 45 minutes or until puffed and set. Let cool slightly. Spoon into bowls and serve warm, with sauce drizzled on top.

For sauce, warm rum with raisins in a small saucepan. Remove from heat and let soak 20 minutes. In a medium saucepan, combine sugar and water. Cook over medium heat until a deep amber caramel forms. Remove from heat. Slowly and carefully add a little cream to stop the cooking. Stir in remaining cream. Add raisins and rum. Serve warm over pudding.

*12 to 15 servings*

*The pudding may be refrigerated overnight. Cover with foil and rewarm in 325°F oven 15 to 25 minutes. The sauce may be refrigerated 1 week. Reheat gently, stirring occasionally.*

# Chocolate Brownie Cobbler

*Wonderful and easy*

| | | | |
|---|---|---|---|
| 2 | cups unsalted butter | 1⅔ | cups all-purpose flour |
| 10 | (1-ounce) squares semisweet chocolate, chopped | 1 | teaspoon salt |
| | | 2½ | cups walnuts, toasted, coarsely chopped |
| 4 | cups sugar | | Cocoa powder, optional |
| 8 | large eggs | | Vanilla ice cream |
| 1 | teaspoon vanilla | | |

Preheat oven to 350°F. In a heavy large saucepan over medium low heat, stir butter and chocolate until melted and smooth. Remove from heat. Whisk sugar into chocolate mixture. Whisk in eggs one at a time. Whisk in vanilla. Stir in flour and salt. Stir in walnuts. Transfer to a buttered 15x10-inch baking dish. Bake 50 minutes or until top is crisp and tester inserted into center comes out with wet crumbs attached. Do not overcook. Cool 15 minutes. Dust with cocoa powder. To serve, spoon warm cobbler into bowls and top with vanilla ice cream.

*12 servings*

# QUEEN CITY FAVORITES

## Bread Pudding with Whiskey Sauce

### Whiskey Sauce

½ cup butter

1½ cups powdered sugar

1 egg yolk

¼-½ cup bourbon

In a saucepan over medium heat, stir butter and sugar until melted and dissolved. Remove from heat. Stir in egg yolk. Pour in bourbon, stirring constantly. Sauce will thicken as it cools.

*1½ cups*

| | | | |
|---|---|---|---|
| 1 | (10-ounce) loaf stale French bread, cubed or torn | 1 | cup flaked coconut |
| 4 | cups milk | 1 | cup chopped pecans |
| 2 | cups sugar | 1 | teaspoon ground cinnamon |
| ½ | cup butter, melted | 1 | teaspoon ground nutmeg |
| 4 | eggs, beaten | | Whiskey Sauce (see accompanying recipe) |
| 2 | tablespoons vanilla | | |
| 1 | cup raisins | | |

Preheat oven to 350°F. Combine all ingredients. Mixture will be very moist but not soupy. Pour into a buttered 13x9-inch baking dish. Bake 1 hour 15 minutes or until top is golden brown. Serve warm with Whiskey Sauce.

*12 servings*

# Lemon Ice Box Cake

*Delicious and beautiful*

### Filling

| | | | |
|---|---|---|---|
| 2 | (14-ounce) cans sweetened condensed milk | ⅔ | cup fresh lemon juice |

### Cake

| | | | |
|---|---|---|---|
| 1 | (18.25-ounce) box yellow cake mix | ⅓ | cup vegetable oil |
| 1 | (8-ounce) carton sour cream | ⅓ | cup sugar |
| 4 | eggs | ⅓ | cup water |
| | | 1 | teaspoon vanilla |

### Icing

| | | | |
|---|---|---|---|
| ¾ | cup filling mixture | 1 | (8-ounce) carton frozen nondairy whipped topping, thawed |

Preheat oven to 350°F. In a bowl, combine filling ingredients. Place in refrigerator to thicken while preparing cake. Combine all cake ingredients. Pour into 4 greased and floured 8-inch round cake pans. Bake 20 to 22 minutes. Let cool. Set aside ¾ cup filling mixture. Spread cake layers with remaining filling mixture. For icing, combine reserved filling mixture and whipped topping. Use wooden skewers if necessary to secure cake layers while icing. Ice cake. Keep cake refrigerated.

*12 servings*

A school for the orphaned daughters of French military officers became famous for its cooking lessons. The school's symbol was a blue ribbon, and eventually the "cordon bleu" - French for "blue ribbon" - became the emblem of a good cook.

# Orange Ice Box Cake

A favorite dessert recipe for the holidays, H.P.'s grandmother prepared it with great love and everyone looked forward to it. She loved the kitchen and always went to great lengths to insure that everyone enjoyed their meal and had their favorites... truly the trait of a "Southern Lady."

| | | | |
|---|---|---|---|
| 1 | tablespoon unflavored gelatin | 3 | dozen ladyfingers, divided |
| 1½ | cups cold water, divided | 1 | cup chopped pecans, divided |
| 1 | cup sugar | | Sweetened whipped cream, for garnish |
| 1 | pound miniature marshmallows | | Finely chopped pecans, for garnish |
| 1 | cup orange juice with pulp | | |
| 1½ | pints whipping cream, divided | | |

Dissolve gelatin in ½ cup cold water in the refrigerator. In a saucepan, boil sugar in remaining water 20 minutes. Remove from heat. In a food processor on pulse, process marshmallows until finely chopped but not mushy. Add gelatin, orange juice and processed marshmallows to sugar mixture. Place orange mixture in the refrigerator, stirring at intervals, until it begins to congeal. Whip 1 pint whipping cream. Fold whipped cream into orange mixture.

Split 1 dozen ladyfingers into halves and crumble remaining ladyfingers. In a 13x9-inch glass baking dish, sprinkle the bottom with half of crumbled ladyfingers. Line the sides with halved ladyfingers. Pour half of orange mixture over crumbled ladyfingers. Top with ½ cup pecans. Sprinkle remaining crumbled ladyfingers. Cover with remaining orange mixture. Top with ½ cup pecans. Cover tightly with plastic wrap. Refrigerate until congealed. Slice cake and top with a spoonful of whipped cream and pecans.

*15 servings*

*Best if made 1 day prior to serving.*

*May substitute freshly squeezed juice of 6 oranges for orange juice.*

# Orange Poppy Seed Cheesecake with Lemon Glaze

*For neater slices, slice cheesecake with waxed unflavored dental floss.*

### Crust

| | | | |
|---|---|---|---|
| ¾ | cup crushed graham crackers | 1 | tablespoon sugar |
| ¾ | cup ground almonds | ¼ | cup butter, melted |

### Filling

| | | | |
|---|---|---|---|
| 2 | (8-ounce) packages cream cheese, softened | 3 | tablespoons all-purpose flour |
| 1 | cup sugar | ¼ | cup orange juice |
| 4 | eggs | ¾ | cup whipping cream |
| 1 | teaspoon orange zest | 2 | tablespoons poppy seeds |

### Glaze

| | | | |
|---|---|---|---|
| 2 | eggs | 2 | tablespoons orange juice |
| ¾ | cup sugar | 2 | tablespoons butter |
| 1 | teaspoon lemon zest | | Poppy seeds |
| 1 | teaspoon orange zest | | Lemon slices |
| ¼ | cup fresh lemon juice | | Orange slices |

Preheat oven to 350°F. For crust, combine all crust ingredients. Press mixture onto the bottom and 1½ inches up the sides of a 9-inch springform pan. Bake 8 minutes. Let crust cool.

For filling, preheat oven to 450°F. In a large bowl, using an electric mixer beat cream cheese and sugar until very smooth. Add eggs, one at a time, beating until just blended. Beat in remaining filling ingredients. Pour mixture over crust. Bake 10 minutes. Reduce heat to 250°F. Bake 35 to 45 minutes or until center is just set. Remove from oven. Run a knife around the rim to prevent cracking. Cool thoroughly at room temperature. Chill overnight.

For glaze, whisk eggs until foamy in a small saucepan. Add sugar, zests, juices and butter. Cook over low heat until smooth and thickened. Cool. May be refrigerated overnight. Return to room temperature prior to serving. To serve, spread glaze evenly over cheesecake. Garnish with poppy seeds and fruit slices.

*16 servings*

Note: Must be refrigerated 8 hours.

# Lemon Mousse
# with Raspberry Sauce
*Perfectly suited for a luncheon - so light!*

### Raspberry Sauce

**1½ cups fresh raspberries**

**2 tablespoons sugar**

**1 tablespoon
fresh lemon juice**

**1 tablespoon orange or
cherry liqueur (optional)**

In a blender or food
processor, purée ingredients.
Pour through a fine sieve into
a bowl, pressing solids. Cover
and refrigerate.

*1 cup*

*May substitute thawed, frozen
raspberries without syrup for
fresh raspberries.*

*Raspberry sauce is also
wonderful served over vanilla
ice cream and garnished with
fresh raspberries.*

## *Mousse*

| | | | |
|---|---|---|---|
| 1 | (¼-ounce) envelope unflavored gelatin | 8 | tablespoons sugar, divided |
| 2 | tablespoons white wine | 1 | cup whipping cream, whipped |
| 1½ | tablespoons lemon zest | | Raspberry Sauce (see accompanying recipe) |
| ⅓ | cup fresh lemon juice | | |
| 3 | eggs, separated | | |

In the top of a double boiler, soften gelatin in wine. Add lemon
zest and juice. Stir over simmering water until gelatin dissolves.
In another bowl, beat egg yolks with 3 tablespoons sugar. Slowly
add to gelatin mixture, stirring constantly. Cool. Fold in whipped
cream. Beat egg whites until stiff, gradually adding 5 tablespoons
sugar. Fold into lemon mixture. Pour into a lightly greased 6 to
8-cup mold. Chill 2 hours or overnight. When ready to serve,
unmold mousse onto a serving platter. Serve with Raspberry
Sauce.

*8 servings*

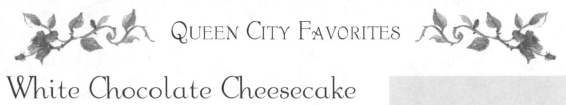
# White Chocolate Cheesecake

### Crust

| | | | |
|---|---|---|---|
| ¼ | cup butter, melted | 1 | ounce white chocolate, grated |
| 2 | cups shortbread cookies, finely ground | ¼ | cup sugar |

### Filling

| | | | |
|---|---|---|---|
| 4 | (8-ounce) packages cream cheese, softened | ⅛ | teaspoon salt |
| | | 4 | eggs |
| 1¼ | cups sugar | 3 | ounces white chocolate, grated |

### Topping

| | | | |
|---|---|---|---|
| 2 | cups sour cream | 1 | ounce white chocolate, shaved |
| ¼ | cup sugar | | |
| 1 | teaspoon vanilla | | |

For crust, in a small bowl, combine all crust ingredients. Press evenly into a 10-inch springform pan.

For filling, preheat oven to 350°F. In a mixing bowl, combine cream cheese and 1¼ cups sugar, beating with electric mixer until fluffy. Add salt and mix well. Add eggs, one at a time, beating with mixer on lowest speed. Add white chocolate and pour into crust. Bake 40 to 45 minutes. Remove from oven and cool 10 minutes.

For topping, combine sour cream, ¼ cup sugar and vanilla in a small bowl. Spread on cooled cake. Bake 10 minutes. Place in refrigerator immediately. Top with white chocolate shavings before serving.

*12 servings*

*Serve with Raspberry Sauce (see index) for a delightful surprise.*

# New York Style Cheesecake

## Crust

| | |
|---|---|
| ¾ cup graham cracker crumbs | ¾ cup chopped nuts |
| ¼ cup sugar | 3 tablespoons margarine, melted |

## Filling

| | |
|---|---|
| 4 (8-ounce) packages cream cheese, softened | 1 tablespoon fresh lemon juice |
| 1½ cups sugar | 2 teaspoons vanilla |
| | 4 eggs, room temperature |

## Topping

| | |
|---|---|
| 2 cups sour cream | 1 teaspoon vanilla |
| ⅓ cup sugar | |

Preheat oven to 350°F. For crust, in a small bowl, mix all crust ingredients. Press into a 10-inch springform pan. For filling, in a mixing bowl, beat cream cheese until smooth. Add 1½ cups sugar, lemon juice, 2 teaspoons vanilla and eggs. Beat until smooth. Pour into crust. Bake 40 to 45 minutes. Cool 10 minutes. For topping, mix all topping ingredients in a small bowl. Spread over cake. Bake 10 minutes. Cool slowly. Refrigerate until serving.

*12 servings*

# Fresh Apple Cake with Hot Buttered Rum Sauce

*A wonderful warm dessert for cold weather*

| | | | |
|---|---|---|---|
| ½ | cup butter, softened | ½ | teaspoon ground cinnamon |
| 2 | cups sugar | | |
| 2 | eggs | 3 | cups pared, cored, chopped Golden Delicious apples |
| 2 | cups sifted all-purpose flour | | |
| 1 | teaspoon baking powder | 1½ | cups chopped nuts |
| ¾ | teaspoon baking soda | | Hot Buttered Rum Sauce (see accompanying recipe) |
| ½ | teaspoon salt | | |
| ½ | teaspoon ground nutmeg | | |

Preheat oven to 325°F. In a mixing bowl, cream butter. Gradually add sugar and beat until light and fluffy. Beat in eggs, one at a time. Sift together flour, baking powder, baking soda, salt, nutmeg and cinnamon. Gradually add to egg mixture. Stir in apples and nuts. Pour into a buttered and floured 13x9-inch baking pan. Bake 45 to 50 minutes. Serve with Hot Buttered Rum Sauce.

*12 servings*

## Hot Buttered Rum Sauce

1 cup sugar

½ cup butter

½ cup whipping cream or half-and-half

1 teaspoon rum extract or ½ cup rum

In a saucepan over low heat, combine sugar, butter and cream, stirring occasionally until hot. Stir in extract or rum. Serve warm over each serving of Fresh Apple Cake.

*1½ cups*

Fresh Apple Cake with Hot Buttered Rum Sauce was a favorite recipe of S.W.'s aunt. She serves it in the fall, especially for Thanksgiving dinner.

## George Washington Gingerbread with Old-Fashioned Lemon Sauce

### Old-Fashioned Lemon Sauce

½ cup butter, softened

1 egg, well beaten

¼ cup water

Zest of 1 lemon

3 tablespoons lemon juice

In a saucepan, combine all ingredients. Cook over medium heat, stirring constantly until boiling. Serve warm over individual servings of gingerbread. May be refrigerated and reheated.

*1⅓ cups*

| | | | |
|---|---|---|---|
| 2¼ | cups all-purpose flour | ¾ | cup firmly packed brown sugar |
| 1½ | teaspoons ground ginger | | |
| 1½ | teaspoons ground cinnamon | ¾ | cup molasses |
| ½ | teaspoon ground cloves | ¾ | cup vegetable oil |
| ½ | teaspoon ground nutmeg | ½ | teaspoon baking soda |
| ½ | teaspoon salt | 1 | cup boiling water |
| 2 | teaspoons baking powder | | Old-Fashioned Lemon Sauce (see accompanying recipe) |
| 2 | eggs | | |

Preheat oven to 350°F. Sift together flour, ginger, cinnamon, cloves, nutmeg, salt and baking powder. In a mixing bowl, beat eggs. Add sugar, molasses and oil. Beat until creamy. Add flour mixture, stirring until well blended. Dissolve baking soda in boiling water. Stir into mixture. Pour into a greased and floured 13x9-inch pan. Bake 35 minutes. Serve with Old Fashioned Lemon Sauce.

*12 servings*

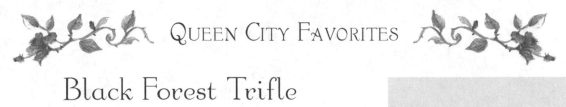

# Black Forest Trifle

| | | | |
|---|---|---|---|
| 4½ | cups milk, divided | 2 | teaspoons vanilla |
| 3 | (1-ounce) squares unsweetened chocolate | 2 | cups cookie crumbs (vanilla wafer, shortbread or chocolate chip) |
| ⅓ | cup cornstarch | | |
| ½ | cup sugar | 1 | (21-ounce) can cherry pie filling |
| ¼ | teaspoon salt | | |

In a heavy saucepan, combine 4 cups milk and chocolate. Cook over moderate heat until bubbles form on milk around edges of pan. Remove from heat. Set aside. In a small bowl, combine cornstarch, sugar, salt and ½ cup milk. Whisk until well moistened and smooth. Gradually add cornstarch mixture to hot milk mixture stirring constantly. Return to moderately high heat, stirring until mixture begins to boil. Boil 1 minute while continuing to stir. Remove from heat. Stir in vanilla. Spoon ⅓ of mixture into a 2-quart soufflé dish or trifle bowl. Top with ⅓ cookie crumbs. Set aside ½ cup pie filling. Gently spoon half of remaining filling onto crumb layer. Repeat layering with another ⅓ of chocolate mixture, ⅓ of crumbs, remaining pie filling and remaining chocolate mixture. Spoon remaining crumbs around top edge of bowl to form a border. Place reserved pie filling in center. Refrigerate covered 5 to 6 hours or until pudding is well chilled.

*8 servings*

## White Chocolate Sauce

**4 ounces white chocolate**

**¾ cup whipping cream**

In the top of a double boiler, melt white chocolate. In a separate saucepan, heat cream to boiling point. Whisk cream into melted chocolate until smooth. Refrigerate until ready to serve.

*1 cup*

## Dark Chocolate Sauce

**1 cup half-and-half**

**½ cup sugar**

**¼ cup cocoa**

**3 tablespoons butter**

**1 teaspoon vanilla**

In a small heavy saucepan, combine half-and-half, sugar, cocoa and butter. Whisk over low heat until sugar dissolves and butter melts. Increase heat to medium and whisk until sauce just begins to simmer. Remove from heat. Stir in vanilla. Refrigerate until ready to serve.

*1½ cups*

# Tiramisu Trifle with White and Dark Chocolate Sauces

| | | | |
|---|---|---|---|
| 1 | (18.25-ounce) butter recipe cake mix, prepared according to package directions | ½ | cup espresso or strong brewed coffee |
| 6 | egg yolks | | Cocoa |
| 1¼ | cups sugar | | Powdered sugar |
| 2 | (8-ounce) packages cream cheese | | White Chocolate Sauce (see accompanying recipe) |
| 1 | pint whipping cream, whipped | | Dark Chocolate Sauce (see accompanying recipe) |
| 3 | ounces coffee flavored liqueur | | |

Bake prepared cake mix in 2 round layers. Cool. Slice each layer in half to make 2 layers per round. Place wax paper between layers. Refrigerate until ready to assemble.

In the top of a double boiler, beat egg yolks and sugar until smooth and lemon colored. Bring water to a boil. Reduce heat to low. Cook 10 minutes, stirring constantly. Remove from heat. Stir in cream cheese, beating well. Cool to room temperature. Fold into whipped cream. Refrigerate 1 hour.

Combine liqueur and espresso. Place one cake round in a trifle bowl, trimming to fit. Brush with ¼ of espresso mixture. Spread with ¼ of cream mixture. Repeat layers using all 4 cake rounds. Dust top with cocoa and powdered sugar. Refrigerate. To serve, top individual servings with White Chocolate Sauce and Dark Chocolate Sauce.

*12 to 15 servings*

*Whoever was responsible for naming tiramisu surely got it right! The name actually means "carry me up" ...straight into a light, fluffy version of heaven.*

# Black and White Crème Brûlée

| | | | |
|---|---|---|---|
| 2½ | cups whipping cream, divided | ½ | cup sugar |
| 5 | (1-ounce) squares semisweet chocolate | 1 | teaspoon vanilla |
| 6 | egg yolks | 6 | tablespoons light brown sugar |

Preheat oven to 325°F. In a heavy saucepan over low heat, cook ½ cup cream and chocolate stirring constantly until chocolate melts and mixture is smooth. Remove from heat and set aside. In a mixing bowl, whisk remaining cream, egg yolks, sugar and vanilla until sugar dissolves and mixture is smooth. Whisk 1 cup egg mixture into chocolate mixture. Cover and chill remaining egg mixture. Pour chocolate mixture evenly into 6 (8-ounce) custard cups. Place cups in a 13x9-inch baking pan. Add hot water to pan to a depth of ½ inch. Bake 30 minutes or until almost set. Slowly pour remaining egg mixture evenly over custards. Bake 20 to 25 minutes or until set. Cool custards in water in pan on a wire rack. Remove from pan, cover and refrigerate at least 8 hours.

Sprinkle each custard with 1 tablespoon brown sugar. Place in a pan. Broil 5½ inches from heat with oven door slightly open for 2 minutes or until sugar melts. Let stand 5 minutes to allow sugar to harden.

*6 servings*

*Note: Must be refrigerated 8 hours.*

Crème brûlée is a rich custard, sprinkled with sugar, and broiled just before serving. The caramelized topping contrasts with the smooth texture of the custard. The name, which means "burnt cream," simply doesn't do it justice!

# Black and White Tartlets

### Chocolate Pastry

| | | | |
|---|---|---|---|
| 1 | cup plus 2 tablespoons all-purpose flour | ½ | cup butter or margarine, cold and cut into 8 pieces |
| ⅓ | cup sugar | | |
| 3 | tablespoons unsweetened cocoa | 1 | egg |
| | | ½ | teaspoon vanilla |

### White Chocolate Cream

| | | | |
|---|---|---|---|
| 6 | ounces white chocolate | 1 | egg, room temperature |
| ½ | cup butter or margarine, softened | 2 | teaspoons light crème de caçao |
| ⅓ | cup powdered sugar | 1 | teaspoon vanilla |

For chocolate pastry, in a food processor fitted with the metal blade or in a mixing bowl with a pastry blender, mix flour, ⅓ cup sugar and cocoa powder. Add ½ cup butter and pulse or mix until dough is in small pieces. Add 1 egg and ½ teaspoon vanilla. Pulse or mix until dough holds together and resembles wet sand. Small pieces of butter will be visible. Remove to a sheet of plastic wrap and shape into a ball. Pastry may be used immediately or refrigerated up to 2 days. Preheat oven to 375°F. Spray 1½-inch muffin tins with nonstick cooking spray. Break off small pieces of dough and press thinly into bottom and up sides of tins. Bake 12 minutes or until set. Turn out on a wire rack and cool.

For white chocolate cream, melt chocolate in a double boiler or in a microwave. Cool slightly. In a small mixing bowl with an electric mixer, beat ½ cup butter until fluffy. Mixing on high speed, slowly add powdered sugar. Beat 2 minutes. Mix in white chocolate. Add 1 egg and mix on high speed 2 minutes. Scrape sides of bowl. Mix in crème de caçao and 1 teaspoon vanilla, beating until the mixture is very thick and smooth. Spoon or pipe cream into baked shell. Refrigerate until serving. Shells will not become soggy.

*30 to 36 tartlets*

# Chocolate Charlotte Rousse

| | | | |
|---|---|---|---|
| 2 | (3-ounce) packages ladyfingers | 1 | teaspoon vanilla |
| ¼ | cup coffee flavored liqueur | 1¾ | cups sifted powdered sugar |
| 1 | (2.6-ounce) box whipped topping mix | 1 | cup unsweetened cocoa |
| 1½ | cups cold fat-free milk, divided | 2 | (8-ounce) packages fat-free cream cheese, softened |

Split ladyfingers in half lengthwise. Brush cut sides of ladyfinger halves with liqueur. Arrange, cut sides up, in bottom and along sides of a 10-inch springform pan. Cover with plastic wrap. Prepare whipped topping according to package directions using 1 cup cold milk and vanilla. Set aside. In another bowl, combine sugar, cocoa and cream cheese with an electric mixer on medium speed until well blended. Mixture will not be completely smooth. Beat in remaining milk until well blended. Gently fold in whipped topping. Pour mixture into prepared pan. Cover and freeze 4 hours or until firm.

*12 servings*

# Easy Chocolate Trifle

| | | | |
|---|---|---|---|
| 1 | (18.25-ounce) box chocolate cake mix, prepared according to package directions | 1 | (8-ounce) carton frozen nondairy whipped topping, thawed |
| 2 | (3.9-ounce) boxes instant chocolate pudding mix, prepared according to package directions | 6 | (1.4-ounce) chocolate covered toffee candy bars, crushed |

Let cake cool completely. Cut into bite-size pieces. Do not chill pudding. Fold cake pieces into pudding. In a trifle bowl, layer half of cake mixture and half of whipped topping. Repeat layers. Sprinkle toffee bar crumbs on top. Refrigerate 2 hours before serving.

*20 servings*

# Flan de Queso

*Cheese Custard*
*Golden caramel drips down*
*the sides forming a delicious sauce*

| | | | |
|---|---|---|---|
| 1¼ | cups sugar | 1 | (12-ounce) can evaporated milk |
| 1 | (8-ounce) package cream cheese, softened | 1 | (14-ounce) can sweetened condensed milk |
| 1 | teaspoon vanilla | | |
| 6 | eggs | | |

Preheat oven to 300°F. In a small skillet over low heat, heat sugar until foamy and golden. Be careful not to burn sugar. Immediately pour into a 1½-quart baking dish and quickly coat the bottom by rotating and tilting the baking dish until completely coated. Allow to set. This will only take a few seconds. In a mixing bowl, combine cream cheese and vanilla. Beat until fluffy. Add 1 egg at a time, beating well after each addition. Slowly pour in evaporated milk and condensed milk. Beat well until lumps disappear. Pour cheese mixture into the baking dish. Place the dish in a shallow pan of hot water. Bake 1 hour or until custard is set. Do not cover. Test for doneness by inserting a knife into center of custard. When it comes out clean, it is done. The crust should be a rich golden color. Allow to cool. Refrigerate for several hours. To remove, run a knife around the edges and shake gently. Invert onto a shallow serving platter.

*1½ quarts*

# Hummingbird Cake

| | | | | |
|---|---|---|---|---|
| 3 | cups all-purpose flour | 1½ | teaspoons vanilla |
| 1 | teaspoon baking soda | 1 | (8-ounce) can crushed |
| ½ | teaspoon salt | | pineapple, undrained |
| 1 | teaspoon ground | 1 | cup chopped pecans |
| | cinnamon | 1¾ | cups mashed bananas |
| 2 | cups sugar | | Cream Cheese Frosting |
| 3 | eggs, beaten | | (see accompanying |
| ¾ | cup vegetable oil | | recipe) |

Preheat oven to 350°F. In a large bowl, combine flour, soda, salt, cinnamon and sugar. Add eggs and oil, stirring until flour mixture is moistened. Do not beat. Stir in vanilla, pineapple, pecans and bananas. Pour batter into 3 greased and floured 8-inch round pans. Bake 23 to 28 minutes or until a toothpick inserted in the center comes out clean. Cool in pans 10 minutes. Invert onto wire racks and let cool completely. Frost with Cream Cheese Frosting.

*16 to 20 servings*

## Cream Cheese Frosting

1 (8-ounce) package cream cheese, softened

½ cup margarine, softened

1 teaspoon vanilla

1 (1-pound) box powdered sugar

½ cup nuts, chopped

Mix all ingredients. Beat until smooth. Frost cooled cake.

*3 cups*

# Pumpkin Cake

| | | | | |
|---|---|---|---|---|
| 2 | cups sugar | 2 | teaspoons baking soda |
| 1½ | cups vegetable oil | 4 | teaspoons ground |
| 1 | (15-ounce) can | | cinnamon |
| | pumpkin | 1 | teaspoon salt |
| 4 | eggs | | Cream Cheese Frosting |
| 2 | cups self-rising flour | | (see index) |

Preheat oven to 350°F. Combine sugar, oil, pumpkin and eggs. Sift together flour, soda, cinnamon and salt. Pour into pumpkin mixture. Stir well. Pour mixture into 3 greased and floured 8 or 9-inch round cake pans. Bake 30 minutes. Remove from pans and cool. Frost with Cream Cheese Frosting.

*16 to 20 servings*

# Carrot Cake

| | | | |
|---|---|---|---|
| 1½ | cups all-purpose flour | 1 | cup cooked mashed carrots, at room temperature |
| 1½ | cups sugar | | |
| 1 | teaspoon baking powder | ¾ | cup vegetable oil |
| 1 | teaspoon salt | 1 | (8-ounce) can crushed pineapple, drained |
| ½ | teaspoon baking soda | | |
| ½ | teaspoon ground cinnamon | 3 | eggs |
| | | 1 | tablespoon hot water |
| ½ | teaspoon ground ginger | ½ | cup chopped walnuts |
| ½ | teaspoon ground nutmeg | ¼ | cup raisins |
| | | | Cream Cheese Frosting (see index) |

Preheat oven to 350°F. In a large bowl, mix flour, sugar, baking powder, salt, baking soda, cinnamon, ginger and nutmeg. In a separate bowl, combine carrots, oil, pineapple, eggs and water. Stir in flour mixture, mixing just until smooth. Stir in walnuts and raisins. Pour into 2 greased and floured 9-inch round cake pans. Bake 15 to 20 minutes or until cake springs back when lightly touched. Remove from pans and cool. Frost with Cream Cheese Frosting.

*12 to 16 servings*

# Applesauce Date Cake

| | | | |
|---|---|---|---|
| 2 | cups all-purpose flour | 2 | eggs |
| 2 | teaspoons baking soda | 1 | cup firmly packed light brown sugar |
| 1 | teaspoon ground cinnamon | ½ | cup butter, softened |
| ½ | teaspoon ground allspice | 2 | cups hot applesauce, divided |
| ½ | teaspoon ground nutmeg | 1 | cup chopped dates |
| ¼ | teaspoon ground cloves | ¾ | cup coarsely chopped walnuts |
| ¼ | teaspoon salt | | |

Preheat oven to 350°F. In a large bowl, sift flour, baking soda, spices and salt. Add eggs, brown sugar, butter and 1 cup hot applesauce. On low speed, beat just until ingredients are combined. On medium speed, beat 2 minutes, occasionally scraping the side of the bowl. Add remaining applesauce, dates and walnuts. Beat 1 minute. Pour into a greased and floured 9x9-inch cake pan. Bake 50 minutes or until cake tests done with a toothpick inserted in center comes out clean. Let cool in pan 10 minutes. Remove from pan and cool on a wire rack.

*9 to 12 servings*

*May be frosted with ½ recipe of Cream Cheese Frosting (see index).*

# Apple Cake

### Cake

| | | | |
|---|---|---|---|
| 3 | eggs | 2 | medium apples, cored, peeled and chopped |
| 1¼ | cups vegetable oil | | |
| 2 | cups sugar | 1 | cup flaked coconut |
| 2½ | cups self-rising flour | 1 | cup finely chopped nuts |

### Glaze

| | | | |
|---|---|---|---|
| ¼ | cup margarine | ⅓ | cup milk |
| ½ | cup firmly packed brown sugar | | |

Preheat oven to 350°F. Blend eggs, oil and sugar. Add flour, a small amount at a time. Mix well after each addition. Fold in apples, coconut and nuts. Bake in a greased and floured Bundt or tube pan. Bake 1 hour 15 minutes. In a saucepan, mix all glaze ingredients. Boil 3 minutes. Pour over cake.

*16 to 20 servings*

# Upside Down German Chocolate Cake

*A great cake for travel*

| | | | |
|---|---|---|---|
| 1 | cup flaked coconut | ½ | cup margarine, melted |
| 1 | cup pecans | 1 | (8-ounce) package cream cheese, softened |
| 1 | (18.25-ounce) box German chocolate cake mix, prepared according to package directions, unbaked | 1 | (1-pound) box powdered sugar |

Preheat oven to 350°F. Place coconut and pecans in the bottom of a greased and floured 13x9-inch baking pan. Pour prepared cake mix over coconut and pecans. Combine margarine and cream cheese. Blend in powdered sugar. Spread over cake mix mixture. Bake 35 to 40 minutes. Let cool and cut into squares.

*15 servings*

To test baking powder, drop ½ teaspoon into a glass of warm water. If it foams to the top, the baking powder is still active.

To test baking soda, pour a couple of tablespoons of vinegar into a small bowl, add 1 teaspoon baking soda. Stand back. If it froths like mad it is good.

# Mississippi Mud Cake

### Cake

| | | | | |
|---|---|---|---|---|
| 1 | cup margarine | 1 | cup flaked coconut (optional) |
| ½ | cup cocoa | | |
| 2 | cups sugar | 4 | eggs |
| 1½ | cups all-purpose flour | 7 | ounces miniature marshmallows |
| 1 | cup pecans, chopped | | |

### Icing

| | | | | |
|---|---|---|---|---|
| ½ | cup margarine | 1 | (1-pound) box powdered sugar |
| ½ | cup cocoa | | |
| | | ½ | cup evaporated milk |

Preheat oven to 350°F. Melt margarine and place in a large bowl. Separately add cocoa, sugar, flour, pecans, coconut and eggs, beating well after each addition. Pour mixture into a greased 13x9-inch baking pan. Bake 35 to 45 minutes. Prepare icing while cake is baking. In a saucepan, mix icing ingredients. Heat almost to a boil. Simmer until ready to use. Remove cake from oven. Immediately top with marshmallows. Pour hot icing over cake. If desired, swirl marshmallows and icing for a marbled effect.

*15 servings*

E.D.'s husband professed his undying love for her after their second date and her Mississippi Mud Cake. Every girl should have the recipe!

# Brownie Sheet Cake

*Teenagers love this!*

### Cake

| | | | | |
|---|---|---|---|---|
| 2 | cups sugar | 1 | cup water |
| 2 | cups all-purpose flour | ½ | cup buttermilk |
| ½ | cup margarine | 2 | eggs |
| ½ | cup vegetable oil | 1 | teaspoon vanilla |
| 4 | tablespoons cocoa | 1 | teaspoon baking soda |

### Frosting

| | | | | |
|---|---|---|---|---|
| ½ | cup margarine | 1 | (1-pound) box |
| 4 | tablespoons cocoa | | powdered sugar |
| ⅓ | cup milk | ¼ | teaspoon vanilla |
| | | ½ | cup chopped pecans |

Preheat oven to 400°F. Sift 2 cups sugar and flour. Set aside. In a saucepan, combine ½ cup margarine, oil, 4 tablespoons cocoa and water. Bring to a boil. Pour over flour mixture and stir. Add buttermilk, eggs, 1 teaspoon vanilla and baking soda. Mix well. Pour into a greased 17x11-inch jelly-roll pan. Bake 20 minutes. For frosting, combine margarine, cocoa and milk in a saucepan. Bring to a boil. Remove from heat. Add powdered sugar and vanilla. Beat until smooth. Stir in pecans. Spread over hot cake.

*24 servings*

## Never-Fail Caramel Icing

2½ cups sugar, divided

1 egg, lightly beaten

½ cup butter

¾ cup milk

2 teaspoons vanilla

In a cast iron skillet, slowly melt ½ cup sugar, stirring constantly, until brown and well melted. In a saucepan over low heat, combine egg, butter, remaining sugar and milk. Cook until butter melts. Increase heat to medium, stir in browned sugar. Cook 10 to 15 minutes or until reaches soft ball stage (235°F.) Mixture should not stick to sides of pan. Remove from heat. Let cool slightly and add vanilla. Beat until proper consistency to spread. If necessary, add cream to thin.

*2 cups*

# Easy Red Velvet Cake

### Cake

| | | | | |
|---|---|---|---|---|
| 1 | (18.25-ounce) box butter recipe yellow cake mix | ½ | cup sugar |
| | | ¾ | cup vegetable oil |
| | | 4 | eggs |
| 3 | tablespoons cocoa | 1 | (1-ounce) bottle red food coloring |
| 1 | (8-ounce) carton sour cream | | |

### Frosting

| | | | | |
|---|---|---|---|---|
| 1 | (1-pound) box powdered sugar | ½ | cup margarine, softened |
| 1 | (8-ounce) package cream cheese, softened | 1 | teaspoon vanilla |

Preheat oven to 350°F. Combine cake mix and cocoa. Add sour cream, ½ cup sugar, oil and eggs. Add red food coloring. Pour batter into a greased and floured tube pan. Bake 1 hour. For frosting, combine and beat ingredients until smooth. Frost cooled cake.

*16 to 20 servings*

## Never-Fail Chocolate Icing

2 cups sugar

½ cup cocoa

½ cup milk

½ cup butter

1 teaspoon vanilla

⅛ teaspoon salt, or to taste

In a heavy saucepan or the top of a double boiler, mix sugar, cocoa, milk and butter. Bring to a boil, stirring constantly. Boil 1½ minutes. Cool. Add vanilla and salt. Beat with a wooden spoon until desired consistency. While warm spread over a two-layer cake or brownies.

*2 cups*

*May easily double recipe.*

# Coca-Cola Cake

A.W. loves her grandmother's Coca-Cola Cake recipe. Now, she makes it for her friends on special occasions.

## Cake

| | | | | |
|---|---|---|---|---|
| 2 | cups sugar | 1 | cup Coca-Cola carbonated beverage |
| 2 | cups all-purpose flour | | |
| 1 | teaspoon baking soda | 1½ | cups miniature marshmallows |
| ½ | cup margarine | | |
| ½ | cup vegetable oil | ½ | cup buttermilk |
| 3 | tablespoons cocoa | 2 | eggs |
| | | 1 | teaspoon vanilla |

## Frosting

| | | | | |
|---|---|---|---|---|
| ½ | cup margarine | 1 | (1-pound) box powdered sugar |
| 6 | tablespoons Coca-Cola carbonated beverage | | |
| | | 1 | teaspoon vanilla |
| 3 | tablespoons cocoa | 1 | cup pecans, chopped |

Preheat oven to 350°F. In a mixing bowl, combine 2 cups sugar, flour and baking soda. Set aside. In a saucepan, mix ½ cup margarine, oil, 3 tablespoons cocoa and 1 cup cola. Bring to a boil. Remove from heat, stir in marshmallows until melted. Pour over sugar mixture. Add buttermilk, eggs and 1 teaspoon vanilla. Beat well. Pour into a greased and floured 13x9-inch baking pan. Bake 45 minutes.

For frosting, combine margarine, cola and cocoa in a saucepan. Bring to a boil. Pour over powdered sugar and beat. Stir in vanilla and pecans. Frost cooled cake.

*15 servings*

# Strawberry Wine Cake

### Cake

| | |
|---|---|
| 1 | (18.25-ounce) box white cake mix |
| 4 | eggs |
| 1 | cup strawberry wine |
| ½ | cup vegetable shortening |

| | |
|---|---|
| 1 | (3-ounce) box strawberry flavored gelatin |
| 1 | cup finely chopped pecans |
| ½ | cup strawberries |

### Frosting

| | |
|---|---|
| 1 | (8-ounce) package cream cheese, softened |
| 1 | (1-pound) box powdered sugar |

| | |
|---|---|
| ½-¼ | cup strawberry wine |
| ¼ | cup strawberry preserves (optional) |

Preheat oven to 350°F. Combine all cake ingredients except pecans and strawberries. Mix well. Fold in pecans and strawberries. Pour into 2 greased and floured 8-inch round cake pans. Bake 20 to 25 minutes. For frosting, combine ingredients. Frost cooled cake and keep refrigerated.

*12 to 16 servings*

When splitting cake layers, a long piece of waxed, unflavored dental floss may be looped around the cake horizontally. The ends of the floss are then crossed and slowly pulled.

# Mandarin Orange Cake

### Cake

1    (18.25-ounce) box butter recipe yellow cake mix

4    eggs

½    cup vegetable oil

1    cup Mandarin oranges, undrained

### Frosting

1    (16-ounce) carton frozen nondairy whipped topping, thawed

1    (3.4-ounce) box vanilla instant pudding mix

1    (20-ounce) can crushed pineapple, drained

Preheat oven to 350°F. Combine cake ingredients and mix well. Pour into a greased and floured 13x9-inch baking pan. Bake 35 to 40 minutes, or until done. For frosting, beat ingredients, mixing well. Frost cooled cake.

*16 to 20 servings*

*Refrigerate for a few hours before serving to allow the flavors to blend.*

# Easy Peach Cake

### Cake

| | | | | |
|---|---|---|---|---|
| 1 | (18.25-ounce) box yellow cake mix | 1 | (3-ounce) package peach flavored gelatin |
| 4 | eggs | | |
| 1 | cup vegetable oil | 1 | cup mashed fresh peaches (2 large peaches) |

### Glaze

| | | | | |
|---|---|---|---|---|
| 2 | cups sifted powdered sugar | ¼ | cup margarine, softened |
| ¼ | cup peach juice | 1 | teaspoon vanilla |

Preheat oven to 325°F. Combine cake mix, eggs, oil and gelatin. Beat 4 minutes. Blend in peaches with a spoon. Spread in a greased 13x9-inch baking pan. Bake 40 minutes. Combine glaze ingredients. Spread over cooled cake.

*15 servings*

## Pecan Pie Cake

2 cups sugar

1 cup margarine, softened

4 eggs

1½ cups self-rising flour

1 teaspoon vanilla

2 cups pecans, chopped

Preheat oven to 350°F. In a bowl, cream sugar and margarine. Add remaining ingredients. Mix well. Pour into a greased and floured 13x9-inch baking pan. Bake 30 minutes.

*15 servings*

# Buttermilk Pound Cake

| | | | | |
|---|---|---|---|---|
| 1 | cup butter, softened | 1 | cup buttermilk, divided |
| 3 | cups sugar | 1 | teaspoon almond extract |
| 5 | eggs | | |
| 3 | cups all-purpose flour, sifted 3 times | 1 | teaspoon vanilla |
| | | ⅓ | teaspoon baking soda |

Preheat oven to 325°F. Cream butter and sugar until light and fluffy. Add eggs one at a time, beating well after each addition. Add flour alternately with ¾ cup buttermilk. Add almond extract and vanilla. Mix ¼ cup buttermilk with baking soda. Fold into cake batter. Pour into a greased and floured 10-inch tube pan. Bake 1 hour 10 minutes. Cool slightly. Invert onto a wire rack.

*16 to 20 servings*

# 7-Up Pound Cake

| | | | |
|---|---|---|---|
| 3 | cups sugar | 3 | cups cake flour |
| ½ | cup vegetable shortening | 1 | cup 7-Up carbonated beverage |
| 1 | cup butter or margarine, softened | 1 | teaspoon almond extract (optional) |
| 5 | large eggs | 1 | teaspoon vanilla |

Preheat oven to 325°F. Cream sugar, shortening and margarine. Add eggs one at a time, beating well after each addition. Add flour alternately with 7-Up, mixing well. Stir in almond extract and vanilla. Pour into a greased and floured tube pan. Bake 1 hour 5 minutes.

*16 to 20 servings*

*Bake pound cake in a 16x4-inch loaf pan and serve on a long pewter tray. Impressive!*

Long before mothers were scheduled to bring "teacher treats," J. & D.'s mother baked countless 7-Up Pound Cakes for Lamar School teachers. She became known for her specialty. Somehow, she always served it hot…right out of the oven.

# Powdered Sugar Pound Cake

| | | | |
|---|---|---|---|
| 1 | cup vegetable shortening | ½ | teaspoon baking powder |
| 1 | (1-pound) box powdered sugar | ⅛ | teaspoon salt |
| 4 | eggs | 1 | cup milk |
| 3 | cups all-purpose flour | 1 | teaspoon vanilla |
| | | 1 | teaspoon lemon extract |

Preheat oven to 350°F. Beat shortening and sugar until very creamy. Add eggs one at a time, beating well after each addition. Sift flour, baking powder and salt. To creamed mixture, add flour mixture alternately with milk, mixing well after each addition. Add vanilla and lemon extract. Pour into a greased and floured tube pan. Bake 1 hour 15 minutes.

*16 to 20 servings*

# Eat The Whole Thing Chocolate Chip Bundt Cake

### Cake

| | | | |
|---|---|---|---|
| 1 | (18.25-ounce) box yellow cake mix | ½ | cup water |
| 1 | (5.9-ounce) box chocolate instant pudding mix | 4 | eggs |
| | | 1 | (8-ounce) carton sour cream |
| ½ | cup vegetable oil | 1 | (11.5-ounce) bag milk chocolate morsels |

### Icing

| | | | |
|---|---|---|---|
| 1 | cup powdered sugar | 4 | tablespoons evaporated milk |

Preheat oven to 350°F. Combine cake ingredients, stirring in chips last. Pour into a greased and floured tube or Bundt pan. Bake 1 hour. Invert onto a cake plate. Combine icing ingredients. Drizzle over slightly cooled cake.

*16 to 20 servings*

When a cake recipe calls for flouring the baking pan, use a bit of the dry cake mix instead...no white mess on the outside of the cake.

# Chocolate Pound Cake

## Chocolate Glaze

¼ cup cocoa

¼ cup butter or margarine

1 cup sugar

¼ cup milk

½ teaspoon vanilla


In a saucepan, combine cocoa, butter, sugar and milk. Boil 1 minute. Cool. Add vanilla and beat. Drizzle over cake.

| | | | |
|---|---|---|---|
| 1 | cup margarine, softened | 1 | (16-ounce) can chocolate syrup |
| 2 | cups sugar | 6 | (1.55-ounce) milk chocolate candy bars |
| 4 | eggs | | |
| 2½ | cups all-purpose flour | 1 | teaspoon vanilla |
| ½ | teaspoon baking soda | | Chocolate Glaze (see accompanying recipe) |
| ¼ | teaspoon salt | | |
| 1 | cup buttermilk | | |

Preheat oven to 325°F. Cream margarine and sugar until well blended. Add eggs one at a time, beating well after each addition. Sift together flour, baking soda and salt. To creamed mixture, add flour mixture alternately with buttermilk. Stir in chocolate syrup. In the top of a double boiler, carefully melt chocolate bars. Add to cake mixture and mix well. Add vanilla and blend. Pour into a greased and floured tube pan. Bake 1 hour 15 minutes or until toothpick inserted in center comes out clean. Cool slightly and invert onto a cake plate. Drizzle Chocolate Glaze over cake, if desired.

*16 to 20 servings*

# Weidmann's Black Bottom Pie

### Crust

| | | | |
|---|---|---|---|
| 14 | ginger snaps, finely crushed | 5 | tablespoons butter, melted |

### Chocolate Layer

| | | | |
|---|---|---|---|
| 2 | cups milk, scalded | 1½ | (1-ounce) squares unsweetened chocolate, melted |
| 4 | egg yolks, well beaten | | |
| ½ | cup sugar | | |
| 1½ | tablespoons cornstarch | 1 | teaspoon vanilla |

### Bourbon Layer

| | | | |
|---|---|---|---|
| 1 | tablespoon gelatin | ½ | cup sugar |
| 2 | tablespoons cold water | | Sweetened whipped cream |
| 2 | tablespoons bourbon | | |
| 4 | egg whites | | Unsweetened chocolate shavings |
| ¼ | teaspoon cream of tartar | | |

Preheat oven to 325°F. For crust, combine cookie crumbs with butter and press into a 9-inch deep-dish pie plate. Bake 10 minutes and allow to cool.

For chocolate layer, mix small amount of scalded milk into egg yolks, then stir yolks into remaining milk. In the top of a double boiler over medium heat, combine sugar and cornstarch. Stir in milk mixture. Cook, stirring often, 20 minutes or until custard coats the back of a spoon. Remove from heat. Combine 1 cup custard with melted chocolate, reserving remaining custard. Add vanilla to chocolate custard. Pour into crust and chill.

Prepare bourbon layer by dissolving gelatin in cold water. Add reserved custard and cool. Stir in bourbon. Beat egg whites with cream of tartar until foamy. Slowly beat in sugar until stiff. Fold beaten egg whites into cooled custard. Carefully spoon mixture over chocolate layer. Chill until set. Serve topped with whipped cream and chocolate shavings.

*8 servings*

Weidmann's Restaurant, Meridian, MS

Birthday tradition in R.T.'s family has always included black bottom pie. It requires two. One is for the family and the other is for the birthday boy. In fact, her husband always says two of the reasons he married her were that she could ride a horse and make black bottom pie. R.T. is glad that she can still make the pie!

# Old-Fashioned Chocolate Pie

| | | | |
|---|---|---|---|
| ⅓ | cup cocoa | 4 | eggs, separated |
| ⅓ | cup all-purpose flour | ¼ | cup butter or |
| 1½ | cups sugar, divided | | margarine, softened |
| ¼ | teaspoon salt | 1 | teaspoon vanilla |
| 2 | cups milk | 1 | (8-inch) pie crust, baked |

Preheat oven to 350°F. In a saucepan, mix cocoa, flour, 1 cup sugar and salt. Add milk and egg yolks. Blend well. Add butter. Over medium heat, cook stirring constantly, until thick. Add vanilla. Pour into crust. Beat egg whites until fluffy. Add remaining ½-cup sugar and beat until peaks form. Spread over pie. Bake 10 minutes or until golden brown. Refrigerate.

*6 to 8 servings*

## Single Pie Crust

1⅓ cups sifted all-purpose flour

½ teaspoon salt

½ cup shortening

3 tablespoons water

Combine flour and salt in a mixing bowl tossing with a fork. Add shortening a little at a time and cut in with a pastry blender or 2 knives. Mixture should resemble a coarse meal. Sprinkle water over mixture one tablespoon at a time, blending with a fork after each tablespoon. Work dough into a uniform mixture, but be careful not to work too much. With your hands, work into a ball. Turn out onto a lightly floured surface and press down into a flat circle. Roll out to about 1½-inches larger than inverted pie plate. Gently place crust into pie plate and tuck excess dough under edge and flute.

If baking with filling, bake according to recipe directions. If baking without filling, preheat oven to 425°F. Prick bottom and side thoroughly with a fork. Bake 10 to 15 minutes or until golden brown. May double recipe for 2 crusts.

*1 pie crust*

# Hot Fudge Pie

*Serve warm with vanilla or mint chocolate chip ice cream.*

| | | | |
|---|---|---|---|
| ½ | cup sugar | ½ | cup evaporated milk |
| 3 | tablespoons cocoa | ¼ | cup butter, melted |
| 1 | teaspoon vanilla | 1 | (8-inch) pie crust, |
| 2 | eggs | | unbaked |

Preheat oven to 325°F. In a mixing bowl, combine sugar, cocoa and vanilla. Add eggs, evaporated milk and butter. Pour into pie crust. Bake 50 minutes. Middle of pie will not be firm.

*6 to 8 servings*

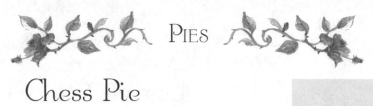

# Chess Pie

| 2 | cups sugar | 3 | eggs, beaten |
| 3 | tablespoons all-purpose flour | ½ | cup buttermilk |
| 4 | teaspoons yellow cornmeal | 2 | teaspoons vanilla |
| ½ | cup butter, melted | 1 | (9-inch) deep-dish pie crust, unbaked |

Preheat oven to 425°F. Combine sugar, flour and cornmeal. Mix well. Stir in butter. Add eggs and mix well. Add buttermilk and vanilla, blending thoroughly. Pour into crust. Bake 10 minutes. Reduce heat to 325°F. Bake 45 minutes or until pie is firm.

*6 to 8 servings*

# Old-Fashioned Egg Custard Pie

| 4 | egg yolks | ¼ | teaspoon ground nutmeg |
| ¾ | cup sugar | 1 | (9-inch) deep dish pie crust, unbaked |
| 2 | tablespoons butter | | Perfect Meringue (see index) |
| 2 | cups milk, scalded | | |
| ¼ | teaspoon salt | | |
| ¾ | teaspoon vanilla | | |

Preheat oven to 400°F. Beat egg yolks and add sugar. Beat thoroughly. Add butter to hot milk. When melted, slowly pour milk mixture over egg mixture, stirring constantly. Add salt, vanilla and nutmeg. Pour into pie crust. Bake 15 minutes. Reduce heat to 250°F. Bake 45 minutes or until custard is firm. Top with Perfect Meringue, if desired.

*6 to 8 servings*

## No Cholesterol Pie Crust

**1⅓ cups all-purpose flour**

**⅓ teaspoon salt**

**⅓ cup canola oil**

**3 tablespoons ice water**

Mix flour and salt. Whisk together oil and water. Pour into flour mixture. Stir with a fork until blended. Form into a ball and roll out between 2 sheets of wax paper. Use as an unbaked or baked pie crust.

For a baked pie crust, preheat oven to 425°F. Prick bottom and sides with a fork. Bake 10 to 15 minutes or until brown as desired. Recipe may be doubled.

*1 pie crust*

## Lemon Chess Pie

| | | | | |
|---|---|---|---|---|
| 2 | cups sugar | | ¼ | cup milk |
| 1 | tablespoon all-purpose flour | | 1 | tablespoon lemon zest |
| 1 | tablespoon cornmeal | | ¼ | cup fresh lemon juice |
| 4 | eggs | | 1 | (9-inch) deep-dish pie crust, unbaked |
| ¼ | cup butter or margarine, melted | | | |

Preheat oven to 375°F. Combine sugar, flour and cornmeal, tossing with a fork. Add eggs, margarine, milk, lemon zest and juice. Beat until smooth. Pour into pie crust. Bake 35 to 45 minutes or until set.

*8 servings*

### Fruit Cream Cheese Pie

1 (8-ounce) package cream cheese, softened

1 (14-ounce) can sweetened condensed milk

⅓ cup fresh lemon juice

1 teaspoon vanilla

1 (9-inch) graham cracker crumb crust

1 (21-ounce) can pie filling, any flavor


Whip cream cheese until fluffy. Gradually add condensed milk, lemon juice and vanilla. Pour into crust. Chill. Top with pie filling and serve.

*6 to 8 servings*

## Frozen Coconut Caramel Pies

| | | | | |
|---|---|---|---|---|
| ½ | cup butter or margarine | | 1 | (16-ounce) carton frozen nondairy whipped topping, thawed |
| 2 | (7-ounce) packages flaked coconut | | | |
| 1 | cup chopped pecans | | 2 | (9-inch) pie crusts, baked |
| 1 | (8-ounce) package cream cheese, softened | | 1 | (12-ounce) jar caramel ice cream topping |
| 1 | (14-ounce) can sweetened condensed milk | | | |

In a large skillet, melt butter. Stir in coconut and pecans. Cook until golden brown, stirring frequently. Set aside. In a bowl, beat cream cheese and condensed milk until smooth. Fold in whipped topping. In each pie crust, layer ¼ cream cheese mixture, ¼ caramel topping, ¼ coconut. Repeat layers. Cover and freeze until firm. To serve, let stand at room temperature 5 minutes before slicing.

*2 pies*

# Sonny's Light Southern Pecan Pie

| | | | |
|---|---|---|---|
| ⅓ | cup butter, softened | 3 | eggs, lightly beaten |
| ½ | cup firmly packed brown sugar | 1 | cup chopped pecans |
| 1 | cup light corn syrup | 1 | (9-inch) pie crust, unbaked |
| 1 | teaspoon vanilla | | |

Preheat oven to 450°F. Cream butter. Gradually add brown sugar, mixing well. Blend in syrup and vanilla. Add eggs and pecans. Pour into pie crust. Bake 10 minutes. Reduce temperature to 350°F. Bake 30 minutes.

*6 to 8 servings*

The Honorable G. V. "Sonny" Montgomery,
United States House of Representatives, retired

# White Chocolate Pecan Pie

| | | | |
|---|---|---|---|
| 1 | (14-ounce) can sweetened condensed milk | ⅓ | cup butter, melted |
| | | 3 | tablespoons milk |
| ⅓ | cup crème de cacao | 2 | teaspoons vanilla |
| 2 | eggs, beaten | ¼ | teaspoon salt |
| 4 | ounces white chocolate, melted | 1 | (10-inch) deep-dish pie crust, unbaked |
| 2 | cups chopped pecans, toasted | | White chocolate curls, for garnish |

Preheat oven to 425°F. In a bowl, mix condensed milk, crème de cacao and eggs. Stir in white chocolate, pecans, butter, milk, vanilla and salt. Spoon into pie crust. Bake 12 minutes. Reduce heat to 350°F. Cook 30 to 35 minutes longer. Before serving, top with white chocolate curls.

*6 to 8 servings*

*May arrange pecan halves around the outer edge of pie before baking for decorative touch.*

## Japanese Fruit Pie

½ cup butter, softened

1 cup sugar

2 eggs, beaten

1 teaspoon vanilla

½ cup raisins

½ cup nuts, chopped

½ cup flaked coconut

1 (9-inch) deep-dish pie crust, unbaked

Preheat oven to 300°F. Cream butter and sugar. Add eggs and beat well. Stir in vanilla, raisins, nuts and coconut. Pour into pie crust. Bake 45 to 50 minutes.

*6 to 8 servings*

# French Coconut Pie

| | | | |
|---|---|---|---|
| 1¼ | cups sugar | 1¾ | cups flaked coconut |
| 6 | tablespoons margarine | 1 | teaspoon vanilla |
| ¼ | cup sour cream | 1 | (9-inch) deep-dish pie |
| 3 | eggs, lightly beaten | | crust, unbaked |

Preheat oven to 375°F. Cream sugar and margarine. Stir in sour cream and eggs. Add coconut and vanilla. Pour into pie crust. Bake 10 minutes. Lower temperature to 300°F. Bake 35 to 40 minutes or until top is golden brown.

*6 to 8 servings*

## Pineapple Pie

1 (14-ounce) can sweetened condensed milk

1 (8-ounce) carton frozen nondairy whipped topping, thawed

1 (8-ounce) can crushed pineapple, drained

½ cup chopped walnuts

1 tablespoon almond extract

¼ cup lime juice

1 (8-inch) prepared graham cracker crumb pie crust

Fold condensed milk and whipped topping together. Stir in pineapple. Add walnuts, almond extract and lime juice. Mix well and pour into pie crust. Refrigerate 8 hours.

*6 to 8 servings*

*Roasted chopped almonds may be substituted for walnuts.*

*Note: Must be refrigerated 8 hours.*

# Peanut Butter Pie

| | | | |
|---|---|---|---|
| 1 | (3-ounce) package cream cheese, softened | 1 | (9-inch) chocolate cookie or graham cracker crumb pie crust |
| ½ | cup powdered sugar | | Sweetened whipped cream |
| 1 | cup creamy peanut butter | | Chocolate syrup |
| ½ | cup milk | | Roasted peanuts |
| 1 | (8-ounce) carton frozen nondairy whipped topping, thawed | | |

In a mixing bowl, beat cream cheese and sugar until creamy and smooth, scraping sides often. Add peanut butter and milk beating slowly 3 minutes or until smooth. Blend in whipped topping until no streaks appear. Pour into pie crust. Freeze until firm. To serve, top with whipped cream and chocolate syrup. Sprinkle with roasted peanuts.

*8 servings*

PIES

# Lemon Ice Box Pie

| | | | |
|---|---|---|---|
| 3 | egg yolks | 1 | (8-inch) graham |
| 1 | (14-ounce) can | | cracker crumb crust |
| | sweetened | | Perfect Meringue |
| | condensed milk | | (see accompanying |
| ½ | cup fresh lemon juice | | recipe) |

Preheat oven to 350°F. Lightly beat egg yolks. Add milk and lemon juice. Mix thoroughly. Pour into pie crust. Top with Perfect Meringue. Bake 12 to 15 minutes or until lightly browned. Refrigerate.

*6 to 8 servings*

*For a thicker pie, use a 9-inch graham cracker crust, 4 egg yolks, 2 (14-ounce) cans condensed milk and ¾ cup lemon juice.*

*For Lemon Almond Pie, add ¼ teaspoon almond extract to filling. Top with sweetened, whipped cream. Sprinkle with toasted almond slivers.*

# French Strawberry Pie

| | | | |
|---|---|---|---|
| 6 | ounces cream cheese, softened | 1 | quart fresh strawberries, washed and hulled, divided |
| 2 | teaspoons milk | 3 | tablespoons cornstarch |
| 1 | (8-inch) pie crust, baked | 1 | cup sugar |
| | | | Sweetened whipped cream for topping |

Combine cream cheese and milk. Spread onto crust. Slice 1 pint of strawberries in half. Layer over cream cheese mixture. Mash remaining strawberries. In a saucepan, cook mashed strawberries, cornstarch and sugar until clear and thick. Pour into pie crust. Chill and serve with whipped cream.

*6 to 8 servings*

## Perfect Meringue

**3 egg whites**
**½ teaspoon vanilla**
**¼ teaspoon cream of tartar**
**6 tablespoons sugar**

Preheat oven to 350°F. In a deep bowl, beat egg whites with vanilla and cream of tartar until soft peaks form. Add sugar gradually, beating until stiff glossy peaks form and sugar is dissolved. Test by rubbing a small amount between fingers. You should not feel any sugar granules. Spread meringue over hot filling. Seal to edges. Bake 12 to 15 minutes or until golden.

*Meringue for 1 (9-inch) pie*

*Note: The number of egg whites may be increased. As a rule of thumb, add two tablespoons of sugar for each additional egg white.*

All the adults who have attempted to make E.W.'s mother's traditional brownies without licking the bowl have failed miserably!

# Rich and Easy Homemade Brownies

| | | | |
|---|---|---|---|
| 4 | eggs | 1 | cup all-purpose flour |
| 2 | cups sugar | 1 | (6-ounce) package semisweet chocolate chips |
| 1 | cup butter | | |
| 4 | (1-ounce) squares unsweetened chocolate | | |

Preheat oven to 350°F. Beat eggs and sugar until thick and light. In a saucepan over low heat, melt butter and unsweetened chocolate. Cool. Add chocolate mixture to egg mixture. Beat until mixed. Stir in flour and chocolate chips. Spread in a greased and floured 13x9-inch baking pan. Bake 35 to 40 minutes. Cool completely before cutting into small squares.

*30 to 40 small brownies*

# Apricot Bars

| | | | |
|---|---|---|---|
| ½ | cup butter, softened | ½ | teaspoon baking powder |
| 1½ | cups sugar, divided | 1 | cup apricot jam |
| 4 | eggs, separated | 1 | cup chopped pecans |
| | Zest of 2 lemons | | Powdered sugar, for topping |
| 2 | cups all-purpose flour | | |
| 1 | teaspoon salt | | |

Preheat oven to 350°F. In a large mixing bowl, cream butter and 1 cup sugar. Add egg yolks and lemon zest. In a separate mixing bowl, mix flour, salt and baking powder. Blend into creamed mixture. Spread into a well-greased 17x11-inch jelly-roll pan. Spread apricot jam over mixture.

In a small mixing bowl, blend egg whites with remaining sugar. Fold in pecans. Pour on top of apricot jam. Bake 30 to 35 minutes. After baking, but while still warm, sift a light cover of powdered sugar over dessert. Cut into 4x1-inch strips.

*4 to 6 dozen*

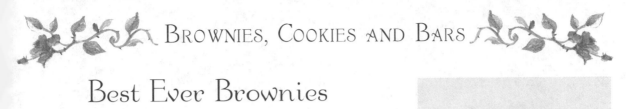

## Best Ever Brownies

### Brownies
| | | | |
|---|---|---|---|
| ½ | cup margarine, softened | 1 | cup all-purpose flour |
| 1 | cup sugar | 1 | teaspoon vanilla |
| 4 | large eggs, beaten | ½ | cup chopped nuts |
| 1 | (16-ounce) can chocolate syrup | | |

### Frosting
| | | | |
|---|---|---|---|
| 6 | tablespoons margarine | 1 | cup semisweet chocolate chips |
| 6 | tablespoons milk | | |
| 1½ | cups sugar | | |

For brownies, preheat oven to 350°F. In a medium bowl, cream ½ cup margarine and 1 cup sugar. Add eggs and chocolate syrup. Mix well. Fold in flour, vanilla and nuts. Pour into a greased and floured 13x9-inch baking pan. Bake 25 to 35 minutes. Let cool in pan.

For frosting, bring margarine, milk and sugar to a boil in a saucepan. Boil 1 minute. Remove from heat and add chocolate chips. Stir until well blended. Spread evenly over brownies. Let stand at room temperature until frosting hardens.

*24 brownies*

## Chess Squares

1 (18.25-ounce) box yellow cake mix

½ cup butter, melted

4 eggs, divided

1 (8-ounce) package cream cheese, softened

1 (1-pound) box powdered sugar

Preheat oven to 350°F. In a mixing bowl, combine cake mix, butter and 1 beaten egg. Press into a 13x9-inch baking pan. Beat remaining eggs. Beat in cream cheese and sugar. Pour over crust. Bake 40 to 45 minutes.

*30 to 40 squares*

## Cinnamon Cookies

1 cup shortening

1 cup plus 2 tablespoons
sugar, divided

2 eggs

2¼ cups self-rising flour

2 tablespoons
ground cinnamon

Preheat oven to 350°F.
In a mixing bowl, cream
shortening and 1 cup sugar.
Add eggs and flour. Mix well.
On wax paper, mix remaining
sugar and cinnamon. Roll
dough into small balls. Roll in
cinnamon mixture. Place on
ungreased cookie sheets.
Bake 10 to 15 minutes.

*30 to 35 cookies*

# Danish Apple Bars

| | | | |
|---|---|---|---|
| 2½ | cups sifted all-purpose flour | 10 | tart apples, peeled, cored and sliced |
| 1 | teaspoon salt | ⅓ | cup crushed cornflake cereal |
| 1 | cup vegetable shortening | ¾ | cup sugar |
| 1 | egg, separated | 1 | teaspoon ground cinnamon |
| ½ | cup milk, or less | | |

Preheat oven to 375°F. In a mixing bowl, combine flour and salt. Cut in shortening. In a measuring cup, beat egg yolk. Add enough milk to make ⅔ cup liquid. Mix well and stir into flour mixture. On a floured surface, roll out half of dough to a 17x12-inch rectangle. Place in a jelly-roll pan.

Combine apples, cereal, sugar and cinnamon. Spread on top of crust. Roll out remaining dough and place over apple mixture. Seal edges. Brush top with beaten egg white. Make slits in crust. Bake 40 to 50 minutes.

*15 to 20 servings*

# Pecan Pie Surprise Bars

| | | | |
|---|---|---|---|
| 1 | (18.25-ounce) box yellow cake mix | ½ | cup firmly packed brown sugar |
| ½ | cup margarine, melted | 1½ | cups dark corn syrup |
| 4 | eggs, divided | 1 | teaspoon vanilla |
| | | 1 | cup chopped pecans |

Preheat oven to 350°F. Set aside ⅔ cup cake mix. In a mixing bowl, combine remaining cake mix, margarine and 1 egg. Mix until crumbly. Press into a 13x9-inch baking pan. Bake 15 to 20 minutes. In a mixing bowl, combine reserved cake mix, 3 eggs, brown sugar, corn syrup and vanilla. With an electric mixer on medium speed, beat 1 to 2 minutes. Pour over crust and sprinkle with pecans. Bake 30 to 35 minutes. Cool and cut into bars.

*3 to 4 dozen*

# Favorite Chocolate Caramel Bars

| | | | |
|---|---|---|---|
| 1 | (14-ounce) bag caramel candy cubes | ½ | cup butter or margarine, melted |
| 1 | (5-ounce) can evaporated milk, divided | 1 | cup semisweet chocolate chips |
| 1 | (18.25-ounce) box German chocolate cake mix | 1 | cup chopped pecans or walnuts (optional) |

Preheat oven to 350°F. In the top of a double boiler or in the microwave, melt caramels and ⅓ cup evaporated milk, stirring until melted and smooth. In a mixing bowl, combine cake mix, melted butter and remaining evaporated milk. Press half of cake mixture into a greased 13x9-inch pan. Bake 8 to 10 minutes. Sprinkle chocolate chips and nuts over crust. Pour melted caramel mixture evenly over top. Top with spoonfuls of remaining cake mixture, pressing gently to flatten. Return to oven. Bake 15 to 18 minutes. Cool. Chill 30 minutes. Cut into small bars and store at room temperature. Freezes well.

*48 bars*

# Peanut Cookie Bars

| | | | |
|---|---|---|---|
| 12 | cups crushed cornflake cereal | 1½ | cups light corn syrup |
| 1 | (16-ounce) jar dry roasted peanuts (optional) | 1 | cup sugar |
| | | 1 | cup firmly packed brown sugar |
| | | 1 | cup peanut butter |

In a large mixing bowl, combine cornflakes and peanuts. Mix well. In a saucepan, combine corn syrup and sugars. Bring to a boil and boil 1 minute. Remove from heat. Stir in peanut butter. Pour over corn flake mixture and mix gently. Press into a greased 15x10-inch baking pan. Cool slightly. Cut into bars.

*24 bars*

## Easy Cake Mix Cookies

1 (18.25-ounce) box cake mix, any flavor

½ cup vegetable oil

2 eggs

⅔ cup chopped nuts, chocolate chips or toffee chips

Preheat oven to 350°F. In a mixing bowl, combine cake mix, oil and eggs. Mix well. Stir in nuts or chips. Drop by spoonfuls onto ungreased cookie sheets. Bake 8 to 10 minutes.

*2½ dozen cookies*

## Cookie Icing

*Icing dries to a shiny, hard finish*

**1 cup sifted powdered sugar**

**2 teaspoons milk**

**2 teaspoons light corn syrup**

In a mixing bowl, combine sugar and milk. Stir until mixed thoroughly. Add corn syrup and mix well. Icing may be thinned with corn syrup. Spread icing on completely cooled cookies.

*¾ cup*

# Roll Out Sugar Cookies

| | | | |
|---|---|---|---|
| ½ | cup margarine, softened | 2 | cups all-purpose flour |
| 1 | cup sugar | 1 | teaspoon baking powder |
| ½ | teaspoon vanilla | | |
| 1 | egg | ¼ | teaspoon salt |

In a mixing bowl, cream margarine and add sugar gradually. Add vanilla and egg. Continue beating until light. Sift together flour, baking powder and salt. Blend flour mixture into margarine mixture, mixing well. Cover and chill at least 2 hours or until firm enough to roll out.

Preheat oven to 325°F. Roll out ¼ of the dough at a time on a lightly floured surface to ⅛ to ¼-inch thickness. Cut out with cookie cutters. May be sprinkled with sugar, if desired. Bake on ungreased cookie sheets 10 to 12 minutes.

*3 to 4 dozen cookies*

# Sunflower Seed Cookies

| | | | |
|---|---|---|---|
| 1 | cup butter, softened | 1 | teaspoon baking soda |
| 1 | cup firmly packed brown sugar | ½ | teaspoon salt |
| | | 1 | teaspoon vanilla |
| 1 | cup sugar | 3 | cups quick cooking oats |
| 2 | eggs | 1 | cup shelled, salted sunflower seeds |
| 1½ | cups all-purpose flour | | |

In a mixing bowl, cream butter and sugars. Add eggs, one at a time, mixing well after each addition. In a separate bowl, combine flour, baking soda and salt. Add to creamed mixture, mixing thoroughly. Add vanilla. Fold in oats and sunflower seeds. Divide dough into thirds. Roll each section into a 1-inch diameter roll. Wrap in plastic wrap and freeze 2 hours.

Preheat oven to 350°F. Remove dough from the freezer and slice into ¼-inch rounds. Place on greased cookie sheets at least 1-inch apart. Bake 10 minutes. Cool on wire racks.

*4 dozen cookies*

# The Ultimate Chocolate Chip Cookie

| | | | | |
|---|---|---|---|---|
| ¾ | cup sugar | 1 | teaspoon baking soda |
| ¾ | cup firmly packed brown sugar | ½ | teaspoon salt |
| 1 | cup butter or margarine, softened | 1 | cup coarsely chopped nuts |
| 1 | egg | 1 | (12-ounce) package semisweet chocolate chips |
| 2¼ | cups all-purpose flour | | |

Preheat oven to 375°F. In a large bowl, mix sugars, butter and egg. Stir in flour, baking soda and salt. Stir in nuts and chocolate chips. Drop dough by rounded tablespoonfuls about 2-inches apart onto ungreased cookie sheets. Bake 8 to 12 minutes or until light brown. Centers will be soft. Cool slightly. Remove from cookie sheets and cool on wire racks.

*4 dozen cookies*

# Favorite Oatmeal Cookies

| | | | | |
|---|---|---|---|---|
| 1 | cup firmly packed brown sugar | ⅛ | teaspoon ground ginger |
| 1 | cup sugar | ⅛ | teaspoon ground cloves |
| ½ | cup shortening | ½ | teaspoon salt |
| ½ | cup margarine, softened | 1 | teaspoon baking powder |
| 2 | eggs | 1 | teaspoon baking soda |
| 2 | cups all-purpose flour | 1 | teaspoon vanilla |
| 1½ | teaspoons ground cinnamon | 2 | cups oatmeal |
| ⅛ | teaspoon ground allspice | 2 | cups granola |
| | | 1 | cup chopped nuts |

Preheat oven to 350°F. In a large mixing bowl, cream sugars, shortening and margarine. Add eggs and beat. In a separate bowl, stir together flour, spices, salt, baking powder and baking soda. Stir into creamed mixture. Add vanilla and stir. Stir in oatmeal, granola and chopped nuts. Drop by teaspoonfuls onto greased cookie sheets. Bake 10 minutes.

*5 to 6 dozen cookies*

## Polish Balls

1 cup margarine, softened
4 tablespoons sugar
2 cups all-purpose flour
1 teaspoon vanilla
1 cup pecans, finely chopped
Powdered sugar

Preheat oven to 350°F. In a mixing bowl, combine all ingredients except powdered sugar. Roll into small balls. Place on a cookie sheet. Bake 8 to 10 minutes. After baking, roll cookies in powdered sugar. Store in a container with excess powdered sugar.

*36 balls*

C.W.'s grandmother has always made Polish Balls as a special treat for the beach. They have become so popular that now C.W. has to make them for her friends whenever anyone goes to the beach. Maybe they should be called "Beach Balls."

# Buffalo Chip Cookies

| | | | | |
|---|---|---|---|---|
| 1 | cup margarine, softened | 2 | teaspoons baking soda |
| 1 | cup shortening | 2 | cups oatmeal |
| 1 | (1-pound) box brown sugar | 1 | (6-ounce) package semisweet chocolate chips |
| 2 | cups sugar | | |
| 4 | eggs | 1 | cup pecans, chopped |
| 2 | teaspoons vanilla | 2 | cups puffed rice cereal |
| 4 | cups all-purpose flour | 1 | cup flaked coconut |
| 2 | teaspoons baking powder | | |

Preheat oven to 350°F. In a large bowl, cream margarine and shortening. Add sugars, eggs and vanilla. Sift together flour, baking powder and baking soda. Add to mixture, stirring well. Add oatmeal, chocolate chips, pecans, cereal and coconut. Use an ice cream scoop to spoon out cookies onto ungreased cookie sheets, 6 scoops per sheet. Bake 15 minutes. Cool on cookie sheets 5 minutes before removing to wire racks.

*30 to 40 cookies*

Use light colored metal pans for baking unless otherwise specified. If using dark metal pans, including nonstick, your baked goods will likely brown more and the cooking times may be shorter.

# Lemon Satin Pie

| | | | |
|---|---|---|---|
| 6 | tablespoons butter, melted | 1 | (9-inch) baked pie crust or graham cracker crumb crust |
| 1 | tablespoon lemon zest | | |
| ⅓ | cup fresh lemon juice | 1 | cup whipping cream |
| ⅛ | teaspoon salt | ¼ | cup powdered sugar |
| 1 | cup sugar | 8-10 | lemon slices, for garnish |
| 2 | eggs plus 2 egg yolks, lightly beaten | | Fresh mint leaves, for garnish |
| 1 | quart vanilla ice cream, softened | | |

Combine butter, lemon zest, lemon juice, salt and sugar in top of a double boiler. Add eggs and egg yolks. Cook over boiling water, beating constantly with a wire whisk, until thick and smooth. Cool. Spread half of ice cream onto pie crust. Freeze until hard. Spread half lemon sauce over frozen ice cream. Freeze until hard. Repeat layers, ending with sauce. Freeze until hard. Beat whipping cream with powdered sugar until peaks form. Spread over pie before serving. Garnish each serving with twisted lemon slice and mint leaves.

*8 to 10 servings*

# Cooked Custard Ice Cream

| | | | |
|---|---|---|---|
| 6 | eggs, separated | 1 | quart milk |
| 2¼ | cups sugar | 1 | (12-ounce) can evaporated milk |
| 5 | tablespoons all-purpose flour | 1 | tablespoon vanilla |
| | Pinch of salt | | |

Combine egg yolks, sugar, flour and salt. In a saucepan, scald milk and evaporated milk. Add a little scalded milk to egg mixture. Mix well. Pour egg mixture into scalded milk. Stirring constantly, cook over medium heat until mixture thickens and coats the spoon. Do not overcook or it will curdle. Fold in beaten egg whites and vanilla. Cool and freeze in a 1-gallon ice cream freezer according to manufacturer's directions.

*1 gallon*

## Vanilla Ice Cream

4 eggs

2½ cups sugar

8 cups half-and-half

2 cups whipping cream

2 tablespoons vanilla

½ teaspoon salt

In a mixing bowl, beat eggs until light. Gradually add sugar, beating until thick. Add remaining ingredients. Mix thoroughly. Freeze in an ice cream freezer according to manufacturer's directions.

*1½ gallons*

Nothing cools off a hot lazy summer day better than a bowl of ice cream with your favorite topping. The following is a list of recipes for sauces just perfect for ice cream. Try one or create your own combination!

**Blueberry Sauce**

**Caramel Rum Raisin Sauce**

**Cinnamon Chocolate Sauce**

**Dark Chocolate Sauce**

**Fig Preserves**

**French Hot Fudge Sauce**

**Hot Buttered Rum Sauce**

**Mocha Sauce**

**Old-Fashioned Lemon Sauce**

**Praline Sauce**

**Raspberry Sauce**

**White Chocolate Sauce**

*Please see index for recipe.*

Want to add a little crunch to your ice cream? Try one of these toppings:

**Peanut Brittle**

**Southern Pralines**

**Sugar and Spice Pecans**

**White Chocolate Peppermint**

*Please see index for recipe.*

# Nutty Ice Cream Balls

| | | | |
|---|---|---|---|
| 2 | pints vanilla ice cream | 2 | tablespoons margarine, melted |
| 2 | cups chopped toasted pecans or walnuts | | Chocolate syrup, for garnish |
| 1 | (3.9-ounce) chocolate instant pudding mix | | Raspberries or strawberries, for garnish |
| 1 | cup light corn syrup | | |
| 2 | tablespoons water | | |

Scoop ice cream into 6 balls. Roll each ball in nuts. Freeze. In a small bowl, combine pudding mix, corn syrup, water and margarine. To serve, spoon about 3 tablespoons of sauce on a dessert plate. Place ice cream ball on top of sauce. Garnish with chocolate syrup and fruit.

*6 servings*

*Make nut covered ice cream balls in advance. Keep in the freezer until serving time. Looks like you have worked for days!*

# Peach Ice Cream

| | | | |
|---|---|---|---|
| 2 | (29-ounce) cans sliced peaches, diced and reserve juice | 2 | (14-ounce) cans condensed milk |
| 3 | (3-ounce) packages peach flavored gelatin | 2 | cups sugar |
| | | | Milk |
| | | ½ | teaspoon vanilla |

Combine peaches, reserved juice and gelatin and stir well. Pour into a 4-quart ice cream freezer. Stir in condensed milk and sugar. Add milk until mixture reaches the fill line on the container. Stir in vanilla. Freeze according to manufacturer's directions.

*1 gallon*

*Strawberries and strawberry gelatin may be substituted for peaches and peach gelatin.*

# Banana and White Chocolate Ice Cream Torte

### Crust

| | | | |
|---|---|---|---|
| 3 | cups walnuts | ¼ | cup unsalted butter, melted and cooled |
| 1 | cup whole almonds | | |
| ⅓ | cup firmly packed dark brown sugar | | |

### Ice Cream Layer

| | |
|---|---|
| 1 | quart vanilla ice cream, softened |
| 8 | (1-ounce) squares white chocolate, chopped |
| 2 | tablespoons whipping cream |
| 3 | bananas, peeled |
| 3 | tablespoons fresh lemon juice |

French Hot Fudge Sauce (see index)
Bananas, peeled, cut on diagonal into ¼-inch wide slices, for garnish
Strawberries with stems, for garnish

To prepare crust, preheat oven to 350°F. In the food processor, chop all nuts with sugar. Add butter and blend until well combined. Press firmly onto sides and bottom of a 9-inch springform pan. Freeze 10 minutes. Bake 20 minutes or until light brown. Cool on a rack.

For ice cream layer, melt white chocolate with whipping cream until smooth in a small saucepan. Cool. Purée bananas with lemon juice. Stir chocolate mixture and banana mixture into ice cream. Spread into prepared crust. Smooth top. Cover and freeze overnight. Before serving, remove sides of springform pan. Arrange bananas and strawberries in rows atop ice cream. Serve with French Hot Fudge Sauce.

*12 servings*

## Cinnamon Chocolate Sauce

¾ cup whipping cream
⅓ cup firmly packed light brown sugar
3 (1-ounce) squares semisweet chocolate, chopped
3 (1-ounce) squares unsweetened chocolate, chopped
¼ cup unsalted butter, softened
½ teaspoon ground cinnamon

In a small heavy saucepan over medium high heat, combine cream and brown sugar. Bring to a boil while whisking occasionally until sugar is dissolved. Remove from heat. Add chocolates and whisk until melted. Whisk in butter and cinnamon until sauce is smooth. Cool slightly. Serve over ice cream.

*1½ cups*

*May refrigerate, covered, 1 week. To serve, reheat sauce over very low heat. Stir occasionally until warm.*

# Chocolate Delight

| | | | |
|---|---|---|---|
| 28 | chocolate sandwich cookies, crushed | 1 | (5-ounce) can evaporated milk |
| ⅓ | cup butter, melted | ½ | cup sugar |
| ½ | gallon chocolate ice cream, softened | 6 | tablespoons butter |
| 12 | (1.4-ounce) chocolate-covered toffee candy bars, crushed (optional) | 1 | teaspoon vanilla |
| 4 | (1-ounce) squares semisweet chocolate | | Whipped cream or frozen nondairy whipped topping, thawed |
| | | | Chopped pecans, for garnish |

Combine crushed cookies and melted butter. Press into the bottom of a well-buttered 13x9-inch pan. Spread ice cream over crust. Top with crushed candy bars, if desired. Freeze until hard. In a saucepan, melt chocolate squares with evaporated milk, sugar, 6 tablespoons butter and vanilla. Cook until thickened. Cool. Pour over ice cream layer. Freeze. To serve, cut into squares. Top with whipped cream or whipped topping. Sprinkle with pecans.

*15 servings*

*Vanilla, chocolate chip, mint chocolate chip or peppermint ice cream may be substituted for chocolate ice cream.*

*May omit frozen chocolate layer and whipped topping. Serve with French Hot Fudge Sauce. (See index)*

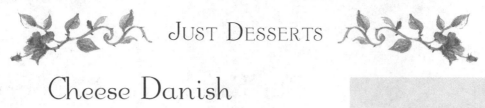
# Cheese Danish

| | | | |
|---|---|---|---|
| 1 | tablespoon sugar | 1 | (8-ounce) package cream cheese, softened |
| 1 | teaspoon ground cinnamon | | |
| 5 | (6 to 7-inch) flour tortillas | 2 | cups frozen nondairy whipped topping, thawed |
| | Nonstick cooking spray | | |
| 1 | cup cold skim milk | 1 | (1-ounce) square semisweet chocolate |
| 1 | (3.4-ounce) package vanilla instant pudding and pie filling | | |

Preheat oven to 350°F. Combine sugar and cinnamon. Spray each side of tortillas with nonstick cooking spray. Sprinkle each side with cinnamon sugar. Cut each tortilla into 4 wedges. Place wedge in muffin cup, curling sides in to fit cup. Bake 10 minutes or until crisp and lightly browned. Cool in muffin pan.

In a large mixing bowl, combine milk and pudding mix. With an electric mixer on low speed, beat 2 minutes. On medium speed, beat in cream cheese until smooth. Gently stir in whipped topping. Refrigerate at least 1 hour or until chilled. When ready to serve, fill each shell with 3 tablespoons filling mixture. Place chocolate in a freezer weight zip-top plastic bag. Microwave on high 1 minute or until chocolate is melted. Snip off tip of one corner of bag. Drizzle chocolate over desserts. Refrigerate 5 minutes or until chocolate sets.

*20 servings*

*Desserts may be frozen and thawed in refrigerator before serving.*

*May use fat-free, sugar-free pudding and pie filling and light cream cheese.*

## Easy, Easy Peach Cobbler

½ cup butter or margarine

1 (29-ounce) can peach slices, drained, reserve ½ cup juice

1 cup self-rising flour

1¼ cups sugar

¾ cup milk

Preheat oven to 400°F. In a 13x9-inch baking dish, melt butter. Add peaches. In another bowl, mix flour, sugar, milk and reserved juice. Pour over peaches. Bake 40 minutes or until browned on top.

*6 to 8 servings*

*This works for any fruit - blackberry, blueberry, etc.*

## Quick and Easy Banana Pudding

1 (14-ounce) can sweetened condensed milk

1½ cups cold water

1 (3.4-ounce) box instant vanilla pudding

2 cups whipping cream, whipped

36 vanilla wafer cookies

4-5 bananas, sliced

In a mixing bowl, combine milk, water and pudding. Beat well. Chill 5 minutes. Fold in whipped cream. In a 2-quart baking dish, layer pudding, vanilla wafers and bananas. Refrigerate until ready to serve.

*8 to 10 servings*

# Old-Fashioned Apple Crisp

| | | | |
|---|---|---|---|
| 8 | large, tart apples, peeled, cored and sliced | 1 | cup sugar |
| | | 1 | cup all-purpose flour |
| | | 1 | egg |
| 1 | tablespoon ground cinnamon | ½ | teaspoon salt |
| | | 1 | teaspoon baking powder |
| 1 | cup firmly packed brown sugar | ½ | cup butter, melted |

Preheat oven to 350°F. In a buttered 13x9-inch baking dish, place sliced apples. Combine cinnamon and brown sugar. Sprinkle apples with half of cinnamon mixture. In a mixing bowl, combine sugar, flour, egg, salt and baking powder. Spread over apples. Sprinkle remaining cinnamon mixture over dough. Drizzle butter over top. Bake 40 to 45 minutes.

*8 to 10 servings*

*For a little extra crunch, substitute ½ cup regular cooking oatmeal for ½ cup flour.*

# Banana Pudding

| | | | |
|---|---|---|---|
| 6 | eggs, separated | ½ | cup margarine, softened |
| 2 | cups plus 6 tablespoons sugar, divided | 4½ | cups milk |
| | | ¼ | teaspoon salt |
| | | 1½ | teaspoons vanilla |
| 8 | tablespoons all-purpose flour | 30-36 | vanilla wafer cookies |
| | | 5 | bananas, sliced |

Preheat oven to 350°F. In the top of a double boiler, not over heat, beat egg yolks and 2 cups sugar. Add flour, margarine, milk and salt. Place over medium heat and cook until thick, stirring constantly. Add vanilla and cool. In a 2-quart baking dish, layer cookies, bananas and filling. In a separate bowl, beat egg whites with remaining sugar until stiff peaks form. Place on top of pudding and seal edges. Bake 8 to 10 minutes or until lightly browned. Refrigerate.

*8 servings*

# Cheesecake Dreams

| | | | |
|---|---|---|---|
| ⅓ | cup firmly packed light brown sugar | ½ | cup sugar |
| 1 | cup all-purpose flour | 2 | eggs |
| ½ | cup pecans, chopped | 3 | tablespoons milk |
| ⅓ | cup butter, melted | 1 | tablespoon lemon juice |
| 2 | (8-ounce) packages cream cheese, softened | 2 | teaspoons vanilla |

Preheat oven to 350°F. In a mixing bowl, combine brown sugar, flour, pecans and butter until well mixed. Reserve ⅓ cup. Pat remaining crumb mixture gently into a greased 8x8-inch pan. Bake 12 to 15 minutes.

With an electric mixer on medium speed, beat cream cheese and sugar until smooth. Beat in remaining ingredients. Pour over crust. Sprinkle with reserved crumb mixture. Bake 25 minutes or until set. Cool on a wire rack. Cut into 2-inch squares and then cut diagonally.

*32 bars*

# Fresh Apple Rings

| | | | |
|---|---|---|---|
| 1 | cup sugar | ½ | teaspoon salt |
| ½ | cup firmly packed brown sugar | ½ | cup vegetable shortening |
| ½ | cup margarine | 5-6 | apples, peeled, cored and chopped |
| 2 | cups plus 4 to 5 tablespoons water, divided | | Ground nutmeg |
| 1½ | cups all-purpose flour | | Ground cinnamon |

Preheat oven to 400°F. In a saucepan, combine sugars, margarine and 2 cups water. Bring to a boil. Pour into a 13x9-inch baking dish. In a mixing bowl, combine flour and salt. Cut in shortening. Add remaining water and mix until dough holds together. On a floured surface, roll out to ¼-inch thickness. Spread apples over dough. Sprinkle with nutmeg and cinnamon. Roll up jelly roll style. Cut into 2-inch rings. Place apple rings in hot syrup. Bake 25 to 30 minutes.

*8 to 10 servings*

"Aunt Alice" always brings banana pudding to family gatherings. She is either extremely fond of banana pudding, or it is her culinary triumph. Unfortunately, every time the banana pudding appeared, P.M. informed her that he did not care for bananas in the pudding. In desperation, Aunt Alice created Banana Pudding Sans Bananas. It is now known by her family as "Cookie Pudding."

## Refrigerator Custard

2 (5.1-ounce) boxes instant vanilla pudding

1 (14-ounce) can sweetened condensed milk

2 teaspoons vanilla

1 (8-ounce) carton frozen nondairy whipped topping, thawed

½ gallon milk

In a mixing bowl, blend all ingredients. Pour into a 3-quart serving dish and refrigerate.

*2½ quarts*

# Lemon Coconut Tartlets

### Pastry

| | | | | |
|---|---|---|---|---|
| ¾ | cup butter, softened | 1 | teaspoon lemon zest |
| 4 | ounces cream cheese, softened | ⅛ | teaspoon salt |
| 2 | tablespoons sugar | 1½ | cups all-purpose flour |

### Filling

| | | | | |
|---|---|---|---|---|
| ½ | cup flaked coconut | 2 | tablespoons butter, melted |
| ¾ | cup sugar | | |
| 3 | eggs, beaten | 1 | teaspoon lemon zest |
| | | 2 | tablespoons lemon juice |

Preheat oven to 325°F. In a mixing bowl, combine all pastry ingredients except flour. Beat well. Add flour. Shape dough into a ball. Divide into 36 equal pieces. Press into greased miniature muffin tins. To prepare filling, place ½ teaspoon coconut in bottom of each shell. Combine remaining filling ingredients until well blended. Spoon evenly into shells. Bake 22 minutes.

*36 tartlets*

# Hot Cranberry Bake

*A cranberry syrup bubbles beneath this streusel-topped dessert*

| | | | | |
|---|---|---|---|---|
| 4 | cups peeled, cored, and chopped cooking apples | 1 | cup chopped walnuts |
| | | ⅓ | cup firmly packed brown sugar |
| 2 | cups fresh cranberries | ½ | cup butter or margarine, melted |
| 1½ | teaspoons lemon juice | | |
| 1 | cup sugar | | Vanilla ice cream |
| 1⅓ | cups quick-cooking oats, uncooked | | |

Preheat oven to 325°F. In a lightly greased 2-quart baking dish, combine apples and cranberries. Sprinkle with lemon juice. Top with sugar. In a separate bowl, combine oats, walnuts, brown sugar and butter until ingredients are moistened and mixture is crumbly. Sprinkle over fruit. Bake 1 hour. Serve warm with vanilla ice cream.

*8 servings*

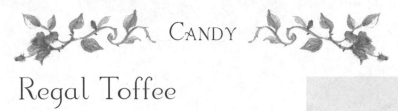

# Regal Toffee

| | | | |
|---|---|---|---|
| 1 | cup margarine | 4 | (1.55-ounce) milk |
| 1½ | cups firmly packed light brown sugar | | chocolate candy bars, broken into pieces |
| ⅔ | cup coarsely chopped toasted almonds | ½ | cup finely chopped toasted almonds |

In a heavy 2-quart saucepan over low heat, cook margarine and sugar. Stirring until the mixture comes to a full boil, being careful not to burn. Continue to boil, stirring occasionally, until mixture reaches hard crack stage or 300°F on a candy thermometer. Remove from heat. Quickly stir in ⅔ cup almonds. Pour into a greased 13x9-inch baking pan. Let stand until set but still very warm. Place candy bar pieces over top. As candy softens, spread evenly with a spatula. Immediately sprinkle with finely chopped almonds. Lightly press almonds into chocolate. Cool until completely hardened. Break into irregular pieces. Store in a covered container.

*1⅓ pounds*

*Note: Margarine works better than butter in this recipe. May be frozen or prepared ahead.*

## Peanut Butter Balls

*Kids love this as an after-school snack.*

1¼ cups powdered sugar

1 cup peanut butter

1 cup dry milk powder

1 cup honey

Combine all ingredients. Roll dough into 1-inch balls. Place on wax paper. Refrigerate until firm.

*30 to 36 balls*

# Peanut Butter Fudge

| | | | |
|---|---|---|---|
| 4 | cups sugar | 6 | tablespoons butter or margarine |
| 6 | tablespoons cocoa | ½ | cup crunchy peanut butter |
| 1½ | cups evaporated milk | | |
| ¼ | cup plus 2 tablespoons corn syrup | 2 | teaspoons vanilla |

In a saucepan, combine sugar, cocoa, evaporated milk, and corn syrup. Boil until mixture reaches soft ball stage or 235°F on a candy thermometer. Add butter, peanut butter and vanilla. Beat until thickened and pour into a greased 13x9-inch pan.

*40 to 50 pieces*

# Peanut Brittle

*A high quality peanut brittle easy for anyone to make.*

| | | | |
|---|---|---|---|
| 2 | cups sugar | 1 | tablespoon butter |
| 1 | cup light corn syrup | 1 | teaspoon vanilla |
| 2 | cups raw shelled peanuts | 2 | teaspoons baking soda |

Combine sugar, corn syrup and raw peanuts. Cook over high heat while constantly stirring until peanuts turn beige in color. Remove from heat and quickly stir in butter and vanilla. Immediately stir in baking soda and mix thoroughly. Quickly pour onto a buttered piece of wax paper. Works best if wax paper is directly on a marble or granite slab, but will work on a cookie sheet. Cool and break into pieces.

*10 to 15 pieces*

### Peanut Brittle Sundaes

Mix 2 cups broken peanut brittle into 1 quart softened vanilla ice cream. Top with chocolate sauce, whipped cream and more chopped brittle.

*8 servings*

*May break peanut brittle by placing it in a zip-top plastic bag and tapping it lightly with a kitchen mallet.*

# Trent's Favorite Chocolate Candy

| | | | |
|---|---|---|---|
| 8 | (1-ounce) squares semisweet chocolate | 1 | (14-ounce) can sweetened condensed milk |
| 4 | (1-ounce) squares unsweetened chocolate | 1 | teaspoon vanilla |
| | | 1 | cup chopped pecans |
| | | 1 | cup pecan halves |

In the top of a double boiler over medium-low heat, melt chocolate squares, stirring constantly. Add condensed milk, vanilla and chopped pecans. Stir well and drop by spoonfuls onto wax paper. Top with pecan halves.

*30 to 40 pieces*

The Honorable Trent Lott, United States Senate, Mississippi

*Note: Candy does not get very firm. Place in an airtight container to keep fresh.*

# Southern Pralines

| | | | | |
|---|---|---|---|---|
| 1 | (1-pound) box light brown sugar | | Pinch of salt | |
| 1 | (5-ounce) can evaporated milk | 2 | cups broken pecans | |
| 2 | tablespoons light corn syrup | ¼ | cup butter, sliced | |
| | | 2 | teaspoons vanilla | |

In a heavy saucepan, combine brown sugar, evaporated milk, corn syrup and salt. Cook over low heat, stirring constantly until it reaches soft ball stage (235°F). Remove from heat and stir in pecans. Place sliced butter on top of mixture and allow to stand 10 minutes. Add vanilla and stir until mixture is creamy. Drop on wax paper and allow to harden.

*3 dozen*

Pralines were once J.E.'s contribution to her son's school fundraising project. Now, another generation enjoys this traditional southern candy.

# Creamy Chocolate Fudge

| | | | | |
|---|---|---|---|---|
| ¾ | cup butter or margarine | 1 | (12-ounce) package semisweet chocolate chips | |
| 1 | (12-ounce) can evaporated milk | | | |
| 2 | cups sugar | 2 | cups chopped pecans | |
| 2 | (7-ounce) jars marshmallow cream | 2 | teaspoons vanilla | |

In a heavy saucepan over medium heat, cook butter, milk and sugar until sugar is dissolved. Bring mixture to a boil. Boil until mixture reaches 235°F on a candy thermometer or soft ball stage. Remove from heat. Add marshmallow cream, chocolate chips and pecans. Stir until chocolate has melted. Add vanilla. Pour into a buttered 13x9-inch pan. Let cool and slice.

*40 to 50 pieces*

# Tiger Butter

| | | | |
|---|---|---|---|
| 1 | pound white chocolate or white chocolate chips | 1 | (6-ounce) package semisweet chocolate chips, melted |
| 1 | (12-ounce) jar chunky peanut butter | | |

In the top of a double boiler, combine white chocolate and peanut butter. Bring water to a boil. Reduce heat to low. Cook, stirring constantly, until white chocolate and peanut butter are melted. Pour into a 15x10-inch jelly-roll pan that has been lined with wax paper. Pour melted semisweet chocolate over peanut butter mixture. Swirl through with a knife. Freeze 15 minutes. Break into pieces. Store in refrigerator.

*50 pieces*

# Buttermilk Fudge

| | | | |
|---|---|---|---|
| 1 | teaspoon baking soda | ½ | cup butter |
| 1 | cup buttermilk | 1 | teaspoon vanilla |
| 2 | cups sugar | 1 | cup chopped pecans |
| 2 | tablespoons light corn syrup | | |

Dissolve baking soda in buttermilk. In a large saucepan, combine sugar, corn syrup and butter. Mix well and add buttermilk. Stir frequently over medium heat until it reaches soft ball stage (235°F). Remove from heat. With an electric mixer on fast speed, beat and stir around 10 times. Add vanilla and resume beating on medium speed about 15 to 20 times around until heavy lines appear. Blend in pecans and pour into a buttered 9x9-inch pan. Let cool 15 minutes. Cut into squares.

*1½ pounds*

## White Chocolate Peppermint

*Great Christmas gifts!*

**1 (1.5-pound) package almond bark**

**1 cup hard peppermint, crushed**

Melt almond bark in microwave. Add crushed peppermint. Pour into a 15x10-inch jelly-roll pan that has been lined with wax paper. Place in freezer 15 minutes. Break into pieces. Store in the refrigerator.

*50 pieces*

Angela Lang gave P.R. this recipe for White Chocolate Peppermint. P.R. finds it refreshing and vibrant…just like our memories of Angela.

# Parties

# A Crowning Attraction

*Meridianites have the rare privilege of treating their children and grand-children to an actual childhood memory—a ride on the horses, goats, deer, giraffes, lion, and tiger of the colorful Highland Park Carousel. This National Historic Landmark features twenty-eight restored hand-carved animals and original oil paintings across its top crown.*

*In the 1890's, Gustav Dentzel built the carousel, which eventually appeared at the 1904 World's Fair held in St. Louis, Missouri. In 1909, the city of Meridian acquired the carousel, and it has operated here since that year. The Highland Park Carousel holds two distinctions: it is the only existing two-row stationary carousel in the world, and it is housed in the only exist-ing original carousel building built from a Dentzel blueprint. Certainly, the Highland Park Carousel's bright colors and delightful music make it the Queen City's crowning attraction for old and young alike.*

# Off To The Circus

*Ages 2 to 8*

## Invitations

Blow up a balloon but do not tie it. Using a permanent marker, write the party details on the balloon. Deflate the balloon and place it in an addressed envelope with confetti.

## Decorations

Balloons, streamers and animals cut from poster board. Circus signs, such as Popcorn for 5 cents, Don't Feed the Elephants, Clown Crossing, etc., from poster board. To create the illusion of a "big top" circus tent, start streamers in the center of the room moving outwards toward the walls. Use a general color scheme of multi-color and for the big top, use red and white.

## Refreshments

- Hot dogs
- Chips
- Cracker Jacks (not recommended for children under 5)
- Popcorn (not recommended for children under 5)
- Cotton candy (machines may be rented at party centers)
- Sandwiches, cut into animal shapes
- Animal crackers

## Games

As the guests enter the big tent, have a trunk with an assortment of clothes, hats, face paint, shoes, etc., so the guests may dress up as circus people. Those who wish may perform a trick or tell a funny story or joke.

Balloon Race! Choose partners. Standing back-to-back, place a balloon between each set of partners. They must keep the balloon squished between their backs as they race to the finish line. On your mark, get set, go!

Set up a circus ring with obstacles for the guests to complete. For tightrope walkers, place a long board or rope on the floor. In the center ring is the lion tamer using a stuffed lion and a whip made from a stick with a string attached. Next come the jugglers tossing rubber balls or plastic fruit and the acrobats playing leap frog.

---

In a box of animal crackers, you will find the following crispy critters:

1 lion

1 buffalo

2 sheep

2 monkeys

2 tigers

3 rhinoceros

5 bears

6 gorillas

Young children may be afraid of clowns.

The popular rule for how many guests to invite to a preschooler party is as many as the age of the child.

# Bow Wow, Calling All Puppies
*Ages 2 to 6*

### Puppy Chow

1 cup peanut butter

½ cup margarine

1 (12-ounce) package semisweet chocolate chips

1 (12.3-ounce) package crispy rice cereal squares

1 (16-ounce) box powdered sugar

In a saucepan, melt peanut butter, margarine and chocolate chips. In a large bowl, pour cereal. Pour peanut butter mixture over cereal. Stir with a wooden spoon. Coat with powdered sugar. Serve in a new dog dish!

*12 cups*

*Games for toddlers need to be kept short and simple. It is best for children under the age of seven to be entertained with non-competitive games. Children seven years and older like to play team games.*

### Invitations
Fold a sheet of white construction paper. Cut a circle on the folded edge, leaving the two circles connected when complete. Decorate the front as a puppy face. Cut puppy ears from brown construction paper. Using brads so the ears move, attach two ears to each puppy face. On the inside, write all party details.

### Decorations
Using a large cardboard box, create a giant doghouse. Cover the walls with dog spots, fire hydrants and paw prints made from construction paper. Use a general color scheme of black, white and red.

### Refreshments
Peanut butter and jelly sandwiches, cut into bone shapes
Bologna and cheese sandwiches, cut into bone shapes
Puppy Chow (see accompanying recipe)
Kibbles and bits - No Bake Snack Mix (see index)
Round cake decorated to match invitations, use licorice for ears, candy covered chocolate pieces for eyes and red rolled fruit for collar

### Games
As the guests arrive, transform them into puppies by painting their faces with acrylic paint. Puppy ears may be made from headbands, pipe cleaners and felt.

Dog Tags! Let the children create their own collars of string beads or colored pasta. Add on nametags and licenses. Prior to party, prepare tags and licenses using shaped pieces of fun-foam.

Bite the Bone! Using string, hang bone shaped cookies from the ceiling. The children, with hands behind their backs, try to eat a bone. The first one finished gets the prize!

Pin the Tail on the Puppy! Using poster board and puppy tails cut from construction paper, create this variation of the old standard game. If you need assistance in drawing the puppy, enlarge a picture from a coloring book.

Off to the Pound! Unique game of chase! Appoint one child dogcatcher. Have a specific area designated as the pound. The dogcatcher chases the puppies. When one is tagged, the puppy is escorted to the pound. The last puppy caught becomes the new dogcatcher.

# Wild Wild West

*Ages 3 to 8*

## Invitations

Using brown paper with burned edges, create Wanted Posters! Sheriff (your child's name) is on the lookout for desperate outlaws. The sheriff's office is located at the party's address. Office hours are the party times. For RSVP, if you have seen any outlaws, send a telegraph (call your phone number) to reserve a spot in the jail. Roll up and tie with jute. If you wish, indicate that they may come dressed in costumes!

## Decorations

Sheriff's badges, construction paper or crepe paper bars on windows, bandanas, cowboy hats, cactus cutouts, horses and checkerboard tablecloths.

## Refreshments

Crockpot Barbecue (see index)
Cowboy Bean Stew (see index)
Hearty Nacho Dip (see index)
Oven Dried Beef Jerky (see index)
Horseshoe shaped cake or decorate cake with plastic horses and cowboys

Serve refreshments in aluminum pie plates with bandanas as napkins.

## Games

Horseshoes! Be sure guests stay back while horseshoes are being tossed. Plastic horseshoes may be used.

Potato Sack Races! Hop in a sack and go!

Horse Roping! Using a sawhorse, secure a mop head for the head. Don't forget to add a tail of yarn. Have the children take turns roping the horse from varying distances. Round 'em up cowboys!

Dancing and Singing! Learn a pioneer dance and or song. Music and instructions may be found in books at your local library.

Sheriff Says! A variation of Simon Says.

Pan for Gold! Fill a wading pool with water and sand. Bury pennies. Using hole punched aluminum pie plates, guests may pan for gold!

Pony Rides! For the more adventurous!

## Dirt Cake

1 (16-ounce) package chocolate sandwich cookies, crushed

1 (8-ounce) package cream cheese, softened

½ cup margarine or butter, softened

1 cup powdered sugar

1 (8-ounce) carton frozen nondairy whipped topping, thawed

2 (3.4-ounce) packages vanilla instant pudding

3 cups milk

1 teaspoon vanilla

In a greased 13x9-inch pan, place half of cookie crumbs. In a mixing bowl, beat cream cheese and margarine until smooth. Mix in powdered sugar. Fold in whipped topping. In a separate bowl, combine pudding, milk and vanilla. Fold in cream cheese mixture. Pour over cookie crumbs. Sprinkle top with remaining cookie crumbs.

*10 to12 servings*

*For dirt cake, a clean, new flowerpot may be used in place of the pan. Garnish cake with gummy worms or artificial flowers.*

# Going Buggy
*Ages 3 to 8*

## Snazzy Snail Snacks

**6 tablespoons sugar**

**3 teaspoons ground cinnamon**

**¼ cup cream cheese, softened, divided**

**4 slices whole wheat bread, crusts removed**

**¼ cup butter, melted**

**Licorice laces, cut into 24 (½-inch) pieces**

**Mini candy-coated chocolate pieces**

Preheat oven to 350°F. Combine sugar and cinnamon. Set aside. Spread 1 tablespoon cream cheese on each bread slice. Roll slices up with cream cheese on the inside. Carefully cut each roll into 3 pieces. Dip into butter and roll in cinnamon mixture. Place rolls, seam side down, on a cookie sheet. Bake 7 minutes or until lightly browned. Attach licorice piece for antennae. Using cream cheese, attach candy pieces for eyes.

*12 snails*

### Invitations
Create ladybugs from black and red construction paper. The wings should open with brads to reveal the party details. Pipe cleaners become the antennae.

### Decorations
Giant ladybugs created from construction paper, plastic bugs, giant paper flowers, paper leaves and green streamers hanging down. Use all the colors of nature as the color scheme.

### Refreshments
**Caterpillars under wraps: Wrap sticks of cheese with bologna and a lettuce leaf. Secure them with dabs of mayonnaise.**
**Ants on a log: Celery sticks with peanut butter topped with raisins**
**Snazzy Snail Snacks (see accompanying recipe)**
**Dirt Cake (see index)**

### Games
As the guests arrive, let each create his own antennae using headbands, pipe cleaners and Styrofoam balls.

Fuzzy Centipede Race! Have the guests lie down on their bellies. Ready, get set, go! Moving like centipedes, race toward the finish line!

Hungry Frog! A variation of the good old-fashioned game of Blind Man's Bluff. Blindfold one child as the frog. The other children become flies, trying not to be caught by the frog.

Leap Frog! Don't forget this traditional game.

# Tea Time

*Girls Ages 3 to 8*

### Invitations

Using ivory colored paper, paper dollies and pressed flowers create old-fashioned invitations.

Write the party details in your best handwriting.

### Decorations

Lace tablecloths, fresh cut flowers and china tea services. Don't worry if they don't match. The young ladies will still love it. Use a general pastel color scheme with white for an air of elegance. For atmosphere, play soft background music.

### Refreshments

> Pimiento Cheese finger sandwiches (see accompanying recipe)
> Cucumber Tea Sandwiches (see index)
> Chocolate Fondue (see index)
> Variety of fruit, for dipping
> Delicate teacakes or petit fours
> Iced Tea Punch (see index)

### Games

Dress-up! Have a collection of old bridesmaids' dresses, dress shoes and costume jewelry. Adult volunteers may do the ladies' hair and make-up.

Prior to the party, create bonnets out of papier mâché using a large round bottom bowl as the base. Make one bonnet per guest. Let each guest practice her millinery skills. The bonnets may be decorated with paint, silk flowers, beads, ribbon etc. Have an adult assist if using a glue gun is necessary.

Tiffany's! Set up a jewelry store using play jewelry, old costume jewelry or even Mardi Gras beads! Have plenty of play money on hand for the big spenders!

## Pimiento Cheese

8 ounces Colby cheese, shredded

8 ounces sharp Cheddar cheese, shredded

1 (4-ounce) jar chopped pimiento, drained

1 cup mayonnaise

1 tablespoon fresh lemon juice

1 teaspoon dry mustard

½ teaspoon Worcestershire sauce

¼ teaspoon cayenne pepper (optional)

1-2 cloves garlic, crushed (optional)

In a food processor, combine all ingredients. For children you may want to omit pepper and garlic.

*4 cups*

*For finger sandwiches, spread pimiento cheese onto bread slice. Top with another bread slice. Trim crust. Cut into thirds or with cookie cutters.*

### Graduation Party Ideas

Pajama breakfast

Progressive dinner party

Ice cream party

Lake party with fish fry

Mexican cuisine

50's sock hop

60's hippie

70's disco

Western party with hayride and barbeque

Karaoke sing-a-long party

Skating party

Bowling party

Paint ceramic graduation memento

Pedicures or manicures

Skeet shooting

Tea party for young ladies

Wild game party for young men

# The Hunt for King Tut

*Ages 4 to 8*

## Invitations

Using gold paint, fabric, pipe cleaners and glitter, decorate old-fashioned clothespins as King Tut. Cut long strips of white fabric. Write all the party details on the cloth strips. Wrap each clothespin with the cloth strips. Attach a tag with instructions to unwrap King Tut for party details.

## Decorations

Rope off the party area as in a real archaeological dig. Complete the dig with shovels, buckets, sand, mummy pictures and trunks of jewels and gold. Use a general color scheme of brown, beige, dark greens, black and gold.

## Refreshments

Mummy wrapped sandwiches - Mexican Rollups (see index)
Flavored gelatin jigglers in jewel shapes
Yummy mummy dip with chips (French Onion Dip)
Round cake, striped with white frosting in various directions to create the effect of mummy wrapping. Fun facial features may be added with colored frosting.

## Games

Mummy Wrap! Divide the guests into teams. One child from each team is chosen to be the mummy. Each team is given a roll of tissue paper or white crepe paper. The object of the game is to be the first team to completely wrap the mummy.

Archaeological Dig! Using a small wading pool or other large container, create a sand pit. In the sand hide various treasures such as gold plastic coins, costume jewelry and a small King Tut made from clay and painted gold. Using magnifying glasses and brushes, have the children carefully dig for treasure. You may also make fossils to hide. Follow the directions on a box of plaster of Paris, using shells, leaves, flowers, etc. to make indentions into the plaster of Paris.

Homemade Fossils! You could have the children create their own fossils with plaster of Paris.

# Backward Fun

*Ages 5 to 12*

### Invitations

Fold the invitations so they open left to right instead of the traditional right to left. Print all party details backwards. Note on the back that the invitation may be read by holding it up to a mirror. Include in the party details a request for guests to wear their clothes backwards and/or inside out.

### Decorations

Make birthday banners with the words spelled backwards. Turn the table upside down and have the chairs facing backwards. Or let the guests eat under the table. Hang balloons upside down. For a color scheme, choose holiday colors, such as red and green or orange and black.

### Refreshments

Upside Down German Chocolate Cake (see index) or
Your favorite cake turned upside down
Inside/outside sandwiches, place one slice of bread
   between two slices of cheese and bologna
Holey Burgers served on hot dog buns (see index)

*Serve breakfast instead of dinner! Remember to serve the meal backwards! Dessert before main course!*

### Games

Seek and Hide! One child hides and the other guests try to find him. As guests find him, they hide in the same place. Eventually, everyone is hiding in the same place!

Not Follow the Leader! Guests do the opposite of the leader.

What's Wrong with This Picture! Before the party, create some changes in the room. The guests name as many abnormalities as possible.

*Remember to greet your guests with "Goodbye" and tell them "Hello" as they leave.*

---

## Crispy Rice Cereal Squares

**1 cup sugar**

**1 cup light corn syrup**

**1 cup peanut butter**

**5 cups crispy rice cereal**

In a heavy saucepan over medium heat, combine sugar and corn syrup. Bring to a boil. Boil 1 minute. Remove from heat. Mix in peanut butter. Fold in cereal. Press into a well buttered 13x9-inch baking dish. Cut into squares.

*15 servings*

## Paskettie

You get some of those long things and a pan and lots of water, and some of that red stuff and you boil it - three degrees, I think, and you have paskettie!

*Recipe for spaghetti by a 4 year old*

# Drive-In Movie

*Ages 5 to 12*

### Invitations
Design invitations to look like oversized movie tickets. Include all party details.

### Decorations
Turn your deck or patio into a drive-in movie theater complete with concession stand. Put a large TV outside. When it gets dark, show a movie at the drive-in. The children will drive to the movie in their cardboard cars.

### Refreshments
    **Popcorn**
    **Hot dogs**
    **Candy**
    **Colas**
    **Cupcakes**

### Games
Create A Car! Prior to the party, spray paint large boxes in different colors. For each box, cut off the bottom and cut a hole in the top. Cut doors on the sides. From poster board, cut out headlights, tail lights, grills, etc. Guests may decorate their cars or they may be decorated prior to the party. Make vanity plates using each child's name. Be as elaborate as you wish. Use small chairs as car seats. Guests may take their cars home as favors.

Concession Stand! Instead of serving refreshments, set up a concession stand. Guests purchase refreshments with play money.

Ticket Booth! Sell movie tickets as guests arrive.

---

## No Drip Ice Cream Tip

Before scooping ice cream onto the cone, place a miniature marshmallow in the tip of each cone.

When planning your games, always consider how much room you will need to safely complete the activities. It is not very fun when someone gets hurt or something gets broken.

Adults need to be present during teen parties to help set limits. Planned activities are essential.

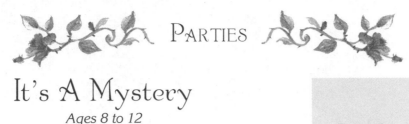

# It's A Mystery
*Ages 8 to 12*

## Invitations

Cut the invitations in the shape of a file folder. Mark the outside "Top Secret" and "your child's name" Detective Agency requests your assistance in solving the Crime of the Century. Using a white crayon, inside write the party details. On the back, instruct your guests to use a cotton swab dipped in colored water to reveal the secret message. You may also create a secret code. Just be sure to enclose the "key"!

## Decorations

Empty jewelry boxes, construction paper footprints, police "do not cross" banners, question marks. Use a general color scheme of brown, black and white.

## Refreshments

- Pizza cut into puzzle piece shapes. Momma Purdy's Pizza Dough recipe (See index)
- Pretzels
- Fruit Kabobs, alternate fruit on party toothpicks
- Cake in the shape of a question mark or
- Rectangular cake decorated with question marks made from frosting or candies

## Games

Fingerprints! As each guest arrives, make a set of his fingerprints on white paper using water-soluble inkpad. Mark the back of the paper with the child's initials. Later take the child's prints again. Using a magnifying glass, each child must compare his new set of prints with all of the first sets of prints until he finds his match.

Find the Clues! Make mini-briefcases out of construction paper. Each detective is given a list of items to find. This may be done as individuals or as a team. Things to find include a penny of a certain year, a rock, a feather, a card, a pinecone, a key, an old birthday candle, a paper clip, a leaf, a clothespin, a colored ribbon, etc. Found items are put into the briefcase.

What's in the Box? While opening gifts, the birthday person tries to guess what it is. Guests provide helpful clues.

## Easy Brownie Pizza

### Pizza

¾ cup butter or margarine, melted

1½ cups sugar

1½ teaspoons vanilla

3 eggs

¾ cup all-purpose flour

½ teaspoon baking powder

¼ teaspoon salt

### Toppings

Semisweet chocolate chips

White chocolate chips

Peanut butter chips

Mini candy-coated chocolate pieces

Flaked coconut

Almond toffee bits

Preheat oven to 350°F. In a mixing bowl, beat margarine, sugar, vanilla and eggs with a spoon. Stir in flour, baking powder and salt. Spread into a 12-inch greased pizza pan or a greased 13x9-inch baking pan. Bake 20 to 22 minutes or until top springs back when touched lightly. Serve plain or sprinkle any combination of toppings over hot brownie.

*10 to 12 servings*

# The Great Pretenders
## Ages 8 to 13

### Buttery Brown Sugar Fruit Dip

1¾ cups firmly packed brown sugar

1 cup butter

1 cup whipping cream

1 cup plus
1 tablespoon chopped toasted pecans, divided

In a heavy saucepan over medium heat, combine all ingredients except 1 tablespoon pecans. Cook until butter melts, stirring occasionally. Reduce heat and simmer 15 minutes, stirring occasionally. Transfer to a serving dish. Sprinkle with remaining pecans. Serve warm with fruit.

*4 cups*

### Cola Punch

3 cups sugar

5 pints water

Zest of 3 - 4 lemons

Juice of 12 lemons

40 ounces cola-flavored carbonated beverage

In a saucepan, boil sugar with water until sugar is dissolved. Add zest and juice. Refrigerate. To serve, add chilled cola.

*20 servings*

### Invitations
Create "back stage passes" from construction paper. Instruct the guests to come dressed as their favorite music stars excluding hair and make-up. They will also need to bring CDs of their favorite music stars.

### Decorations
Old 45 records and albums, blow-up guitars, stars, tinsel, music posters. Use a general color scheme of purple, gold, silver.

### Refreshments
Barbecued Sloppy Joes (see index)
Buttery Brown Sugar Fruit Dip (see accompanying recipe)
Cola Punch (see accompanying recipe)
Frosted round cake, use black licorice to encircle the cake. It should resemble a record. Frost the center in a bright color. Personalize the cake by writing with frosting "It's My Party" recorded by "your child's name."
Easy Brownie Pizza (see index)

### Games
Each guest pulls a number 1, 2, or 3 from a hat. All the number 1's go to make-up, 2's go to hair design, and 3's go to the rehearsal hall.

A make-up area should consist of mirrors and a variety of make-up including body glitter.

A hair design area should consist of gels, hairsprays, temporary hair color sprays, brushes, combs, curling irons, blow dryers, barrettes, ribbons, and other hair jewelry.

At the rehearsal hall, the group selects a song from the selection of CDs brought by the guests and create a lip-sync routine.

An adult should be present at each area to supervise and direct.

Each group should spend 30 minutes at each area. After everyone has visited each area, all guests return to the rehearsal hall for the main performances. Have an adult act as the evening's master of ceremonies. Invite parents to return early, so they may enjoy the entertainment.

# Tropical Paradise

*Customize to suit any age.*
*Great graduation party.*

### Invitations
Design a small island map. Include all party details. Place in a small plastic water bottle and seal with a cork. Deliver.

### Decorations
Paper flowers, paper palm trees, pineapples, bananas, monkeys, crepe paper vines, etc. Use a general color scheme of green, beige and blue.

### Refreshments
Blueberry Lemonade (see index)
Sailboat sandwiches with Fruit and Chicken Salad (see index), halved pitas filled with chicken salad. Add cheese slices for sails.
Cold Rainbow Tuna Salad (see index)
Tropical fruit - kiwis, bananas, mango, pineapple
Fresh Fruit Dip (see index)
No Bake Snack Mix (see index), use fish shaped crackers instead of snack crackers
Hummingbird Cake (see index)
Tropical island cake, frost a cake using brown sugar for an island surrounded by a blue frosting sea. Top with palm trees and fish.
Sand (see accompanying recipe)

### Games
Limbo! Use a cane fishing pole or a broom handle cut to size.

Necklaces! Using leather straps, create necklaces with beads, shells, seeds, nuts, etc. Some items may need to be pre-drilled.

Frames! Decorate a picture frame with seashells.

Under the Sea! Create sea shell animals with pipe cleaners and wiggle eyes.

Sand Art. To make colored sand, use high quality sand box sand. Place in a plastic bag with a few drops of food coloring, shake.

Coin Toss! Drop "treasure coins" in a fish bowl of water, trying to land in a small glass located at the bottom of the bowl.

## Sand

*Use your plastic sand bucket and shovel to serve this in!*

**1 (8-ounce) package cream cheese, softened**

**½ cup margarine, softened**

**1 cup powdered sugar**

**2 (3.4-ounce) boxes instant French vanilla pudding mix**

**3 cups milk**

**1 (16-ounce) carton frozen nondairy whipped topping, thawed**

**1 (12-ounce) box vanilla wafers, crushed to sand consistency**

In a bowl, combine cream cheese and margarine. Stir in sugar and set aside. In a separate bowl, combine pudding mix and milk until a pudding consistency is reached. Fold in whipped topping. In a 6-inch plastic sand bucket, layer ⅓ of vanilla wafer crumbs, ½ cream cheese mixture and ½ of pudding. Repeat layers. Top with remaining vanilla wafer crumbs. Use a small sand shovel to serve.

*12 to 15 servings*

# Monster Munch

| | | | |
|---|---|---|---|
| 2 | cups crispy rice cereal squares (spiders' webs) | 1 | cup peanuts (monsters' toes) |
| 1 | cup milk chocolate chips (bats' teeth) | 1 | cup miniature marshmallows (ghosts' toes) |
| 1 | cup raisins (cats' eyes) | | |

In a black pot, add appropriate ingredient as you recite the accompanying poem!

*14 servings*

Monster munch, monster munch
A special meal for Halloween lunch.
When you eat this ghoulish treat,
Your spooky look will be complete!
Stir it round, stir it round,

It's the creepiest dish I've found.
Spider webs, so thick and sticky,
Teeth from bats, so sharp and black,
Eyes from cats still glaring, staring,
Monsters' toes with crunchy bones,
Toes from ghosts, a freaky sight!

Stir it round, stir it round,
It's the creepiest dish I've found.
Eat some more on Halloween night,
Go and spread some holiday fright!

Make sure you have a back up plan when scheduling an outside party. Place the alternative location on the invitation in case of bad weather. Plan party activities that can be done outside as well as inside. An age appropriate video is always good to have on hand in good or bad weather.

What do you do if your party does not go as planned? Do not become upset. Sometimes things will happen that are not planned. Just continue on and the odds are good that your guests will never know there is a problem. Remember it is a party! Relax and have fun!

# Christmas Cookies

*Easy for children to make - Start a Christmas tradition!*

| | | | |
|---|---|---|---|
| **9** | tablespoons powdered sugar | **1** | cup butter, melted |
| **2½** | cups all-purpose flour | | Cherry jelly or jam |
| **1** | teaspoon vanilla | | Mint jelly |
| | | | Powdered sugar |

Stir sugar, flour and vanilla into hot melted butter. Shape into 1-inch balls and place onto an ungreased cookie sheet. Flatten and make indentions in tops. Fill indentions with 1 teaspoon cherry jelly or mint jelly. Bake 15 minutes or until top begins to brown. Cool. Roll in powdered sugar.

*2½ to 3 dozen*

Always include the
following information on your invitations:

**Host**
**Location**
**Date**
**Starting Time**
**Ending Time**
**Phone Number**
**R.S.V.P. or Regrets Only**

Send the invitations early.
They should be received at least
one week prior to the party.

J.G.'s 8th grade home economics teacher used this recipe to introduce her students to baking. Wouldn't her teacher be proud to know that her student's grandchildren are still measuring "very carefully."

Don't forget to preserve memories on film! Since you will be busy with the guests, assign someone to act as official photographer. Be sure that he is aware of the shots you most want. Remember the extra film and batteries!

Don't forget to enlist the help of adult volunteers, generally one adult per every five children.

# Recipe for Preserving Children

| 1 | grass-grown field | 1 | brook |
|---|---|---|---|
| ½ | dozen children or more | | Pebbles |
| | Several dogs and puppies, if in season | | |

Into the field pour the children and dogs, allowing to mix well. Pour brook over the pebbles until slightly frothy. When children are nicely browned, cool in a warm tub. When dry, serve milk and freshly baked cookies.

*The World Moves Forward On the Feet of Little Children.*

Have an extra game on hand as a back up in the event the party moves more quickly than you anticipated.

The length of the party for preschoolers should be limited to 1½ hours. Older children can generally be entertained for 2 hours but not longer than 3 hours.

Don't assume that your child is too old for a birthday party. Preteens and teens still love an occasion to get together with friends and be the center of attention.

# ACKNOWLEDGMENTS

More than 1200 recipes were submitted to the cookbook by friends of Lamar School. Each recipe went through an extensive process of testing and evaluation before being selected for this book. The recipes chosen for *Prime Meridian* are indeed the best of the best. We want to acknowledge the contribution of everyone who shared their time, recipes and personal memories. Our deepest gratitude goes to all those listed here and to anyone we may have inadvertently failed to mention. Thank you for your contributions and we hope you will visit *Prime Meridian* often.

Laura Abney
Pat Abrasley
Sherry Purdy Acton
Mary Adams
Frances S. Ainsworth
Tamara Alexander
Nancy Aley
Maxine Alford
Linda Anders
Debra Anderson
Joann Anderson
Julia Anderson
B. B. Archer
Mary Arrington
Karlen Bagley
Michelle Ball
Dot Barber
Lisa Layton Barrett
Janette Batchelor
Cindy Bates
Cindy Bennett
John Jennings Bennett
Lallie Bennett
Lallie Elise Bennett
Wes Bennett
Wesley Bennett
Mary Billups
Bernice Bishop
Mavis Bishop
Frances Blackmon
Cindy Blubaugh
Virginia Boardman
Celia Speed Bois Fontaine
Lesley Peterson Bolton
Virginia Bonner
Lori Booker
Barbara Boone
Lynn Bowers
Denise Boyd
Mary Jo Bozeman
Amy Branning
Doc Braswell
Faith Braud
Kevin Braud
Norma A. Braud
Lilia O. Bresino
Nancy D. Brown
Anne Cherry Buffington
Tony Buntyn
Charlie Busler
Amy Cady
Betty Cady
Calla Grill, Terry Clark
Betty Caldarelli
Cindy Caldwell
Gayle Callahan
Cynthia Calvert

Sandra Cameron
Phyllis Campbell
April Carlson
Andrea Carver
Jamie Cater
Teresa Caudill
Miriam Chesney
Jo Chester
Joyce Church
Bill Clark
Shannon Price Cleveland
Betsy Cobb
Laurie Cobb
Sandra Cobb
The Honorable Thad Cochran,
     United States Senate
Susan Coffin
Dan Coit
Elna Faye Coit
Ann Cook
Kerry Cook
Marjorie Cook
Amy Countiss
Anna Covington
Benn Covington
Catherine Covington
Diana Covington
Leslie Covington
Paula Covington
Roger Covington
Carolyn Cowart
Lisa Cowart
Julie Craven
Juanita Crowe
Penny Parker Cunningham
Theresa Cushing
Roselyn Dabbs
Reitha Davidson
Barbara Davis
Karen Davis
Linda Davis
Mildred Davis
Robin Davis
Stacy Davis
Wendy Davis
Woody Davis
Marcie de Zafra
Angie Denney
Janna Denney
Lea-Ann Denton
Jo Ann Devalcourt
Nancy Donald
Tracey Dooley
Elise L. Dorsey
Bobbie Douglas
Betty Maude Downer
Melissa Duggan

Robin Dungan
Sherry Dungan
Lori Dunlap
Connie Duplantis
Charlotte Eagle
Shazowee Edgerton
Bertha Ellington
Jean Ellis
Ann Epps
Miller Epps
Brad Escouse
Elaine Eure
Cathy Feltenstein
June Ferguson
Jimmie Kay Fisher
Marc Fisher
Sharon Flaccomio
Sue Floyd
Lean Follett
Amy Ford
Kinnie Ford
Jeanne Fort
DeeDee Fouts
Joyce Frank
Angie Ruth Fuller
Cody Fuller
Eddie Fuller
Sharon Futch
Mary Jarvis Futrell
Gerald Gafford
Peggy Gale
Debbie Gardner
Karen Gates
Tara L. Gates
Virginia Gates
Donnie Geddie
Ernestine Geter
Angie Gibson
Harry Gibson
Cheryl Gorges
Linda Grant
Maude Grant
JoAnn Grantham
Ranae Grantham
Vance Grantham
Vickie Graves
Marilyn B. Gray
Joy Greer
Teresa Gregory
Mary Ann Grisham
Linda Grissom
Donna Moss Hacker
Geraldine Hagerty
Deborah Haggard
Virginia Haggard
Cathy Hall
Judy Hammack

Jill Hammes
Evie Hand
Martha Ann Harris
Mary Harris
Richard Harris
Jennifer Harrison
Carol S. Hartvigson
Rod Hartzog
Mona Haskins
Reba Heldreth
Charlotte Herrington
Christine Herrington
Jan Hicks
Karen Hicks
Hazel Higdon
Ashley Hill
Karen Hill
Steve Holifield
Laura Holladay
Barbara Holland
Becky Howard
Richard H. Howarth
Mathilde "Til" Howell
Nell Huff
Penne Huff
Vergie Huggins
Girly Hull
Le Dawn James
Pat Jarrett
Carolyn Johnson
Dianne Johnson
Donna Jill Johnson,
     Lauderdale County Circuit Clerk
Jennie Johnson
Lisa Johnson
Philip Johnson
Robin Johnson
Suzanne Johnson
Debbie Joiner
Angela Allen Jones
Betty Lou Jones
Cynthia Jones
Jennifer Jones
Elsie Jordan
Mrs. James Keller
Alison Sanders Kimbrell
Ann Kimbriel
Lynn Kimbriel
Zulene King
Margaret Knight
Mev Knight
Robbie Knight
Rosanne T. Knight
Shirley Knight
Velma Ruth Kynerd
Sara Lincoln LaCour
Cornelia Laird

 # Acknowledgments

Peggy Lamar
Polly Lashley
Chris Lauderdale
Jim Lauderdale
Dana Lawyer
Lili Lewis
Susan Lockley
Bea Loeb
Lee Loeb
Frances Long
The Honorable Trent Lott,
    United States Senate
Lisa Love
Mary Lawrence Love
Melissa Love
Sara Love
Theresa Love
Shirley Lucas
Kathy Luke
Judy Luquire
Melissa Mabry
Julie Mahoney
Jean Makey
Susan Malloy
Pat Maranto
Don. E. Marascalco
Tricia Marascalco
Alexa Marcello
Jodie Marsalis
Debbie Martin
Joan Martin
Shelly Martin
Frank Matheny
Kim Matheny
Vicki Mathis
Missy McCracken
Cindy McDaniel
Debbie McDaniel
Paige McDonald
Carrie McDonnell
Frances McDonnell
Jenn McDonnell
John McDonnell
Mary McDonnell
Vicky McDonnell
Becky McElroy
Pam McKee
Jane McMullen
Nell McMullen
Sharon McMullen
Rhonda McRae
Shelby McRae
Joyce Meitin
Lalla B. Mellor
Lillian Merritt
Arlene Merson
Gail A. Meyer
Helen Meyer
Angie Miller
Alice P. Mitchell
Jill Mitchell
Joy Mitchell
Melanie Mitchell
Opal Mitchell
Sally Ann Mitchell
Colie Moffett

The Honorable G.V.
    "Sonny" Montgomery,
    United States House of
    Representatives, retired
Angie Moore
Evelyn Moore
Liz Moore
Harriet Morrison
Maye Morrow
Georgette Mosley
Kim Mosley
Mitch Mosley
Regina Myatt
Mrs. Robert E. Nader
Christy Stamper Napoli
Eileen Neunaber
Margaret Nicholson
Nora Nicholson
Deneane Nix
Jeanette Norment
Jeanne Norwood
Gloria Null
Gail Ogg
Olivia O'Hearn
Beth Ohnemus
Randy Olmstead
Dot Owen
Holli Owens
Lallie C. Owens
Reily Ann Owens
Shirley Pace
Peggy Parrish
Claudia Pass
Lynn Payne
Michelle Pearson
Zoe Pearson
Mary Peavey
Debbie Penny
Brenda Perry
Shirley Petkovsck
Cathie Phillippi
Diane Phillippi
Dale Phillips
Hallie Phillips
Leslie Phillips
Rosemary Rogers Piedmont
T. J. Pippin
Teresa Mayatt Pittman
Ree Pollman
Suzie McWilliams Pool
Leigh Poole
Amy Porter
Pretty Presentations,
    Renee Davis,
    Leigh Ann Randall
Sara Purvis
Bob Rea, Jr.
Betty Ready
Debbie Reau
Mitzi Reece
Margaret Remy
Lois S. Rewis
Joan Rhett
Charlotte Rhodes
Carolea Richardson
Cat Richardson
Cheryl Richardson
Earline Richardson

Jody Richardson
Vanessa Roberts
Faye Robinson
Jan Robinson
Barbara Rogers
Boots Rogers
Lela Rosenbaum
Morele Rosenfeld
Karen Rush
Lynn Russell
Shelia Russell
Pam Rutherford
Whitney Salie
Dennis Salley
Linda Sanford
Peachie Saxon
Joyce Scarborough
Jeanne R. Schornitzky
Ann Rogers Scott
Amy Scrivner
Stanley Shannon,
    Lauderdale County Tax Collector
Susan Sheehan
Karen Shelton
Cathy Shields
Phyllis Shields
Carla Shirley
James E. Shults
Bobbie Joe Simmons
Jackie Simpson
Julia L. Skinner
Phyllis Skipper
Jimmy Slay,
    Lauderdale County Tax Assessor
Phyllis B. Slife
Terry Slife
Cheryl Smith
Cindy Smith
Darrel Smith
Fairie Smith
Joyce Smith
Mary Elizabeth Smith
Nancy K. Smith
Susan Smith
Tracy Smith
Dianna Spencer
Billy Stallworth, Jr.
Shirley Standefer
Mary Stanton
Cathy Stone
Donna Story
Gloria Straus
Marie Williams Stuart
Becky Stubbs
Johnnie Stutts
Beth Tartt
Charlotte Tartt
Donis Taylor
Donna Sanders Terry
Carri Thaler
Delores Thomas
Eydie Thomas
Suzanne Thomas
Auzella Thompson
Elyse Thompson
Emily Thompson
Jamie Thompson
Tanya Thompson

Mae Carroll Thornton
Jeanette Thrash
Janet Tinnin
Diana Gilbert Tipton
Beth Touchstone
Aimee Tramontana
Jean Tucker
Mary V. Tucker
Ricki Tucker
Sheila Tucker
Angel Uhl
Donna Ulmer
Eleanor Umphlett
Helen Valentine
Christina Van Den Handel
Carol VanZandt
Laurel VanZandt
Mike VanZandt
Spencer VanZandt
Susan VanZandt
Reece Vaughan
Betty Vise
Jill White Von Edwins
Bernard Waites
Martha Walker
Diane Wallace
Heidi Walters
Maureen Walters
Hallie C. Ward
Kim Ward
Sela Ward
Betty Waters
Cori Waters
Emily C. Waters
Ginny Waters
Josh Waters
Kim Waters
M. L. Waters
Carolyn Watson
Kim Watts
Sheryl Watts
Nellah B. Webb
Sarai Ann Webb
Weidmann's Restaurant,
    Gloria McWilliams Chancellor,
    L. M. "Poo" Chancellor, Jr.
Carol Welch
Julie Wells
Angela Whiddon
Carol Whiddon
Melissa Whiddon
Dorothy B. White
Mrs. Bryan Whitehead
Angelia Wiggins
Francie Wilkinson
Millie Wilkinson
Brenda Williams
Jan Williams
Nancy Coit Williams
Connie Wilson
Dai Waters Wilson
Karen Wilson
Glenda Woodridge
Jo Turner Wright
Ann East Wyche
Drucella Young
Marlinda Young
Pat Young

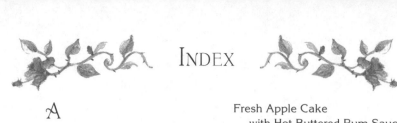

# INDEX

# INDEX

# INDEX

# INDEX

 # INDEX

# INDEX

# INDEX

# INDEX

# INDEX

 INDEX

# INDEX

# INDEX

# INDEX

# INDEX

# INDEX

# INDEX

# INDEX

# INDEX

 # INDEX

P R I M E
# MERIDIaN
*A CULINARY TOUR OF A*
*SOUTHERN QUEEN CITY*

Name _____

Address _____

City _____ State _____ Zip Code _____

Daytime Phone _____

_____Number of Copies at $22.95 each       _____

Mississippi Residents Add 7% Sales Tax     _____

Shipping & Handling at $5.00 per book     _____
*(Add $2.50 for each additional copy to the same address)*

❑ Check Enclosed (Payable to Prime Meridian)

Please Charge to     ❑ VISA     ❑ Master Card

Card Number _____

Expiration Date _____

Total $ _____

Return to: Prime Meridian
P. O. Box 3387 • Meridian, MS 39303 • 601-482-1345 ext 9 (voice mail)

- - - - - - - - - - - - - - - - - - - - - - - - - - - - - - - - - - - - - - -

P R I M E
# MERIDIaN
*A CULINARY TOUR OF A*
*SOUTHERN QUEEN CITY*

Name _____

Address _____

City _____ State _____ Zip Code _____

Daytime Phone _____

_____Number of Copies at $22.95 each       _____

Mississippi Residents Add 7% Sales Tax     _____

Shipping & Handling at $5.00 per book     _____
*(Add $2.50 for each additional copy to the same address)*

❑ Check Enclosed (Payable to Prime Meridian)

Please Charge to     ❑ VISA     ❑ Master Card

Card Number _____

Expiration Date _____

Total $ _____

Return to: Prime Meridian
P. O. Box 3387 • Meridian, MS 39303 • 601-482-1345 ext 9 (voice mail)